DATE DUE

DATE DUE	
APR 1 8 1999	
MAY 1 6 2003	
GAYLORD	PRINTED IN U.S.A.

GEOPOLITICS
OF THE
CARIBBEAN

POLITICS IN LATIN AMERICA,
A HOOVER INSTITUTION SERIES
General Editor, **Robert Wesson**

Copublished with Hoover Institution Press
Stanford University, Stanford, California

GEOPOLITICS OF THE CARIBBEAN

Ministates in a Wider World

by

Thomas D. Anderson

PRAEGER

PRAEGER SPECIAL STUDIES • PRAEGER SCIENTIFIC

New York • Philadelphia • Eastbourne, UK
Toronto • Hong Kong • Tokyo • Sydney

Library of Congress Cataloging in Publication Data

Anderson, Thomas D.
  Geopolitics of the Caribbean.

  (Politics in Latin America)
  Bibliography: p.
  Includes index.
  1. Geopolitics—Caribbean Area. I. Title. II. Series.
F2176.A52 1984   327.1'01'109729   83-21200
ISBN 0-03-070553-3 (alk. paper)

The Hoover Institution on War, Revolution and Peace, founded at Stanford University in 1919 by the late President Herbert Hoover, is an interdisciplinary research center for advanced study on domestic and international affairs in the twentieth century. The views expressed in its publications are entirely those of the authors and do not necessarily reflect the views of the staff, officers, or Board of Overseers of the Hoover Institution.

Published in 1984 by Praeger Publishers
CBS Educational and Professional Publishing
a Division of CBS Inc.
521 Fifth Avenue, New York, NY 10175 USA
© 1984 by Praeger Publishers

56789 052 9876543

Printed in the United States of America
on acid-free paper

FOREWORD

The Caribbean has long been a mecca for tourists, drawn by shimmering beaches and crystalline waters even more than exotic sights and peoples. In past centuries it has also been a prime haven for pirates, who preyed on the rich commerce of Spain with its colonies. Recently, the United States has become acutely aware of the Caribbean region as a primary channel for trade, especially petroleum imports, and as a key strategic locale, beset by swirling currents of revolution. All four of the Marxist–Leninist–inclined states of the Western Hemisphere—Cuba, Nicaragua, Grenada, and Suriname—are here, and it is in this area that the influence of the United States is most fiercely challenged by hostile ideologies and guerrilla assaults.

It is consequently most appropriate that an outstanding geographer, Thomas D. Anderson, presents this study of the geopolitics of the Caribbean. He describes in detail the natural and economic background of the problems of the basin, giving most attention to the smaller islands, which have been relatively neglected. The many ministates form a complex system, with special relationships both among themselves and with external powers.

Most people in the United States would be surprised to learn that, after Western Europe, the Caribbean islands include the most numerous group of democratic polities in the world. This fact adds to the U.S. responsibility and concern for the region dictated by its strategic significance. The problems the Caribbean basin represents for the United States are both political and economic, with many facets and complications. This volume should increase the understanding with which they can be met.

Robert Wesson

ACKNOWLEDGMENTS

Preparation of this book was aided greatly by a travel grant from the Faculty Research Committee at Bowling Green State University. In addition the ready cooperation of many people was a vital help. Of particular significance were the staff of Senator John Glenn; Lewis M. Alexander, Office of The Geographer, and N. Stephen Kane, Office of the Historian at the Department of State; Celso Rodriguez of the Organization of American States; and Raymond D. Gastil at Freedom House. The Series Editor, Robert Wesson, at the Hoover Institution provided a professional blend of prodding and encouragement needed to speed completion of the project. I am grateful also for the good-natured and skillful typing assistance of Marie Derkis and Jo Mahoney.

Thomas D. Anderson
Bowling Green, Ohio
1983.

CONTENTS

LIST OF MAPS

The base projection and the outlines of land, water, and political boundaries for all maps except #2 were adapted from *Gulf of St. Lawrence to Strait of Juan de Fuca*, No. 145, 13th edition, Defense Mapping Agency (Washington, DC, 1938, revised 9/2/74).

LIST OF TABLES

1

INTRODUCTION

The Gulf/Caribbean region long has been regarded in the United States as the foreign area most vital for defense of the homeland. Despite this strategic imperative there has been a history of comparative diplomatic neglect during times when no serious military threat was perceived in the area, a disregard that is puzzling in view of the multitude of economic and other ties that exist. Treatment of the geopolitics of the Caribbean requires attention to a wide range of topics, yet fundamental is a continuing awareness of this almost visceral U.S. apprehension and the policies that it engenders. Relations with and within the region have become more complicated since 1945 as decolonization has led to establishment of a growing number of tiny independent states. What these current relationships seem to be, as well as their significance to the United States and to outside powers, are the main subjects of this study. The focus, then, is on new ministates in a strategic sea and on changes that affect the entire region.

Often termed the American Mediterranean due to its virtual encirclement by land, the western bulge of the Atlantic Ocean consists of the Gulf of Mexico and Caribbean Sea. The island-studded waters intervene between the major land masses of the hemisphere, flanked on the west by the southward taper of the northern continent. The existence of a narrow intercontinental land bridge has contributed to the significance of this flank, as has the presence of many islands added to the importance of the ocean bulge. Since the initial European contacts led by Columbus, the region has been either a focus of interest or a major route. It has never been regarded as a barrier.

Although geopolitics acquired an unsavory connotation through its employment during the 1930s as a rationale for Hitler's expansionist policies, it remains a valid approach to regional analysis. In brief, geopolitics can be regarded as the interaction of geography and politics, with particular attention to strategies associated with those interactions. Child has suggested that elements such as military strategy, national development, expansion, and imperialism are needed to capture the full flavor of the approach (Child 1979, p. 89). These traditional views notwithstanding, there is merit also in a concept of geopolitics that provides a more comprehensive treatment of a region's geography. It should be understood that geography properly includes consideration not only of locational and environmental circumstances but also of demographic, social, and economic conditions. Essential both to geography and politics is appreciation of the legacies of history. In the words of Erhard Rostlund, "The present is the fruit of the past and contains the seeds of the future" (Rostlund 1955, p. 2). In geopolitical analysis how a region functions economically and politically as well as its cultural personality are essential to fuller understanding.

This approach to the geopolitics of the Caribbean ministates gives considerable attention to the elements noted above, and comparatively little to more orthodox topics such as military power, national objectives, and national will. The small size and brief period of independence make the latter features less relevant. Their military power is necessarily slight, and their tenures as sovereign states are too short for distinctive national qualities to have emerged. Attitudes based upon cultural links and colonial ties are examined in some detail, on the other hand. In short, what follows is an unconventional approach to geopolitics.

Geopolitical scrutiny of the Caribbean benefits from perception of two significant facts: (1) no other sector of the ocean has so many different political entities adjoining or facing across a common water surface and (2) the region lies adjacent to the United States. Regardless of which aspect of the region's politics is selected for attention, one or both of these realities can be expected to be pertinent. These two inherent qualities influence circumstances within the area as well as world perceptions of its character.

Natural fragmentation of the land along with the past imperial activities of several European powers contributed to development of a region with little internal sense of cohesiveness. Primary loyalties are confined to one's island, and often on that island to one's own race, social class, or neighborhood. Languages, religions, and political forms largely reflect colonial experiences, yet insularity remains the most pervading basis for identification. As Lowenthal has observed, the social relations network seldom survives the barrier of the sea. Indeed, he referred to the existence of 51 Caribbean islands, each with distinctive social integrity (Lowenthal 1962, p. 188). In economic terms, on the other hand, for most island peoples the sea is regarded not as a barrier but as an opportunity.

The modern consequences of the natural and cultural divisions are numerous independent states and political dependencies. Despite obvious common concerns and the disadvantages of small size, efforts toward political consolidation have thus far failed. Even voluntary cooperation in several sorts of international associations have succeeded only in limited ways. As a result, measures intended to increase intraregional integration remain more of potential than actual benefit. The island realm, as well as portions of the continental rim, is composed of political units small in size and population. Ministates or microstates are appropriate designations. An important aim is to examine the implications of small scale in a region regarded as strategic by larger powers. Although valid distinctions are possible between the categories of mini- and microstates, for the sake of convenience the term *ministates* is used here to describe all.

Fronting on the Caribbean Sea are 20 independent states and 11 dependencies (see Table 1). Inclusion of places commonly considered part of the region despite lack of a Caribbean coastline adds five countries and two dependencies. They are The Bahamas, El Salvador, Guyana, Suriname, and the United States as well as French Guiana and the Turks and Caicos

TABLE 1 Political Entities That Face the Caribbean Sea

Countries	Dependencies
Antigua–Barbuda	Anguilla
Barbados	British Virgin Islands
Belize	Cayman Islands
Colombia	Guadeloupe
Costa Rica	Martinique
Cuba	Montserrat
Dominica	Netherlands Antilles
Dominican Republic	Puerto Rico
Grenada	St. Kitts & Nevis*
Guatemala	Turks & Caicos Islands
Haiti	U.S. Virgin Islands
Honduras	
Jamaica	
Mexico	
Nicaragua	
Panama	
St. Lucia	
St. Vincent & the Grenadines	
Trinidad and Tobago	
Venezuela	

*Became independent on September 12, 1983.
SOURCE: Compiled by the author.

Islands, respectively. Bermuda, which lies much further into the Atlantic, rarely is viewed or views itself as part of a Caribbean region.

Although the islands of the region as a whole have about 29 million people and over 90,000 square miles, 16 of the 23 island political entities have no more than 325,000 inhabitants and do not exceed 700 square miles in area. Of the independent states, Grenada is smallest with 133 square miles and Dominica is least populous with about 90,000 people. Even of the mainland countries, only the United States, Mexico, Columbia, and Venezuela are large in area. Countries on the continent such as Belize and Suriname far exceed the islands in area but are ministates in population terms.

The strategic significance of the Caribbean is not new. Recognition by European powers that access to its lands and waters was valuable developed within a few decades following the Columbian discoveries. For three centuries no overseas region was contested more vigorously by the imperial forces of Britain, France, Spain, and The Netherlands. As European interests began to fade early in the nineteenth century, those of the United States began to grow. For the latter the primary objective was the construction and protection of an interocean canal, although other factors were involved as well. By the twentieth century, United States presence and influence were preeminent. The external forms and future of the hegemony constitute central elements in geopolitical consideration of the region.

A major objective in Washington has been to deny potential enemies access to the islands along the eastern rim of the Caribbean. The chain of islands has been likened to a curving fence with five main gates: the Straits of Florida, the Windward Passage, the Mona Passage, the Anegada Passage, and the Galleon's Passage north of Trinidad (see Map 1). In addition, between the small eastern islands are many smaller gaps, at least 11 of which are deep enough to be used by any ship now afloat. Control of these openings furnished security for sea movement over the gulf and Caribbean. It also offered a buffer for attacks aimed at the Panama Canal. The increased capabilities of modern submarines, aircraft, and missiles have altered some of these relationships. It is not wholly clear, however, to what degree adjustments in geopolitical strategies have kept pace with advances in military technology.

The cultural and economic history of the Caribbean islands has produced a region unique in terms of population composition and human ecology. Prior to the European intrusions, millions of native inhabitants obtained adequate sustenance from ecologically balanced systems of agriculture and from the sea. Indeed, one student of the region's prehistory was persuaded to agree with Columbus that it was "paradise on earth" (Sauer 1981, p. 280). This native support system was aided by the domestication of food plants of greater yield than any of the Old World other

MAP 1

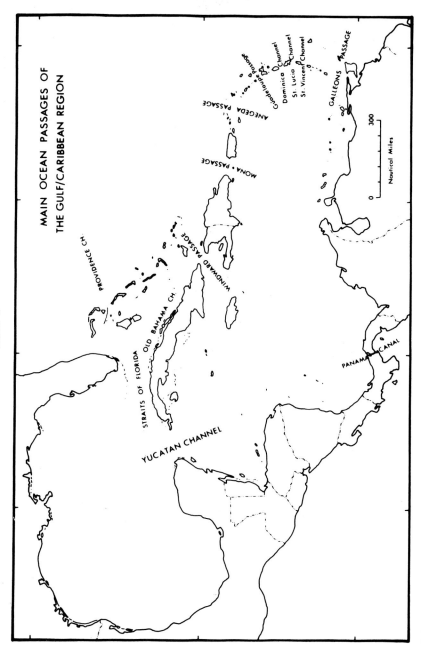

MAIN OCEAN PASSAGES OF
THE GULF/CARIBBEAN REGION

SOURCE: Constructed by the author.

than yams. However, the impacts of conquest—warfare, cruelty, and diseases—combined essentially to wipe out the original island populations in less than half a century.

Introduction of a plantation economy based mainly on sugar cane by the middle 1600s caused a repopulation of the islands by slaves brought from Africa. Emancipation of slaves in the middle 1800s brought an influx of contract workers from British India and Dutch Java that lasted into the twentieth century. Most of this later migration stream went to British and Dutch colonies. A consequence of these movements is the presence of a diversity of races and cultures. Race consciousness and associated social stratifications are cultural qualities of the islands and have political connotations, both domestically and internationally.

An early focus on export agriculture limited popular access to the best soils and fostered a dependence on imported foods. Following emancipation, the former plantation workers sought to establish subsistence agricultural systems away from the plantation but without the cultural foundation of traditional ties to the habitats. As a result their productivity levels and ecological stability were less successful than those achieved by original inhabitants. Two features derived from the plantation era make the Caribbean distinctive. The present population is descended largely from transported peoples who retain little of the cultures of their ancestors, and the Caribbean is less self-sufficient in basic foodstuffs than any other large world region.

Elected governments predominate on the islands of the Caribbean. Arbitrary rulers are in power only in Cuba, Grenada, and Haiti. The fact that the first two of these heads of state proclaim themselves to be Marxist–Leninists has affected U.S. policies toward the region in major ways. This concern (obsession?) in Washington and in the United States as a whole has tended to obscure recognition of the democratic nature of the governments in the other states and dependencies. That the Caribbean is the fourth most democratically ruled region in the world—after Anglo–America, Western Europe, and the Southwest Pacific—is a political reality. The geopolitical implications of this circumstance are treated as an important theme.

Even though economic data suggest that the region's political entities are places of moderate wealth, much unemployment and considerable poverty exist. Important mineral deposits are present only in Jamaica and in Trinidad and Tobago. For most islands, national income depends heavily on exports of tropical crops and on tourism. Less visible but of considerable importance nearly everywhere are remittances from island migrants working abroad. For some islands, and Jamaica in particular, the drug traffic is an income producer of major proportions. Petroleum refining and transshipment constitute the largest single industrial category although it is significant at only a few places. Labor-intensive manufacturers of consumer goods are widely distributed but are everywhere inadequate to meet the demand for employment. Virtually all economic activities depend in some way on outside connections, a circumstance that has increasing political significance.

Disproportionately high rates of emigration exist, with motivations that are primarily economic. Emigration is stimulated by high rates of unemployment and underemployment that are virtually endemic and which in turn reflect high population densities and demographic increases. Because a large proportion of migrants are working-age males, social imbalances have developed on some islands. Most movement is to the United States and Canada and to the metropolitan countries of Europe. The migrant flow has increased greatly since 1950 and has expanded greatly the cultural and economic ties between the islands and the migrants' new home countries. These emerging linkages have added a new dimension to Caribbean international relations.

Two issues of wide concern are related to some extent. They are the historically derived condition of economic dependency and perceptions of the threat of Cuban-sponsored subversion. Speakers on the left have argued that adoption of the Cuban model will resolve the problem of economic dependency. This position lacks credibility in view of the poor economic performance of Cuba under Fidel Castro, yet it persists nonetheless and contributes to Cuban political influence in the region. The strength of this influence has waxed and waned since 1959, and in the early 1980s was on the down side. But regardless of any Cuban role, the inhibitions on national autonomy that stem from pervasive economic dependency is one of the most emotional—and hence most powerful—political issues in the Caribbean region.

Two other matters of interest are primarily maritime. Formal adoption by Caribbean countries of changes in the Law of the Sea established a new framework for international relations. Agreement on new rules has yet to be fully implemented by means of mutually recognized new sea boundaries, and all implications of the changes are yet to be understood. This subject is examined in the context of actual and potential boundaries and of disputes. In addition, the Gulf/Caribbean area is one of the world's busiest ocean routes. The current significance of this fact is assessed with particular emphasis upon the transportation of petroleum. Connections with the Pacific, and the Panama Canal in particular, are examined in some detail.

In addition to the United States, other hemispheric power centers increasingly affect the geopolitics of the Caribbean. Most significant of these are Cuba, Mexico, Venezuela, and Canada but also influential have been Colombia, Panama, Jamaica, Guyana, and recently Brazil as well. The effect is to modify and in some ways to challenge the preeminence long held by the United States and the metropolitan countries in Europe. Each of these is examined from a geopolitical perspective with particular emphasis upon Cuba.

Because the trend away from political dependency has slowed, but apparently not ended, the process of devolution is addressed. As the number of tiny sovereign states increases, the political and economic interrelations of the Caribbean can be expected to become even more complex. Perhaps most significant geopolitically is the fact that independence makes the nature of domestic politics and interstate alliances in the region less predictable. Sudden and sometimes radical changes can necessitate modifications in diplomatic strategies for states with interests in the region. Recent examples of such a circumstance are the coups in Grenada in 1979 and in Suriname in 1980.

Involved in the region also are a number of nonstate actors that still further complicate and diffuse traditional lines of power. These include intraregional associations such as the Caribbean Community as well as agencies of wider scope. Examples are the British Commonwealth of Nations, Organization of American States, United Nations, Nonaligned Nations, World Bank, International Monetary Fund, along with others. Often there is a degree of overlap in their functions even though the role of each organization is different. Collectively they provide for newly independent ministates multiple avenues for action and serve to lessen a common sense of isolation and impotence. A diplomatic consequence of such nonstate actors is to reduce the reliance on bilateral contacts in international matters (Manspach et al. 1976, pp. 32–45).

Recent United States policies toward the region receive considerable attention, with a particular scrutiny of the Caribbean Basin Initiative. Included is a brief assessment of U.S. defense capabilities in the region. The policies are examined in the context of perceptions of the Caribbean that appear to be present in Washington. This attention was thought to be pertinent because such perceptions tend to influence the choice of strategies adopted. The interpretations presented are personal ones based upon research and also based on off-the-record personal contacts in Congress, the State Department, the OAS, and the Pentagon. As such, the interpretations are intended to be instructive or perhaps provocative; they are not presented as being definitive.

Foreign policy options in a region of change is the subject of the final chapter. Speculative in tone, the main concern is with policies formulated in Washington, although attention is also given to the perspectives of the ministates. Circumstances elsewhere in the world necessarily influence policy options for the Caribbean, but the main focus is on policy applications for the region itself. One aim is to examine the affects of changes in the geopolitical components of the Caribbean on perceptions and diplomatic strategies in the United States. It seems proper to explore to what extent geopolitical perception from the past remains valid, and also to what extent adjustments appear needed. Predictions, however, are offered cautiously and recommendations are both personal and tentative.

Although the Gulf/Caribbean area is treated as a geopolitical unit, the small islands are given greatest attention. This volume is part of a series. Details regarding political conditions in countries along the continental rim, as well as in Cuba, Dominican Republic, Haiti, and Puerto Rico, are surveyed by other scholars. The focus here is on the small eastern Caribbean islands, Jamaica, The Bahamas, and Trinidad and Tobago. Other countries in the region are dealt with as geopolitical actors or as influences on the states defined. In that context, however, they appear often. Inherent in a geographical approach is concern with the totality of place. Thus the environmental setting is given short but thorough consideration. A central theme is that comprehensive understanding of a region provides a superior basis for successful policy formulation.

REFERENCES

Child, John. 1979. "Geopolitical Thinking in Latin America." *Latin American Research Review*, 14, pp. 89–111.

Lowenthal, David. 1962. "The Range and Variation of Caribbean Societies." Reprinted in *Readings in Cultural Geography*, edited by Philip L. Wagner and Marvin W. Mikesell, pp. 186–94. Chicago: University of Chicago Press.

Manspach, Richard W. et al. 1976. *The Web of World Politics: Nonstate Actors in a Global System*. Englewood Cliffs, NJ: Prentice-Hall.

Rostlund, Erhard. 1955. *Outline of Cultural Geography*. Berkeley: University of California Press.

Sauer, Carl O. 1981. "The Indian Food Production in the Caribbean." *Geographical Review*, 71, July, pp. 272–80.

2

GEOGRAPHIC SETTING

LOCATIONAL RELATIONSHIPS

The Gulf of Mexico and Caribbean Sea combined are a western bulge of the Atlantic Ocean. The fact that this ocean extension is island-studded and partially separates two continents has contributed to its past and present significance. The area of the combined seas is large, with a total water expanse of roughly 1.35 million square miles. The addition of 92,000 square miles of islands produces for the region a total area nearly half that of the conterminous United States. From Corpus Christi, Texas, to Barbados the distance is over 2,600 miles, whereas about 1,600 miles separate Colombia, at the southern margin of the Gulf of Darien, from Alabama (see Map 2). Location, distance, and area are unvarying geographic realities that affect human activities in a number of ways.

The Gulf/Caribbean area consists of two semienclosed seas joined by the Yucatan Channel. The Straits of Florida provide the only open-sea connection for the Gulf of Mexico. Often included in regional treatments are the Bahama Archipelago and the Turks and Caicos Islands, which lie in the Atlantic along the northeast flank. East of Cuba, a curving chain of islands picket the northern and eastern margins of the Caribbean.

Although not greatly different in size, the Gulf of Mexico and the Caribbean are quite different in geopolitical terms. Only the United States, Mexico, and Cuba—militarily the three strongest countries of the region—face the Gulf of Mexico. Frontage on the Caribbean, on the other hand, is shared by more political entities than any other arm of the sea in the world.

11

Map 2

POLITICAL UNITS OF LATIN AMERICA

SOURCE: Constructed by the author.

Roughly a score of passages connect the Atlantic and the Caribbean, besides the Yucatan link with the gulf. The Panama Canal provides a water passage between the Pacific and the Caribbean. Unlike the gulf, the Caribbean also is important as an ocean route between distant places.

The main island chain is known as the Antilles, a term that predates discovery. It appeared originally on fourteenth-century European maps to designate unseen islands thought to lie west of Portugal. Common usage distinguishes between the Greater Antilles—Cuba, Jamaica, Hispañola, and Puerto Rico—and the Lesser Antilles—the string of small islands extending toward South America. Only the Netherlands Antilles use the term officially, although the French holdings are termed the French Antilles in speech and writing and their inhabitants are known as Antilleans. The strait between Dominica and Guadeloupe divides the Lesser Antilles into the Leeward Islands on the north and the Windward Islands on the south. Despite the fact that climatically there is little sense to the usage as the Northeast Trade Winds affect both groups, the appellation endures. For reasons no more clear, Barbados, Trinidad, Tobago, and the Venezuelan islands of Margarita and Tortuga are not regarded as part of the Antilles despite similarities in size and location.

Other islands, cays (keys), and banks interrupt the water surface of the Gulf/Caribbean. In particular, groups of islands fringe both main coasts of Cuba and lie off Central America from Yucatan to Colombia. The Cayman island group west of Jamaica is the largest of the open-sea islands. A cluster of land fragments east of Nicaragua includes Isla de Providencia (Old Providence Island) and Isla San Andrés (St. Andrews Island). Revival by the Sandinista government of a once-settled dispute with Colombia over ownership of these islands has added another issue to the geopolitics of the western Caribbean.

Unavoidable in a treatment of Caribbean politics is the matter of definition. No original insights are part of the following account of the study's limits, yet omission of a clarification may cause confusion for the reader. Terms and perceptions of its extent differ. G. Etzel Pearcy, for example, considered the best overall name to be the West Indies, adding region or realm to avoid confusion with any political association (Pearcy 1965, pp. 17–19). The term has two handicaps, however. It has a distinctly British connection in origin and use, and it suggests concern primarily with islands rather than with a sea containing islands.

An alternative name for the West Indies is the Caribbean islands, whereas Caribbean America is understood to include the continental rim as well as the sea and islands. In 1982, the Reagan administration employed an equivalent variation, the Caribbean basin. Geographers have been comfortable with Middle America to designate the area between the United States and South America, although some prefer Middle America and the Caribbean to enhance precision. Problems with use of Middle America is that in the United States the term mainly conveys the sense of a mainstream political consciousness, as well as being often interchanged in usage with the regional term *Middle West*.

The continental portion of Middle America includes Mexico and Central America, which consists of seven small countries between Mexico and Colombia. Latin Americans, however, usually distinguish between Central America and Panama. The attitude has a historical basis. Panama was detached from Colombia in 1903 and continues to be regarded by many Latins politically and culturally as part of South American. Belize, independent from Britain only since September 1981, is culturally different from its neighbors. In addition, many Latin Americans regard Belize as having been unfairly seized from Guatemala by the British. Regardless of the Latin American custom, the term *Central America* as used in this book refers to all countries that lie between Mexico and Colombia.

A useful geographical subdivision of the Caribbean region is that of rimland and mainland sectors (Augelli 1962, pp. 119–27). This division recognizes racial and cultural differences resulting from contrasting economic histories. As defined, the rimland includes all Caribbean islands and the western coastal margin from northern Belize to the Panamanian–Colombian border. The area was dominated historically by the institution of the plantation or shows in its present population composition evidence of association with that institution. The peoples are black or partly black, with concentrations of East Indians, and a white upper-class structure. The languages and most of the culture are European in origin. An economy based on agricultural exports—sugar in particular—was dominant. The Bahamas and the Turks and Caicos Islands are excluded from the rimland despite some resemblances due to a lack of a plantation history. Plantations were part of the history of the Central American coastal zone, although the black populations there result as much from the dumping of black and Carib refugees from the islands as from slavery.

The interior area categorized as mainland was dominated culturally by the hacienda, where a white elite minority held political and economic control over majority peoples who were racially indian or mestizo. Unlike the plantation, the hacienda functioned more as a self-sustaining way of life than as a commercial enterprise. A recent manifestation of the contrasts between the two culture realms occurred in Nicaragua in 1981. There, ostensibly in the interests of state security, the Sandinista central government forcibly relocated thousands of the partly black Miskito, Sumus, and Ramas indians. A lack of understanding and trust between the two groups is hardly surprising in light of the fact that the coastal peoples differ from other Nicaraguans in terms of race, language, religion, social organization, and basic economy.

Coastal Venezuela, Colombia, and even parts of Mexico also exhibit at least some of the qualities of the rimland. In fact, on the basis of the above characteristics, the concept of a rimland could with logic be extended even further to encompass the southern United States, the Guianas, and even parts of coastal Brazil. Like any simple scheme intended to divide complex elements, application of the rimland–mainland idea requires adjustments in some circumstances. Yet its thesis seems valid. It is a useful concept in an effort to consider the geopolitics of the Caribbean.

Broad use of the term *Caribbean* must contend with inconsistencies. Unless the term *Gulf/Caribbean* is employed, the United States is a part only through political control of Puerto Rico and several of the Virgin Islands. In a locational sense the Bahamas, Turks and Caicos Islands, and El Salvador also are not a part as none touches the Caribbean Sea. Yet custom and common sense favor the perception that they are part of a Caribbean region or realm.

The Guianas present another problem in classification. Situated on the continent southeast of Venezuela, they neither fringe the Caribbean nor are islands. The name, however, comes from a native American name meaning land of many waters. The sea and rivers do dominate the coastal environment, which was the only portion of the Guianas to receive serious European contacts. Mountain barriers did and do make surface travel difficult between coast and interior.

The British, Dutch, and French colonies in the Guianas were exceptions on a continent conquered elsewhere by the Spanish and Portuguese. A result of this situation is that throughout their history, the Guianas have functioned as islands. All contacts were by sea with distant places.

Plantations established by the English and Dutch were worked by slaves from Africa and later by contract laborers from South Asia. The effect was to create cultures similar to those of the rimland. Plantations, however, never became established in French Guiana, and it remains a backwater place with unique characteristics. For these reasons, inhabitants of Guyana and Suriname, and West Indians as well, regard the Guianas as part of a Caribbean region despite the physical separation. Since independence, both countries routinely have been included in various Caribbean regional organizations.

The sea was not called the Caribbean at first. Prior to the discoveries, the Spanish had called all the western Atlantic the *Mar del Norte*. After the voyages of Columbus the usage was extended to the Caribbean. Following discovery by Balboa the Pacific became known as the *Mar del Sur*, a designation that is logical in light of the fact that the Pacific is indeed south of Panama. To the Spanish the continental rim south of the Caribbean became known as *Tierra Firme*, which the English eventually transmuted into *Spanish Main*. Most wealth in precious metal and gems was transported from mainland sources to Spain, and privateers soon found it easier to attack the treasure ships than the fortified towns. In time the entire sea and its islands came to be known as the Spanish Main. Sailing *to* the Spanish Main evolved to sailing *on* the Spanish Main.

Caribbean as a name for the sea was introduced in 1773 in the *West Indies Atlas* by Thomas Jefferys. His stated view was that it was better to attach this arbitrary name than to leave the ocean space "quite anonymous."

(This historical account is adapted mainly from Sauer 1966, pp. 2–4). Because Carib peoples were native to the islands then held by the British, the association was natural. General acceptance of the name was slow, however, especially in Spanish lands.

In this study, *Caribbean, Caribbean basin*, and *Caribbean region* are employed interchangeably to denote the semienclosed ocean, islands, and fringing mainland. *Island Caribbean* is intended to exclude the countries on the continents. The choices have the merits of convenience and wide public identification in the United States. The major focus is on conditions in the small islands, specifically excluding Cuba, Hispañola, and Puerto Rico. General geopolitical analysis, however, entails attention to the entire region, including the seas and neighboring countries.

Panama Canal

The Caribbean region lies not only south but also largely east of the United States. Trinidad, for example, is about 1,200 miles east of Miami. Even the Panama Canal is east of Miami. This circumstance long has favored sea links between the region and Europe, a relationship that persists despite decolonization and development of closer ties with the United States. Patterns of sea trade and air travel reflect this skewed juxtaposition of the continents. One effect is to make Miami the main focus of air travel between the northern and southern regions. In function as well as present ethnic composition, Miami can logically be viewed as the northern margin of Latin America. Certainly many Latin Americans of wealth regard it so. In terms of ocean trade, on the other hand, Miami is of minor importance.

For about a century following European discoveries the Caribbean islands served mainly as refitting stations for ships from Europe. The main wealth of precious metals and jewels came from the mainland. The Caribbean islands also were part of an outer line of defense, with great fortresses built to guard spacious harbors at San Juan, Puerto Rico; Havana and Santiago, Cuba; and Cartagena, Colombia. The vital destinations were further west at Vera Cruz, Mexico, and Portobelo, Panama (just east of present-day Colon). These latter harbors were the conduits through which flowed the riches of Mexico and Peru, respectively (Mathews 1975, p. 223). Return voyages favored a northern route through the Straits of Florida, where westerly winds were probable and the easterly thrust of the Gulf Stream was certain. Then as now the Providence channels through The Bahamas were a favored route toward Europe.

By 1600 a decline in the flow of mainland treasure coincided with a shifting of power in Europe from the Iberian countries to France, England, and Holland. Spanish hegemony over the Caribbean weakened as a consequence. Several decades of colonial redistribution ensued, accompanied by gradual development of the sugar cane plantation as a socio-economic system and source of profit. After 1650 the main center of wealth generated in the Americas became the region from Jamaica to the Guianas (Sheridan 1970, pp. 10–11). Sugar never was important in the Bahamas, and large-scale development in Cuba is barely a century old. Along with this change in location came a refocus on trade routes. Imports of necessities, including slaves to maintain the economy, were more than matched by exports of sugar and rum. In Europe the Caribbean became renowned as a place of extravagant riches.

Conversely, the relative decline of gold shipments from Peru was not matched by increases in shipment of other goods overland across the isthmus of Panama. The California Gold Rush beginning in 1850 increased Caribbean traffic only slightly, in that most crossings of Middle America by gold seekers followed the Isthmus of Tehuantepec in Mexico which fronts on the gulf. Thus during much of the 1700s and 1800s the western Caribbean was a neglected backwater in terms of trade. Its shores generated few exports, its waters connected few places of importance.

This situation was altered profoundly by completion of the Panama Canal. Sea traffic began to increase in 1907 when the United States renewed work on the earlier French project that had stalled. Besides materials a stream of workers came, mainly from Caribbean islands. Canal traffic commenced on August 15, 1914, with the passage of the *S.S. Ancon.* The event caused a major reorientation of world ocean routes and a striking change in the significance of the Caribbean Sea. The canal became an actual rather than a potentially strategic place for the military and commercial interests of the United States. Plus there was a reappraisal of the strategic significance of other places in and along the Caribbean. This reappraisal had diplomatic consequences that continue to affect events within the region. The geopolitical importance of a canal as well as the strategic qualities of places along its approaches were analyzed clearly in the 1890s by Captain A. T. Mahan. His interpretations and recommendations have been influential in Washington even into the 1980s (see Mahan 1898, 59–107 and 271–314).

Despite the canal's obvious contribution to the naval capabilities of the United States, its publicly stated main purpose was to get vessels from one ocean to another with the least possible delay, efficiently, at moderate tolls, and without discriminating among users (Padelford and Gibbs 1975, p. xii). This objective seems to have been served. Although roughly 66 percent of all cargo through the canal goes to or comes from United States ports, vessels of 60 countries commonly use the canal in a single year. Its presence is an obvious advantage in shortening trade routes. This fact is perhaps best appreciated by noting that sea travel between San Francisco and New York is shortened by 7,860 miles by way of the Panama Canal (Padelford and Gibbs 1975, p. 4).

A measure of the value of the canal to other countries is the percent of national sea-bourne commerce that passes through the canal. Some figures from 1973 are suggestive (Padelford and Gibbs 1975, p. 72, Footnote). Nicaragua had the highest relative dependence on the canal with nearly 77 percent of its ocean trade passing through it. El Salvador had two-thirds; Ecuador over half; Peru two-fifths; Chile, Colombia, and Guatemala roughly a third; and Panama and Costa Rica over a fourth. Significance of the canal for Pacific and Central American countries is obvious. In contrast, Mexico and the United States had almost identical figures of less than 17 percent of total ocean commerce passing by way of Panama. Their total trade volume was much higher, of course. That the Panama Canal is primarily of benefit to Western Hemisphere countries is suggested by the fact that it was used by only about 1.5 percent of trade of the United Kingdom and The Netherlands, two of the world's leading maritime countries.

The presence of locks imposes limits on the size and number of ships that may transit the canal. These consist of the Gatun Locks on the Caribbean side and the Pedro Miguel and Miraflores locks on the Pacific side. Lock chambers are 1,000 feet and 110 feet wide, with a full water depth of 42 feet over the sills (Padelford and Gibbs 1975, p. 31). As a result, maximum dimensions for ships seeking transit have been established. They are: 975 feet long, 106 feet wide, 40 feet draft, with a maximum dead-weight tonnage of 65,000 tons (Padelford and Gibbs 1975, p. 106). As of 1974 no commercial ships with such maximum dimensions had yet transited the canal, although Missouri-class battleships with beams of 108 feet had been squeezed through the locks. The record cargo tonnage was 61,078 long tons of coal (Padelford and Gibbs 1975, p. 45).

For many years ship designers observed a measure known as "Panamax" to produce ships suitable for normal transit through the locks. Since about 1950 this standard has been exceeded often although mainly only fractionally larger ships still are capable of transit. Most prominent of these have been a group of specialized container ships that serve the U.S. East Coast and Japan. These craft crowd the actual maximums in all dimensions (McGinnis 1974, p. 222).

In addition, two of the most important types of ships now in use are generally too large in one or more dimensions to pass through the locks. These are large oil tankers and attack aircraft carriers, although some of the latter such as the U.S.S. *Lexington* can make use of the canal. Several other types of vessels, such as some passenger liners and dry bulk carriers, also are too large. Missile-carrying submarines, with the possible exception of the Trident class, can transit the canal, although both the nature of their cargo and the high visibility involved make them rare users.

As of January 1982 one source reported 1,421 oil tankers of more than 70,000 deadweight tons in commission, each of which was too large to pass through the canal. Though this total does not encompass every oversize tanker, it is suggestive of the disconformity between canal dimensions and the current tanker fleet. Despite a sharp drop in the world demand for large tankers that has essentially ended new construction and caused the scrapping of others, deep-draft craft can be expected to carry most world oil, at least over the next few decades. In this context it is well to remember that petroleum is, in both value and tonnage, the most important commodity in international trade (Bartlett 1982, p. 47). Thus, neither the most valuable cargo nor the most powerful naval craft currently make common use of the canal. In this important sense, its strategic significance has declined sharply since about 1950.

Aside from the restraints of size, the necessity for locks imposes other limitations. Despite an abundant normal rainfall for replenishment, the water-storage capacity of Gatun Lake can sustain little more than a lockage rate of 40 changes per day (McGinnis 1974, p. 219). Lockage water needs vary little regardless of ship size. Drought is uncommon, yet low water does at times restrict the number of lockages possible. Time needed for transit is also a factor that can limit the volume of traffic. The aim of the Canal Company long had been to achieve an average time of 17 hours for a ship to be in canal waters. Of this total, eight to ten hours were needed for actual transit. For a number of reasons, shutdowns for maintenance for example, this goal was not always achieved (Padelford and Gibbs 1975, p. 115). In its present state of development, the maximum rated capacity of the Panama Canal is 26,800 transits per year. This figure should be evaluated in light of annual transits of 14,800 in 1975 and an estimated 21,300 by the year 2000 (Ibid, p. 189). Increases in the volume of traffic are both possible and anticipated.

In 1982 the only serious alternative to the canal for container cargo traffic between East Asia and the U.S. East Coast was the railroad Land Bridge System across the United States. This system also served trade between East Asia and Western Europe, although this latter connection was itself challenged by a different land bridge system by way of the Soviet Trans-Siberian Railroad. An alternative route that offers more direct competition came into operation in 1982. This is the SMT (*Servicio Multimodal Transistmico*) developed by the Mexican government. The SMT makes use of the narrow trough occupied by the Isthmus of Tehuantepec. With a minimum width of 125 miles and a maximum elevation of about 800 feet, Tehuantepec has long served as a comparatively easy interocean connecting route. As developed, a railroad of 189 miles (304 kms.) connects Coatzacoalcos on the gulf with Salina Cruz on the Pacific. A parallel highway also has been improved. Rail transit of 12 hours and highway transit of six hours are planned.

In addition to the upgrading of the railroad and highway routes, development of the SMT involved other improvements as well. At each port two berths of 250 meters (820 feet) in length and 12 meters (39.37 feet) in depth were constructed. Installed in conjunction were cargo cranes, storage areas, specialized rail cars, and highway carriers. Computerized management is involved. A scheduled daily rail run in each direction was designed to provide an annual interocean transportation capacity of 58,400 TEUs (20-foot-long container packages). Trucks provide flexibility to accommodate unusual demands (information from personal correspondence with Fernando Bueno Alvarez, SMT).

Because Tehuantepec is roughly 1,100 miles closer to the United States than is the Panama Canal, interocean connections for container cargo trade with U.S. ports will be shortened at least by 2,000 miles. Development of the SMT then can have several effects. It provides a shorter and speedier alternative route to the Panama Canal for container shipments, a category of cargo of rapidly increasing significance in world trade. As such the competition can be expected to restrain the transit charges established by each government, lessen the rate of increase in canal traffic, and reduce still further the strategic importance of the canal. To some extent there also can be a redirection of ocean traffic, at least of container ships. Vessels connecting North America or Europe with the eastern end of the SMT need not enter the Caribbean at all. A geopolitical consequence of its increased use, then, would be a relative decrease in the volume of traffic in the Caribbean and an increase in traffic through the Straits of Florida.

POLITICAL ENTITIES

There are 23 island political entities in the Caribbean, of which 12 were independent states at the beginning of 1983. The remaining 11 dependencies are self-governing in internal affairs. (St. Kitts–Nevis achieved independence on September 12, 1983, making 13 independent states.) A number of other islands—Cozumel, Turneffe Cay, Corn Island, and Margarita, for example—are politically part of mainland countries. The different units are listed in Table 2 in decreasing order of area. Population estimates and densities as well as political status as of January 1983 are included to provide further perspective. Despite a rough correspondence between population numbers and area, several exceptions illustrate that the Caribbean islands are a collection of contrasts in a sea of surprisingly uniform physical attributes.

The countries of Cuba, Dominican Republic, and Haiti, plus the U.S. Commonwealth of Puerto Rico are outside the declared focus of this study, which is to say that the four most populous Caribbean entities are treated peripherally. Attention is devoted mainly to nine independent states and ten

TABLE 2 Island Political Units in the Caribbean Region

	Area (sq. mi.)	Population (1981 est.)	Population per sq. mi.	Year of independence, political status
Cuba	44,218	9,700,000	219	1902, Socialist, Republic
Dominican Republic	18,704	5,515,000	295	1844, Republic
Haiti	10,714	5,040,000	470	1804, Republic (president for life)
The Bahamas	5,382	250,000	46	1973, Parliamentary State
Jamaica	4,244	2,210,000	521	1962, Parliamentary State
*Puerto Rico	3,435	3,223,000	938	U.S. Commonwealth
Trinidad and Tobago	1,980	920,000	465	1962, Republic
*Guadeloupe	687	320,000	466	French Overseas Department
*Martinique	425	310,000	729	French Overseas Department
*Netherlands Antilles	383	255,000	666	Overseas part of Netherlands Realm
Dominica	290	83,000	286	1978, Republic
St. Lucia	238	124,000	521	1979, Parliamentary State
Antigua–Barbuda	170	75,000	441	1981, Parliamentary State
Barbados	166	275,000	1,657	1966, Parliamentary State
*Turks and Caicos Islands	166	6,700	40	U.K., Colony
St. Vincent and the Grenadines	150	126,000	840	1979, Parliamentary State
Grenada	133	114,000	857	1974, Parliamentary State
*U.S. Virgin Islands	133	100,000	752	U.S. Unincorporated Territory
*St. Kitts–Nevis	104	53,000	510	U.K., Associated State
*Cayman Islands	100	18,000	180	U.K., Colony
*British Virgin Islands	59	14,000	237	U.K., Colony
*Montserrat	40	11,000	275	U.K., Colony
*Anguilla	34	7,700	226	U.K., Dependency Status
Totals	91,955	28,750,400	313	

*Dependency
SOURCE: Area, population, and densities adapted from *Goode's World Atlas*, 16th edition (Chicago: Rand McNally & Company, 1982), pp. 237–41.

21

dependencies, all small in size and population. The miniature dimensions of these entities are part of the region's geopolitics. Ministates and microstates—all termed ministates for convenience here—must contend with political and economic circumstances often different from those of states of more usual sizes (see Reid 1974 for a specific analysis of these situations). Allegiances tend to be insular, autonomy is constrained by external influences (Clarke 1976, p. 8).

Political diversity in the Caribbean has a long history, although the presence of a dozen sovereign states results mainly from changes since 1962. Even Cuba, which with Haiti and the Dominican Republic are relatively old established countries, attained national independence only in 1902.[1] The countries came into being as part of the post-World War II decolonization process that so profoundly altered world politics. Even entities that retain political ties with metropolitan states gained greater self-rule over that span of time.

The first of these postwar changes was the French law of March 19, 1946, that conferred the status of overseas departments (*departements d'autre-mer*, known as DOM) on Guadeloupe and Martinique, along with French Guiana and La Reunion (Lasserre and Mabileau 1972, p. 82). In a legal, if not always in a functional, sense, inhabitants of these islands gained rights comparable to citizens in the metropolitan country. Although Puerto Ricans were granted full U.S. citizenship in 1917, they obtained the right to elect their own chief executive only in 1947. Following a 1951 plebiscite, Puerto Rico become a commonwealth in 1952. Inhabitants of the U.S. Virgin Islands were made citizens in 1927, but were given increasing self-government in a series of measures from 1954 to 1973 (Banks and Overstreet 1981, pp. 521–22). The Netherlands Antilles became an entity constitutionally equal to The Netherlands in 1954, a relationship similar in many ways to that of Guadeloupe and Martinique with France.

In the British-held islands of the Caribbean proper, the first major change toward greater self-rule was the West Indies Federation. This attempt at collective government lasted only from 1958 to 1962. Its failure had several causes but fundamental was a nearly overpowering sense of personal identification with individual islands. Independence of the two largest members, Jamaica and Trinidad and Tobago, came the year of the breakup. The next most populous, Barbados, chose independence in 1966. It was in 1966 that Britain devised the West Indies Act. Under its provisions member islands became internally self-governing Associated States. External dependency with the United Kingdom was voluntary and could be terminated at any time by either party (Abbott 1981, p. 69).

Beginning in 1967, Antigua–Barbuda, Dominica, Grenada, St. Kitts–Nevis, Anguilla, St. Lucia, and St. Vincent became Associated States and held that status for varying periods of time. Most soon opted for sovereignty and as of June 1983 only St. Kitts–Nevis remained an Associated State. The Anguilla Act of September 19, 1980, formally granted to that island the stature of a dependency separate from St. Kitts–Nevis. The effect was to formalize a political detachment that had existed in fact since 1969 (Abbott 1981, p. 87–8).

Remaining as British colonies were Montserrat, the Cayman Islands, the Turks and Caicos Islands, and the British Virgin Islands. Each had internal self-rule, whereas a governor appointed by the Crown retained responsibility for external affairs, defense, and internal security. Despite the status as colonies, within each there was vigorous expression of politics on local issues.

The fragmented nature of the region's land has contributed to a sense of island loyalty that in turn has fostered a trend toward political devolution. This trend was exhibited most strongly in the breakup of the West Indies Federation in 1962. Wherever a political unit comprises more than a single island, a potential for devolution exists. Trinidad and Tobago, for example, were merged into a single Crown Colony in 1888 and passed through various stages of decolonization as a unit. the separateness of Tobago remained an issue, nonetheless, to the point that in September 1980 a House of Assembly for Tobago was established within the governing structure of the country, an obvious device to mollify a sentiment for divergence.

Presence of a centrifugal mood is virtually ubiquitous. Until separation in 1959 the Cayman Islands were a dependency of Jamaica. Anguilla functioned as part of the Associated State of St. Kitts–Nevis for only about two years. In St. Vincent and the Grenadines an armed revolt began on Union Island the day following the new country's first election. Police officers were sent to put down the attempt at detachment. Part of the problem is the fact that despite the small sizes of the region's political entities, most have outlying islands even smaller. These fragments necessarily are subordinate to a central government located elsewhere. Grand Cayman subordinates Little Cayman and Cayman Brac. Antigua subordinates Barbuda and St. Kitts subordinates Nevis. The Grenadines are divided politically between St. Vincent and Grenada. Governed from Guadeloupe are Marie Galante, Desirade, Les Saintes, St. Barthelemy, and the northern part of St. Martin. The Dutch southern third of that island is even spelled differently, St. Maarten.

More complex are The Bahamas and The Netherlands Antilles. The Bahamas are an archipelago with roughly 700 islands and perhaps as many more cays and rocks. Most of these are uninhabited and only about 17 have a population of more than 100. The geographical cohesiveness of an archipelago along with a historical treatment as a single political entity have contributed to a sense of collective national identity stronger than is common in the region (see Lewis 1974). Internal administrative structure is divided on the basis of islands. But other than New Providence (Nassau) and Grand Bahama (Freeport), islands are administered by centrally appointed commissioners.

The Netherlands Antilles consist of far fewer islands than The Bahamas, yet lack the physical coherence of an archipelago and are more widely separated. The political structure is that of a federation, with four island territories: Aruba, Bonaire, Curaçao, and the Netherlands Windward Islands. This last unit consists of St. Eustatius (Statia), Saba, and the part island of St. Maarten. Each territory has a degree of individual internal autonomy, with separate elected Island Councils and Boards. The federal government is in Willenstad on Curacao with most power held by a parliament called the *Staaten*. A governor appointed by the Crown has mainly ceremonial duties (Hoetink 1972, p. 108). The strongest pressures for separation come from Aruba. Despite a conference in February 1981 aimed at mollifying the sentiment for division, the Aruba delegation maintained its insistence on an early independence from the federation. Regardless of the details of the eventual political settlement, continued close cooperation in a commonwealth relationship can be anticipated.

All nine of the newly independent Caribbean states were former parts of the British Empire and each chose to remain part of the British Commonwealth. The prevalent form of government is generally referred to as the Westminster model. In essence this form consists of an appointed representative of the Crown (governor-general), an appointed upper house (called a senate in most cases), and a popularly elected lower house (often termed a house of assembly). The governor-general has limited duties, one of which is to appoint members of the senate, which in turn has limited powers. Legislative authority, particularly on budget matters, is vested in the representative house of assembly, whereas executive powers rest with a prime minister. This latter individual is appointed by the governor-general but is first selected by the lower house and serves at its pleasure.

In general, variations from this model are minor. Dominica and St. Vincent and the Grenadines have no appointed upper house, only an elected unicameral legislature. Dominica and Trinidad and Tobago have presidents rather than governor-generals, though the functions of the positions are similar. The most significant difference is that the presidents are selected domestically rather than appointed by the Crown.

Most different are conditions on Grenada following the coup of March 13, 1979, led by Maurice Bishop. Once in control he suspended the constitution and announced formation of a People's Revolutionary Government. As of January 1983 the political form was of a leftist personal dictatorship governing by means of proclamations and directives. Despite a Marxist and anti-Western tone to his actions and rhetoric, Bishop insisted that no change in Grenada's relationship with the British Crown was planned. Even the Governor-General remained in place, albeit with powers more limited than previously.

Actions toward decolonization were motivated by a mood in London for disengagement overseas as well as by yearnings for independence in the West Indies. It must be recognized that for many island residents, colonial status was as much a state of mind as a political condition. Important to such people are the ceremonial trappings and personal values stemming from colonial ties. One result has been a sense of ambivalence on the islands. Inner personal conflicts between the longstanding appeal of things European and rational desires for a greater sense of West Indian nationhood carry over into domestic politics and international relations. An effect on many islands is the projection of an Afro-Saxon image, an image that may endure depending upon the impact of the aspirations of poor black societies on parliamentary governments (Clarke 1976, p. 13).

PHYSICAL SETTING

Prerequisite to consideration of the geopolitics of a region is awareness of its physical character. In brief, the Gulf/Caribbean region is an island-studded tropical arm of the Atlantic that lies between two continental masses linked by a narrow land bridge. Far more details than these are needed, however, to provide necessary understanding of environmental factors that long have affected human activities there. The following brief description is intended to draw attention to those features and processes thought to be pertinent to the region's geopolitics.

Islands and Sea Floor

The Gulf of Mexico and Caribbean Sea differ in geological origins as well as in location. Most of the sea floor of the gulf consists of sedimentary rock with origins similar to those of the coastal plain in the United States and in Mexico west of the Yucatan Peninsula. The Caribbean Sea and islands, on the other hand, are associated tectonically with the Yucatan, Central America, and the mountain margin of South America. The combined sea floors consist of six large physiographic units (Gulf of Mexico, Yucatan Basin, Cayman Trough, Colombia Basin, Venezuelan Basin, and Grenada Trough) plus several smaller deep basins (Emery and Uchupi 1975, p. 239). These depressions are separated by linear zones of uplift which produce shallow water dividers with clusters of banks and cays as well as a number of small islands.

The processes of geological formation were such that the areas of thick, organic-rich, land-derived sediments lie along the northwest and southeast continental margins. Such strata are favorable for the development of gas and petroleum deposits. The broad belt between is less favorable because of a generally low organic content (Emery and Uchupi 1975, p. 241). The character has not prevented drilling searches and even small finds. Nonetheless, the likelihood that sizable fossil-fuel resources will be found on or near the Caribbean islands is small.

The Gulf of Mexico and the Caribbean Sea are essentially separated by three large limestone platforms—the Yucatan, Cuba, and Florida. The Bahama Bank is similar in form but is composed of a crystalline platform capped by coral islands (Niddrie 1971, pp. 75–76). To the south is a zone termed the Greater Antillean Complex Mountains. These were formed in conjunction with the east–west trending ranges of Guatemala and Honduras and consist of limestone and sandstone strata, underlain by granites and steeply folded and faulted. This zone includes Jamaica, Hispañola, and the Virgin Islands, as well as the Sierra Maestra of southeastern Cuba. The form is of linear ranges with intervening troughs. Two lines of structures extend undersea to connect with Central America. The northern one surfaces in Misteriosa Bank and the Cayman Islands. The other produces shallows, banks, and several small islands between Jamaica and Central America (West and Augelli 1971, pp. 31–32).

Origins of the smaller islands are more complex. Islands and banks flanking Venezuela are geologically related to the ranges on the continent that extend eastward from the Andes. Included are Aruba, Curaçao, Bonaire, Margarita, Trinidad, Tobago, and the eastern part and continental shelf of Barbados. Actually, southern Trinidad is an extension of the sedimentary structures that underlie the Orinoco Basin. A zone of complex folded rock forms an eastern margin of the Lesser Antilles. Where uplifted to form islands (Maria Galante, Antigua, the eastern half of Guadeloupe, and parts of Barbados) these soft sediments have been eroded to form a low-lying surface of only moderate relief. Several islands are more coral than limestone in origin, Anguilla and Barbuda, for example.

Of more recent origin (Pleistocene Period) is an inner volcanic arc of the Lesser Antilles. Present are volcanic peaks, including several of recent activity, with aprons of ash or weathered dark lava that slope gently to the sea. In places waves have reworked this volcanic debris into beaches of black sand. It is islands of this type that conform most closely to the popular image of a tropical island. The string of volcanic islands stretches from Grenada to St. Martin (St. Maarten) and includes the Grenadines, St. Vincent, St. Lucia, Martinique, Dominica, Western Guadeloupe, Montserrat, St. Kitts (St. Christopher), Nevis, St. Eustasius, and Saba. These islands, like most in the region, are fringed by coral reefs (adapted freely from Niddrie 1971, pp. 75–76).

The tectonic activity that produced the islands and bordering continental mountains continues. Earthquakes are common in a zone that surrounds the

Caribbean. The gulf as well as Yucatan, Bahamas, and Cuba except for the Sierra Maestra lie outside the circle of greatest activity.

Shocks usually originate in the deep passages between islands although, as is the case with zones of tectonic instability worldwide, most quakes are mild. Even minor quakes, however, can trigger damaging landslides when steep slopes are soaked by rain. Historically earthquakes have been especially damaged in southern Cuba and Jamaica. Santiago de Cuba was virtually leveled at least five times, most recently in 1947. Kingston, Jamaica, was nearly destroyed in 1907 just as massive shocks essentially obliterated nearby Port Royal centuries earlier. The coasts also are subject at times to tremor-generated ocean waves (*tsunami*). Although severe quakes are infrequent, they are an everpresent potential hazard throughout the Caribbean.

On the volcanic islands the picturesque cones constitute a rarely expressed by constant menace. The most deadly historic eruption was in 1902 when Mt. Pelée on Martinque blew its top and released deadly gases that swept downslope and killed perhaps 30,000 in St. Pierre. Mt. Soufrière on St. Vincent erupted at roughly the same time, causing roughly 2,000 deaths. Both volcanoes have been active since 1902, Mt. Soufrière most recently in 1980.

Climate

Save for the northern Bahamas all the island region lies within the tropics, and even The Bahamas enjoys all-season warmth. It is this lack of winter cold rather than especially high temperatures that contributes so greatly to the appeal of the Caribbean to the inhabitants of higher latitudes. The absence of cold is also significant in terms of crop ecology.

Temperatures also are affected by the fact that most islands are small and the surrounding sea is warm. Ocean temperatures in the region range from 73°F to 84°F and winds from any direction moderate land conditions. Locations sufficiently inland to be little tempered by the sea are present only on the four large islands. Land temperatures range annually from 70°F to 81°F in Nassau, The Bahamas; 76.5°F to 81.5°F in Kingston, Jamaica; and 79.5°F to 82°F in Georgetown, Guyana (Macpherson, 1973, p. 6). Consistent warmth is characteristic everywhere, except on the higher slopes of mountainous islands. The quality of crops such as coffee benefits from the lower temperatures present on these higher elevations.

The entire region is affected by the Northeast Trade Winds which are particuarly persistent in the Lesser Antilles and Caribbean Sea. Only in The Bahamas, the Gulf of Mexico, and at times in Cuba do westerly winds dominate during the winter. Nearly everywhere then, for roughly 90 percent of the time, winds blow from the northeast or east at an average velocity of about 15 miles per hour. Along with the low seasonal temperature variation, this consistency in wind direction is a notable feature of the climate. As a rule, winds in the Caribbean are more east than northeast during the winter months.

Despite the expanse of ocean surface, trade winds are irregular producers of precipitation. Originating in the Bermuda–Azores High Pressure Cell, they consist principally of descending, warming air. As a consequence, although they absorb vast quantities of water vapor from the warm ocean, they are inherently stable. Unless triggered upward by barometric depressions, convection from large land surfaces, or highlands, the trades are drying rather than moistening winds.

Perhaps the only consistent description of rainfall in the Caribbean region is that it is seasonal. For most places the heaviest rainfall begins several weeks following the northward passage of the direct rays of the sun. Thus in more northerly locations the maximum rainfall occurs later in the year. In the Turks and Caicos Islands the rainiest period is the fall (Macpherson 1973, p. 13). For most of the region long dry seasons are normal. Indeed, certain parts of and even whole islands are nearly arid.

Heavier rainfall normally occurs over a period of several months and alternates with dry seasons of differing length. In general there are long dry seasons. In the absence of wide temperature variations, the amount of rainfall distinguishes seasonality. There is a difference in usage between Spanish-speaking lands and those colonized from northern Europe. In Spain, summer (*verano*) is dry and winter (*invierno*) is wet. Similar terms were applied in the Caribbean despite the fact that the months of occurrence were reversed. As a result, January is summer to those on Spanish-speaking islands and winter to the English, Dutch, and French.

The affect of highlands on precipitation patterns is very great. Moisture-laden air from the east forced to rise over land barriers produces very high rates of local precipitation. Thus, although irregular in distribution, the location of orographic wetness is predictably on the eastern and northern slopes of mountainous islands. The opposite sides even of small islands often are quite dry. Rainfall also is small in amount and irregular on low-lying islands such as Anguilla or Aruba. Even the eastern shorelines of islands receive relatively little rain, often in view of rain pelting nearby higher slopes. Regardless of the amount, the rain that does occur usually comes in the form of hard showers of short duration. Generalizations regarding annual amounts are difficult because of sharp variations within short distances. For lowland sites suitable for agriculture, however, yearly totals of 40 to 60 inches are normal.

The climate of the region constitutes an asset with respect to economic development. Continuous warmth permits production of a wide range of tropical crops. Of benefit also is the seasonal nature of precipitation. Sugar cane, cotton, and coffee are three tropical crops that are favored by presence of a dry season. The Caribbean is as well-suited climatologically for sugar cane production as any area in the world. It was these tropical climates in lands controlled by and accessible to Europeans that stimulated development of the plantation economies which have been dominant over much of the period since 1650 A.D.

The most destructive natural hazard is the tropical cyclone known best by the Arawak Indian name of hurricane. Such storms originate over the South Atlantic and western Caribbean, normally during a period from June to November. Strong winds[2] circulate around a center of calm (the "eye") several miles in diameter. Rainfall is very heavy, with much lightning and sometimes tornados as well. The system of wind and rain can extend over 200 miles and moves slowly (15–35 miles per hour), at times stopping and even reversing direction. As a rule their tracks are to the west and northwest, with a movement northward in the western Caribbean. Only rarely do hurricanes affect land south of a line from Trinidad to Central Nicaragua.

Damage on land can be produced by an advance wave, strong winds, or torrential rain, and sometimes by all three. Flooding and landslides usually cause most damage to buildings and roads, whereas tree crops and boats are harmed by strong winds. Hurricanes are predictable only with regard to their season of occurrence, and there are exceptions even to that aspect. They are frequent enough to be regarded as a normal climate element, although only a few a year normally produce damage on land. Some of exceptional size and duration cause damage over most of the Caribbean. Others may affect only a single island or stretch of coast. In recent decades, tracking by aircraft and warning systems do much to reduce loss of life. However, with or without warnings, property damage will result if a hurricane strikes.

In addition to powerful winds and exceptionally heavy rain the surface thrust of a hurricane can produce a surface wave in advance of the storm. Popularly mislabeled as tidal waves, these ocean waves when accentuated by shallow depths can burst without warning upon low-lying shores and cause severe damage.

Measures intended to mitigate the harmful effects of hurricanes vary. Generally structures and crops able to withstand hurricanes are selected, or there is a choice of materials and crops more easily replaced if damaged. Sugar cane, for example, suffers few ill effects from the storms. On the other hand, bananas may be devastated but replanting can restore production within a year. The economic impact of hurricanes is greatest on the crops that require spans of several years between planting and bearing age. Examples are citrus fruits, coffee, cocoa, and coconuts, all crops otherwise well-suited ecologically to the region. Because all Caribbean islands save

Trinidad are threatened annually by hurricanes, decisions regarding building sites, materials and design, and commercial crop selection necessarily take the storm danger into account.

The Sea

Despite several shallow underwater ridges, the gulf and Caribbean both occupy deep structural basins. Soundings of 1,500 to 2,100 fathoms characterize much of the gulf, with the Caribbean even deeper in general. Two exceptionally deep east–west troughs are present. One lies between Jamaica and Cuba and another north of Puerto Rico in the Atlantic. A wide continental shelf rings most of the gulf except for segments along Cuba. In the Caribbean a wide shelf is found only east of Honduras and Nicaragua. The Bahama Bank, as the name suggests, also is a wide area of shallow sea. Elsewhere, and particularly near most islands, the bottom plunges deeply only short distances offshore.

An effect is to provide deep-water passages between islands, even where the channels are rather narrow. Indeed, all major and most lesser passages are quite deep. The Straits of Florida are over 300 fathoms deep, as is the Mona Passage. The Yucatan Channel and Windward Passage exceed 1,000 fathoms in depth. Even the narrow Old Bahama Channel between Cuba and the Bahama Bank exceeds 200 fathoms, whereas the Providence Channel through the northern Bahamas is over 400 fathoms in depth. Depths restrictive for deep-draft ships exist only between the northernmost of the Lesser Antilles and in the area of the Grenadines.

The pattern of surface currents reflects closely the prevailing winds (see Map 3). Between most islands and over the open Caribbean itself there is a steady water movement from east to west. This pattern is complicated somewhat in constricted waters. For example, in the Gulf of Darien, Gulf of Honduras, and the inner curve of Cuba, circular patterns have developed. The main surface flow passes directly northward through the Yucatan Channel into the gulf. In the western gulf, surface currents are weak and indiscriminate, with a net northward orientation. In the eastern gulf, however, the Yucatan Channel currents turn clockwise to join currents moving westward past northern Cuba to form the powerful Gulf Stream. This renowned ocean river passes eastward through the Straits of Florida and increases in power as it moves northward between Florida and The Bahamas and into the Atlantic.

The effects of surface currents are less important in modern times than in the preconquest era or the age of sail. They do have increasing current significance in the matter of the spread of pollution. Oil slicks originating in the main Atlantic tanker lines are an issue of growing concern to governments in the eastern Caribbean. At the same time pollution from tankers,

Map 3

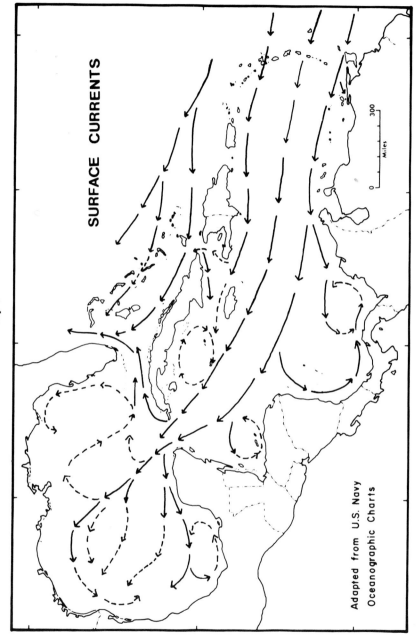

SURFACE CURRENTS

300

Miles

0

Adapted from U.S. Navy
Oceanographic Charts

SOURCE: Adapted from U.S. Navy Oceanographic Charts.

refiners, and chemical works in the eastern and southern Caribbean are carried west and sometimes north into the gulf. The areas of backwater eddies are most susceptible to accumulation of pollutants. The coating of Texas beaches from an uncontrolled well off Mexico has already produced diplomatic repercussions. The eastern islands are perhaps most sensitive in this regard because attractive beaches and clean air constitute vital resources to the tourist industry.

The combined influence of steady winds and currents from the east is reflected in the consistent selection of leeward locations for harbors in the region. In the Lesser Antilles, the main ports, and largest cities, lie on the west or south sides of islands. The pattern is only somewhat less consistent on the large islands. Even exceptions, such as San Juan, Puerto Rico, benefit from a sheltering promontory on the northeast margin. Because the main port has tended to become the capital and largest city, population concentrations also usually are greater on the west sides of islands.

Fishery resources differ greatly between the gulf and the Caribbean. The gulf, especially its northern margins, constitutes a major fishing area. In contrast the sea harvest from the Caribbean is comparatively small. Both environmental and human factors contribute to the difference. The gulf has a broad band of shallow water offshore, with waters enriched by organic sediments from numerous large rivers, the Mississippi in particular. Such conditions attract and sustain sea life. The Caribbean largely lacks such shelves and the only river system of consequence that empties into it is the Magdalena in Colombia. The Orinoco River also contributes a great amount of such materials but only to waters south of Trinidad. Ocean environments suitable to large fish and crustacean populations are uncommon, especially in the eastern Caribbean. Inhibiting also is the fact that worldwide, tropical oceans are less productive fisheries than are waters in higher latitudes.

Although the sea has been exploited as a source of food even in preconquest times (Sauer 1981, pp. 273–275), both water resources and fishing skills declined during colonial times. Neither has improved notably since. The small tidal range in the Caribbean has always hampered the harvest of littoral shellfish. On the other hand, manatee and sea turtles were abundant and a major component of Caribbean diets for Native Americans and during the early stages of conquest. Relentless hunting of both creatures as well as heavy consumption of turtle eggs reduced both populations to levels where their food potential is now slight.

On most islands fishing commonly ranges not far from shore and is small in scale. Small catches and reliance on local markets provide little incentive for greater investment. Much fishing is done primarily to feed one's own family; commercial exploitation is poorly developed. In addition, a taste for salted fish stemming from the days of slavery also reduces the market for fresh fish. Fish salted locally must compete with imports from the North

Atlantic. A preference for salted fish is particularly marked on the large islands.

Entrance into the Caribbean and western Atlantic in recent years by modern fishing craft from countries such as the United States, Poland, South Korea, and Brazil has become an issue within the region. Yet other than Cuba, few Caribbean countries have invested in comparable equipment on either a private or governmental level. Besides a low domestic demand for fresh catch and poorly developed fishing technology, exploitation of the food resources of the sea is hampered by ignorance and habits. Scientific knowledge of the ecology of the Caribbean is not high, not only in Caribbean countries but in the world at large. Logic suggests that more rational approaches, especially cooperative ones, can increase the sustained harvest from the sea. The constraints appear to be more human than environmental.

Population

Collectively the island Caribbean had a population estimated at 28.75 million in 1981. This total was roughly equal to that of Argentina or, put another way, was exceeded in the Americas only by the national populations of the United States, Brazil, and Mexico. Even when viewed solely in terms of numbers of people, the region is a significant part of the hemisphere. Most of the inhabitants, however, live on three main islands: in the countries of Cuba, Haiti, and the Dominican Republic, and in the Commonwealth of Puerto Rico. The remaining 19 political entities had only 5.27 million inhabitants (see Table 2). Within this group distribution was quite uneven. Together Jamaica and Trinidad and Tabago contained roughly 60 percent of the total, whereas Guadeloupe, Martinique, Barbados, the Netherlands Antilles, and The Bahamas had another 25 percent. The remaining 15 percent were divided among 11 different entities, from 121,000 in St. Lucia to only 6,700 in the Turks and Caicos Islands.

Population densities generally are high. The regional average of 313 persons per square mile was roughly comparable to that of Denmark and Czechoslovakia. For the 19 smaller units, however, the average exceeded 354 persons per square mile of total territory.[3] Large proportions of unproductive land make the functional densities much higher. Statistical densities differ greatly, ranging from lows of 40 and 46 in the Turks and Caicos Islands and The Bahamas, respectively, to 1,657 per square mile in Barbados. The latter figure is the highest in the world for largely rural countries. Densities exceed 500 persons per square mile as well on Jamaica, Martinique, Netherlands Antilles, St. Lucia, St. Vincent and the Grenadines, Grenada, the U.S. Virgin Islands, and St. Kitts–Nevis. Except for the Netherlands Antilles and U.S. Virgin Islands, in each of these places a large part of the population depends heavily on agriculture for subsistence. Population pressures are exceptionally severe under such circumstances.

A curious feaure of the region's human geography is a general absence of population concentrations and large cities along the continental rim. The Caribbean flank of Central America in particular is thinly settled. Most inhabitants as well as the political cores of these countries are located in the interior or along the Pacific. From the tip of Yucatan to Cartegena, Colombia, the largest city on the Caribbean is Colon, Panama, which has at best 80,000 people. Even the populous countries of Colombia and Venezuela together have no more than six or seven coastal cities exceeding 100,000 population. Maracaibo, with well over a million people is the only metropolis along the lowland and even it is not actually situated on the sea. Despite important historic and current commercial ties with the Caribbean, in terms of population and economic development Colombia and Venezuela are primarily Andean countries.

The worldwide flight from farm to city is operative also in the Caribbean, although it is not as pronounced as in many areas elsewhere. Venezuela, for example, has an urban percentage even higher than that of the United States. The urban proportions ranged from 90 percent in the virtually nonagricultural Netherlands Antilles to less than 20 percent in Grenada and St. Lucia. About half the population was urban on most islands (Population Reference Bureau 1981). Several factors help to account for comparatively lower rates of urbanization. Where land to farm is available a strongly expressed hunger for property acts to retard abandonment. This circumstance is particularly applicable on small islands where towns are not distant and access to their amenities is not difficult. In addition, economic opportunities in island towns are not that much greater than in the nearby countryside. Those who seriously seek work are likely to migrate toward wealthier countries abroad. (See Harris and Steer 1968 for analysis of this movement on Jamaica.)

Nonetheless, the shantytown is an increasingly prominent part of urban landscapes in the Caribbean. They are especially notable in larger cities such as Kingston and Montego Bay, Jamaica, and Port of Spain, Trinidad. Despite individual differences the main characteristics are consistent: ramshackle structures built of assorted materials by migrants on land for which they hold insecure tenure. The housing pattern is haphazard and infrastructure—roads, water, sewers, electricity—is absent or inadequate. Advantages are proximity to the city, low-cost shelter, and often a pride of possession and accomplishment. The social problems of unemployment, disease, and crime tend to worsen among the newly arrived inhabitants, just as the social needs for education and health care are increased. (See Eyre 1972 and also Clarke 1975 for treatment of shantytowns in Jamaica.)

Despite difficulties, shantytowns tend to develop a sense of community that provides place identity in the context of a freely chosen but unfamiliar environment. Their expansion has created distinctive constituencies within the democratic societies of the Caribbean, constituencies with different needs and aspirations than those of the traditional societal strata. Efforts to exploit their political potential differ according to their comparative size in each country. The 1980 election campaigns of Manley and Seaga in Jamaica, for example, focused heavily on such districts.

The languages of the various peoples reflect the history of colonialism. English is the language of government and education in all Commonwealth members. It also is common speech, except in parts of Dominica, Grenada, St. Lucia, and St. Vincent. On these islands periods of earlier French occupation have left cultural traces. In rural areas on the four islands local *patois* with French roots endures although the spread of improved roads, radio/TV, and formal schooling have caused its users to dwindle. Conditions on Trinidad are most complex due not only to historical occupation by French and Spanish but also to the influx of East Indians from various parts of the subcontinent. Proximity to Venezuela causes Spanish to be a required school langauge, but like most such compulsory experiences functional knowledge is uncommon.

French is the official and functional tongue on Guadeloupe and Martinique. Some creole forms remain in isolated areas but their use is declining. Similarly Dutch is the official language of the Netherlands Antilles. On the southern islands of Aruba, Bonaire, and Curaçao, however, the vernacular is a peculiar speech called *Papiamente*. An uneven mixture of Spanish–Portuguese–Dutch–English (Central Intelligence Agency 1980, p. 142), *Papiamente* is evidence of the complex history of the islands. Throughout the Netherlands Antilles, English is widely understood, a reflection of the close contacts with other islands and the heavy tourist trade. On the shared island of St. Martin/St. Maarten, residents of the Dutch portion are conversant in French.

The common religions derive from the same colonial affiliations and diffusion strains. Yet despite the British ties, Anglicans are dominant only on Barbados, where perhaps 70 percent of the populace express that preference (Central Intelligence Agency 1980, p. 14). Elsewhere other Protestant denominations claim, with the Anglicans, the religious allegiances of the majority. Roman Catholicism is understandably very strong on the French islands (95 percent) and also on Dominica and Trinidad. The faiths on Trinidad are especially mixed, with about 30 percent each of Roman Catholics, Protestants, and religions from South Asia. The last category is split about four to one, Hindu to Moslem (Central Intelligence Agency 1980, p. 196). Aside from Islam and Hinduism, rural church affiliations can be based merely on the denomination of the most accessible church (Ballard 1971, p. 39).

Only on Jamaica are faiths (often denigrated as cults) with African links at all significant. Most widely followed of these are the Ethiopian Zion Coptic Church and the *Ras Tafarian* movement. The latter is best known and potentially of greatest political importance. It developed among itinerant Christian preachers following news stories in 1930 about the ascension as emperor of Ethiopia of Haile Selassie and was stimulated by the Marcus Garvey statement that deliverance of the black man would occur when a black king was crowned in Africa. Its thesis was that blacks in the Americas were Ethiopians, that Ethiopia was the promised land, that Haile Selassie was divine, and that hope lay in a return to that place. The visible manifestations of its followers are a refusal to cut hair or wash bodies, a refusal on principle to accept employment, and smoking of marijuana during rituals.

Regarded as a harmless lunatic fringe until the 1950s, they burst onto public consciousness after several killings by its followers in 1960. Despite a spread in membership in and beyond Jamaica, the faith's reputation exceeds its small numbers. Its potential strength, or danger depending on one's perceptions, lies in its indigenous origins and antiestablishment stance. Its followers are most numerous among the urban poor, particularly in shantytowns. (This account was adopted freely from Naipaul 1963, pp. 216–19).

Social Qualities

According to published data the quality of life of most peoples of the island Caribbean ranks high in terms of usual social indicators when compared with conditions elsewhere in the third world. Admittedly, generalized national statistics tend to conceal gaps in reporting and suffer from the lack of a consistent data base for all countries. Information from the Population Reference Bureau (see Table 3) is quoted here because the organization is highly skilled, has no obvious ideological bias, and published more recent data than did other sources. Information of this sort for the Caribbean is thought to be of reasonable reliability because, except for Cuba, Haiti, and recently Grenada, there are few institutional barriers to data collection. Open and literate societies predominate. Unfortunately for the purposes of this study not all political entities were listed nor are all data available for each place.

Data for the entire region were shown in order to provide comparisons between places with generally similar geography and history. The fact that the data for each were somewhat distinctive illustrates again the region's diversity and the need for caution regarding hasty conclusions.

TABLE 3 Demographic and Social Data

Country	Rate of Natural Increase (annual percent)	Population Under Age 15 (in percent)	Infant Mortality Rate (to age 1 per 1,000 births)	Child Mortality Rate (Ages 1–4 per 1,000 births)
Antigua and Barbuda	1.3*	—	31.5	—
Bahamas	2.0	44	31.9	2
Barbados	.9	31	25.1	1
Cuba	1.2	35	19.3	1
Dominica	1.6	—	19.6	—
Dominican Republic	2.8	45	68.0	10
Grenada	2.2	—	15.4	—
Guadeloupe*	1.1	32	35.0	—
Haiti	2.6	41	115.0	21
Jamaica	2.2	40	16.2	3
Martinique	.9	32	32.0	—
Netherlands Antilles	2.2	38	25.0	1
Puerto Rico	1.7	31	20.4	1
St. Lucia	2.8	50	33.0	—
St. Vincent and the Grenadines	3.0*	—	38.1	—
Trinidad and Tobago	1.9	37	26.4	3
(World)	1.7	35	80.0	12

(continued next page)

37

TABLE 3 *(continued)*

Percent Enrolled in Primary School (boys/girls)	Percent Enrolled in Secondary School (boys/girls)	Percent of Adults Illiterate (male/female)	Per-Capita Calorie Supply as Percent of Requirements	Per-Capita Gross National Product in $U.S.
—	—	10/12	86	1,270
—	—	10/11	96	3,300
100/100	75/82	2/2	133	3,040
100/99	58/63	4/5	118	1,410
—	—	6/6	87	620
69/73	58/59	25/27	93	1,140
—	—	2/2	88	690
100/100	75/92	—	103	2,850
42/37	46/35	67/76	93	270
91/92	54/60	10/7	119	1,030
100/100	78/96	—	103	3,950
—	—	7/8	102	4,290
100/100	91/95	6/8	—	3,010
—	—	19/18	92	850
—	—	4/4	98	520
96/96	49/50	5/10	111	4,370
79/66	47/38	25/39	109	2,620

*U.S. Census Bureau Projected Estimates. This measure combines both natural rates of increase and migration.

SOURCE: Data are adapted from *World Population Data Sheet*, 1979 and 1980 and *World's Children Data Sheet*, 1978 and 1982. Published by Population Reference Bureau, Inc. (Washington, D.C.).

Perhaps the least favorable social indicators in the Caribbean are natural rates of increase. Compared with a world average of 1.7 percent, eight entities had higher rates, six had lower ones, and Puerto Rico was even. Data for Antigua and Barbuda and for St. Vincent and the Grenadines were compiled from a different source and are not strictly comparable. Only the Dominican Republic, Haiti, and St. Lucia had growth rates at levels common to other countries in tropical Latin America, Africa, and the Middle East. It is widely accepted among population specialists that doubling rates of fewer than 35 years—which result from annual growth rates of 2 percent or higher—cause especially great social and economic stress. The category of population under age 15 is a significant indicator in that it reflects the impact of growth rates over the past decade or longer. The category calls attention to the proportion of economically dependent people in a population and to the scale of educational needs. Wherever this statistic exceeds 40 percent, such strains on a society are particularly acute.

In the context of the third world, the educational levels of the island Caribbean generally are quite high. Especially noteworthy are the educational achievements in the dependencies of advanced countries, in Puerto Rico, Guadeloupe, and Martinique, for example. The data suggest that the various governments have succeeded in providing at least primary education to nearly all children. Such schooling ordinarily stresses basic literacy, math skills, training in sanitation, and inculcation of a national ethos. Secondary schools are less widely distributed and less well-attended. The consistently higher secondary school enrollments by girls than by boys presumably reflect an economic motivation for school leavings.

Higher education also is well-established, except in Haiti. Colleges and universities have long existed and are well-attended in Cuba, Dominican Republic, and Puerto Rico. On most of the smaller islands, qualified students have access to the University of the West Indies, which was formed in January 1949 and was granted university status in April 1962 (*Caribbean Year Book 1978*). The university serves all the island commonwealth members and Belize with campuses at Cave Hill, Barbados; Mona, Jamaica; and St. Augustine, Trinidad. Many of its graduates also take advanced degrees in North America and Europe. The University of the West Indies has trained many of the current political leaders and civil servants in the Commonwealth Caribbean. Students from the dependencies of France and The Netherlands are most likely to take higher education in the respective metropolitan country. Unique is St. Georges Medical College on Grenada. Enrollment consists primarily of students from the United States who are unable to find places in medical schools at home.

Of particular consequence for geopolitical analysis is the statistic for percent of adults illiterate (and by inference, those literate). The estimated rates of illiteracy are remarkably low in the context of the third world and only Haiti has percentages above the world average. Such low rates of adult illiteracy offer evidence that nearly universal primary education is not a recent phenomenon. They also indicate populations able to function in the modern world, either at home or as migrants overseas. General adult literacy can enhance democratic government, assuming an open press is functioning. The fact that the past and present political forms have been able to provide at least basic education for nearly all children defuses an issue that has been used effectively by radical leaders to gain popular support in many other places in the world. Published data suggest that regardless of what other social needs a leftist revolutionary may argue are lacking, on most Caribbean islands an effective educational system is already in operation.

The data also add perspective to some common assumptions regarding the Caribbean. Although the data are predictable in that they support the image of Haiti as the most backward country in the hemisphere, they provide scant evidence of superior social conditions in Cuba. One of the major propaganda themes of the government of Fidel Castro is that advances in the human condition in Cuba have been so great since 1959 that its version of socialism merits adoption in neighboring countries. Yet compared on similar measures with places not greatly different in basic ways, Cuba's social qualities rank well but are not exceptional for the Caribbean. This circumstance is especially noteworthy in light of evidence that in the decade before the revolution Cuba was already one of the most literate and economically advanced countries south of the United States. A literacy rate of over 76 percent was reported for 1953, for example (*Britannica Yearbook* 1960, p. 191). Cuban achievements have nonetheless been impressive, especially with respect to the extension of social benefits to the poorest segments of the population.

Under Castro a major redistribution of income also has been accomplished. There now is no wealthy class in Cuba; the nation's wealth is in the hands of the government. A class structure based on income remains, however. For example, in Cuba the wage level of agricultural workers is pegged at less than a fifth that of managers, a differential that was officially increased in July 1980.

Although the data support the view that the general social welfare in Cuba has improved in recent decades, the question arises as to whether they would not have done as well under a less repressive political system. Nearby Caribbean former colonies have comparable social indicators achieved without the loss of individual freedoms.

It seems clear from the published data that continued or recent political association with the United States, United Kingdom, France, and The Netherlands has brought social benefits to the general populations. That other aspects of a dependency relationship were not regarded favorably by Caribbean peoples is evidenced by the surge of choices for independence since 1962. Nonetheless, a main argument against independence was the fact that as a dependency the main financial burden for improving social conditions lay with the metropolitan power. Certainly the well-developed educational and health services on many islands owe their origins to the overseas administrations. Regardless, since independence, even those governments not openly socialist in political stance have maintained and expanded social services.

In assessing the island Caribbean as a whole it is well to recognize that few of the characteristics usually attributed to newly independent former colonial holdings apply. Compared with the third world as a whole the peoples are not as poor, ill-fed, unhealthy, or uneducated. In general there exists a substantial corps of well-trained civil servants, modern skills, and an awareness of their place in the world. Improvements are indeed needed in all socioeconomic aspects but, aside from Haiti, the Caribbean is not a backward region.

Despite its history as a region of transplanted peoples dominated by colonial powers, distinctive cultural elements have developed within the Caribbean. Its music, for example, has rhythms and sounds like none other and is identifiable worldwide. The Calypso, and especially the Calypso of Trinidad, is perhaps the best known of the styles, although there are others. More recent in origin is the Reggae music of Jamaica, popularized first by Bob Marley in the 1960s. Because of its underlying theme of social protest, Reggae has been adopted in some circles as much for its political as for its musical qualities. More so than Calypso, Reggae's appeal has spread well beyond its island of origin. Carribean dance also is distinctive, of which the Limbo has achieved the widest recognition. Although African influences on such expressions are very strong, the origins are Caribbean. They are not imports.

These and other evidences of cultural creativity give to the inhabitants a sense of accomplishment and a regional identity, qualities that also have political implications. Despite the fact that they often are individualistic personally and in matters of island allegiance, West Indians usually use the pronoun *we* when referring to the Caribbean as a whole. This mood of regional consciousness can be expected to have increasing geopolitical consequences.

Race

To an extent greater than any other broad world region, the Caribbean is inhabited by the descendents of transported peoples. Except for a few thousand Caribs, most of mixed race (Gullick 1982, pp. 522–23), Native Americans no longer live on the islands. Destruction of the indigenous peoples occurred within a few decades following European contacts and left few survivors. Other than crop plants, some words, and a few artifacts such as the hammock, few cultural traces endure. Replacement peoples came from many sources over the centuries but two groups were of special significance: white Europeans and black Africans.

Europeans were the earliest migrants. Permanent settlement dates from Columbus's second voyage and in varying numbers has continued to the present day. Overall, several million Europeans have come to the region, not always to stay or to survive. They constitute the second most numerous and culturally the most influential group of people. Spanish, English, French, and Dutch—ranked in sharply decreasing order—were most numerous, yet most of Europe contributed at least some migrants. The region's languages, religions, economies, political forms, standard value systems, indeed, nearly all cultural elements, are derived from or were profoundly influenced by human diffusion agents from Europe.

The number of migrants from Europe, however, was dwarfed by the massive importation of slaves from Africa. This movement began in 1518 (Sauer 1966, p. 207), reached its peak during the 1700s, and although legally ended in 1806 did not dwindle to a halt until perhaps the 1870s (West and Augelli 1971, p. 111). Because almost no Africans have ever come voluntarily, migration from that continent has contributed little to the region's mix of people for over a century.

Precisely how many Africans were transported to the Caribbean as slaves can never be known. Loss of life in transit and the fact that several islands—St. Estatius and Curaçao in particular—served as markets from which slaves were sent to mainland destinations complicate even those records that do endure. Sheridan estimated that over a span of four centuries at least 15 million slaves were sent to the New World. With a maximum of about seven million arriving during the 1700s, it was not until the mid-1800s that immigration to the New World of whites from Europe exceeded that of blacks shipped from Africa (Sheridan 1970, p. 21). Although these totals apply to an area broader than just the Caribbean, they attest to the scale of the slave movement.

The loss of life under slavery was horrendous. It has been estimated that the laboring life of field hands averaged less than seven years, whereas the collective renewal rate for slaves was about 15 years (William Dickson as quoted in Sheridan 1970, p. 20). Thus, although a minimum estimate of the number of Africans who completed the "middle passage"[4] is about five million, actual population totals on the islands were not great. Rates of natural renewal also were quite low. For example, the British islands had an estimated 60,000 slaves in 1906 when the legal trade was abolished. Yet, in 1834 the number emancipated was only 83,176 (Eriksen 1962, p. 32). Assuming that both numbers are reasonably valid, the growth rate involved was very low by present standards. For example, assuming an annual rate of natural increase of only 2.5 percent, the 60,000 population would have doubled in 28 years. The population totals reported for the two dates suggest an increase rate of less than 1 percent.

The conditions under which slaves lived differed between countries. Under Spanish rule the legal framework placed restrictions on conduct for both owner and slave. A major distinction under Spain as compared with other colonial powers was that a slave was legally a person, not merely property. Provisions were made to permit a slave to be freed. Included was the opportunity for a slave to buy freedom, an option offered much more often to those of mixed parentage. Freed slaves also had legal recourse to protection from molestation. Although cruelties remained part of the system, the Spanish islands provided relatively more humane circumstances and attracted runaways from slavery elsewhere. Puerto Rico was noted as a haven.

Treatment was more harsh in non-Spanish colonies, with the Dutch reputed to be especially severe with slaves. Although the Dutch islands were not important plantation areas, Dutch Guiana was. Naipaul called attention to the fact that records for the period of slavery indicate a total of 300,000 slaves were landed in Dutch Guiana, yet in 1960 its black population stood only at 60,000 (Naipaul 1963, p. 24).

The combination of a master–slave relationship and a largely male European poulation early resulted in many racial mixed offspring. Called variously mulatto, colored, or creole (and there are more terms), over time this brown-skinned population became the third major element in the racial and related social composition of the islands. Persons of mixed race constitute a large proportion of nearly all Caribbean islands and commonly occupy an interemediate position in the socioeconomic hierarchy.

East Indians constitute the fourth major Caribbean ethnic element, although they are neither as numerous nor as widely distributed as the other three. These people came principally from India and, for Suriname, from Java. Over a half million Indians came under work contracts between 1850 and 1917, at which point the government in India halted the practice. Far fewer came from Java, but the stream lasted somewhat longer. Most Asians went to the Guianas and Trinidad, although most non-Spanish plantation islands received at least a few. Although many eventually returned home, the great majority, for a variety of reasons, remained (Waddell 1967, p. 87).

As in the case of the term *African*, East Indian is a vague term. Racially, for example, those from British India were Caucasion whereas Javanese were Mongoloid. Religions included Hinduism, Islam, and Buddhism, plus minor faiths. Native languages differed even more. In the context of the Caribbean, however, the fact that they came from South Asia under comparable conditions was sufficient to make them a distinct group. This group perception is part of the regional culture and has important political ramifications in Trinidad, as well as in Guyana and Suriname.

Smaller numbers of immigrants from other places also flavored the ethnic complexity of the Caribbean. Between 1850 and 1890 over 100,000 Chinese indentured laborers came to Cuba (West and Augelli 1971, p. 145). In less organized fashion smaller numbers of Chinese came to the region in later years. Jews from various countries have been a small but economically influential ethnic component since the first century of conquest. They were particularly important in the early development of the Dutch colonies. The Nazis provoked a much larger influx in the years preceding and following World War II. Syrians and Lebanese and other small ethnic groups are especially active in commerce in urban areas; most came after 1900.

Despite this population diversity, in a broad sense the Caribbean may be regarded racially as a black region. This assessment is most true with respect to the non-Spanish islands but depending upon how race is defined, can apply to the entire region. In Cuba, Puerto Rico, and the Dominican Republic, for example, persons of mixed origins who have some white features normally are regarded as white. This attitude is the reverse of normal custom in the United States (Pearcy 1965, p. 9). For the region as a whole, distinctions are recognized between white and colored, and demographic tables commonly show both racial categories.

Thus, Haiti is regarded either as 100 percent or as 95 percent black, depending upon how its colored component is classified. The Dominican Republic has been listed as nearly 75 percent black, even though the combined black and colored inhabitants probably constitute about 85 percent of the total (Macpherson 1980, p. 147). Perceptions vary most with respect to Cuba. West and Augelli (1971, p. 108–09) maintain that Cuba has a white majority and that only a third of the population may be classed as black. On the other hand, Central Intelligence Agency (1980, p. 43) data show Cuba's population as 37 percent white, 11 percent black, and 51 percent mulatto. The basis for such precision was unstated, although other sources also suggest that more than 60 percent of Cubans have perceptible negroid features (Macpherson 1980, p. 137; Pearcy 1965, p. 81). That is to say, such people would be non-white as that category is recognized in the United States.

It is clear that in Spanish–American countries the perception of racial categories is based upon different standards than those employed in the United States. An example of the difference is the manner in which the U.S. Census Bureau treats population data for Puerto Rico. Whereas for the 50 states population data include listings by race, for Puerto Rico no racial classifications are used (Shryock et al. 1973, p. 257).

It can be assumed that this administrative decision reflects recognition of a cultural perception so different that data collected for Puerto Rico could not validly be compared with racial data gathered in the remainder of the United States. No effort is made to ascertain a correct position on this matter. It does seem logical, however, that the interests of interregional comparisons are better served if a consistent classification is employed, in the cases of Cuba and the United States, for example.

Racial data on Table 4 were adopted from the CIA *National Basic Intelligence Factbook* (1980). Estimates from this source are included not because they are necessarily most accurate, but rather because they are

TABLE 4 Racial Composition in the Caribbean

Places	White	Black	Mixed	East Indian	Other
Countries					
Antigua–Barbuda	—	"almost complete"	—	—	—
Bahamas	10	80	10	—	0
Barbados	4	80	16	—	—
Dominica	—	"mostly"	—	—	—
Grenada	—	"mainly"	—	—	—
Jamaica	3.2	76.3	16.3	3.4	.9
St. Lucia	—	"mainly"	—	—	—
St. Vincent and the Grenadines	"few"	"mainly"	"the rest"	"few"	"trace"
Trinidad–Tobago	1	43	14	40	2
Dependencies					
Anguilla	no data				
Cayman Islands	no data				
Guadeloupe	5	90*			5
Martinique	5	90*		1	4
Montserrat	no data				
Netherlands Antilles			"diverse, many mixed"		
St. Kitts–Nevis		"mainly"			
Turks and Caicos	no data				
Virgin Islands (British)	no data				
Cuba	37	11	51		1
Dominican Republic	16	11	73		
Haiti		95	5		

*Black and mixed.

SOURCE: Adapted from *National Basic Intelligence Factbook* (Central Intelligence Agency 1980).

assumed to reflect the perceptions of Caribbean racial composition available to strategic planners in Washington. Lack of precise information for several islands is evident from the use of terms such as "mainly" and "mostly" rather than percentages. In fact, such comparatives are probably as reliable and useful as are the pseudo-precise percentages offered for Jamaica.

The racial makeup of the island populations is related to geopolitics in several ways. On a world scale over half of all present countries formerly were colonies of European powers and most are inhabited by peoples racially different from the imperial center. This legacy has engendered an acute sense of racial consciousness that fosters a sense of unity among states that in other respects have few characteristics or interests in common. In this context it is well to remember that the concept of a third world did not originally have an obvious racial component. Yugoslavia, for example, was a founding member of the movement. Yet an increasing trend within the third world is toward a common identity linked with perceptions of color. In the early 1980s the mood had not yet become a major diplomatic force in the Caribbean. In many countries, however, there was a potential for a greater degree of racial polarization on international issues.

Color consciousness is an integral part of Cribbean cultures. The memory of slavery is indelible and is manifested in countless ways. One reason is that few native-born are unaffected genetically by centuries of racial intermingling. Under slavery, societies consisted essentially of white, black, and colored. Each group had its own interior social hierarchy but the lines between were sharply drawn (Hall 1972, p. 33). Following emancipation gradual changes occurred and the rate of change accelerated sharply with the spread of elective government. Yet social stratifications related to color remain central threads in the regional fabric. Where present in greater than token numbers, East Indians constitute a fourth ethnic element in the complex human mosaic.

Social ranking by color retains much of the hierarchy of the past, with whites highest, blacks lowest, and whoever else is present somewhere in the middle. Of the racially mixed, those with darker skin shades or more obvious negroid features generally occupy lower strata, although distinctions are subtle and not consistent between islands. Naipaul calls the ability of a native West Indian to distinguish persons with even slight black ancestry a "futile skill unconsciously acquired" (Naipaul 1963, p. 196). The facility may indeed be futile but is a widespread trait that affects business and political dealings as well as social relations. Members of the middle social ranks include not just colored and East Indians, but Syrians, Lebanese, Chinese, Portuguese, and others as well.

Economic stratification is comparable but less consistent. It is not rare for whites to have low or only moderate incomes, whereas persons of wealth may be of any race or ethnic group. Merchants in particular are often of East

Indian or Middle Eastern origins. The rural poor are black nearly everywhere, with Trinidad the main exception. There blacks are principally urban and East Indians dominate the countryside. Racial distribution in Tobago, on the other hand, conforms with regional norms.

Several rural poor-white communities are present on different islands. The tiny islands of Les Saintes and St. Barthelemy, dependencies of Guadeloupe, have predominatly white populations. The people came as colonists during colonial times and settled on islands where plantations were impractical. Hence slaves never were numerous. Elsewhere, clusters of whites remain as relict racial enclaves by resisting intermarriage with racial groups outside their society. Among these are English on Grand Cayman, French on Petit Martinique, Germans in Seaford, Jamaica, and Dutch farmers on Saba and St. Maarten (Niddrie 1971, p. 90).

Perhaps best known of the white communities are the "Redlegs" of Barbados, Grenada, and St. Kitts (West and Augelli 1971, p. 108). Descended from indentured laborers sent during the seventeenth and eighteenth centuries, they rank with blacks at the bottom of their island societies. They have a racially mixed distribution and differ from their black neighbors principally in race, not really in culture. Their racial distinctiveness is sustained by an attitude of superiority that will not allow intermarriage. Many of those on Barbados are descended from people expelled from Britain as political prisoners under Cromwell. At one time the practice was so common that to barbado became a verb used to mean transported to the Americas by deportation or deceit (Keagy 1975, p. 14–17).

Never numerous, one category of Caribbean blacks is currently the basis for a popular mythology that has growing political implications. These are the Maroons. The name derives from *Cimarrones* (dwellers of the summits), which was the Spanish term for surviving Indians who withdrew to the forested interiors to escape enslavement. There they retained their ways of life and raided lowland settlements. Escaped slaves later joined such groups and added African culture elements. Racial mixing over time made the groups essentially black, and the term *Maroon* came to mean runaway slaves living independent of white authority (West and Augelli 1971, p. 66).

Most numerous and best known were the Maroons of Jamaica. When the British took the island from Spain in 1655, many slaves of the Spanish used the opportunity to flee to the interior highlands. There they lived as Maroons, raiding constantly the bordering plantations. The problem of the plantation owner was two-fold. In themselves the raids were dangerous and expensive, plus the bands of free blacks attracted a steady stream of runaway slaves. Efforts to subdue the Maroons had little success. Eventually an agreement made in 1739 stipulated that the Maroons would be left in peace if they would return fugitive slaves (Waddell 1967, p. 59). Although later many were rounded up and deported to Central America (Gullick 1982, p. 522), Maroons remaining in Jamaica have retained a degree of autonomy from the national government. Justice in their rural enclaves is administered locally for other than capital crimes (Ericksen 1962, p. 37).

Sizable groups of Maroons also formed in Haiti, Cuba, and the Guianas. Those of the Guianas long were termed Bush Negroes. In Suriname especially, Maroons remain as separate communities with many clearly African customs and considerable racial purity. The antagonisms of the past have largely subsided, however, and they now interact regularly with the national culture (Lenoir 1975, p. 308). They remain distinct, nonetheless.

Rising black consciousness in the Caribbean has renewed interest in these early rebels as Africans who would not accept enslavement. They are viewed as blacks who, although brought forcibly to the New World, were able to resist white domination and live according to their own cultural terms. (See Price 1973 for fuller treatment of this theme.) Currently intellectual circles in the Caribbean have merged this concept with modern perceptions of Western cultural and economic imperialism to present Maroons as folk heroes in a political context. The political effects of this contrived mythology are yet unclear, although there is the chance that a potent political theme of regional scope may emerge.

Besides geopolitical ramifications, racial diversity affects domestic politics. At this level, local history and personalities add complications that make circumstances on each island unique, yet within the general framework outlined above. In the West Indies, race is inseparable from politics just as it permeats virtually all other aspects of society.

Migration

Unlike other regions of the world populated largely by peoples from distant lands—the United States, Argentina, Australia, for example—the Caribbean has also become a major source of migrants to other countries. Indeed, since about 1950 the increase in volume and range of destinations of this outflow has reached such proportions that the term *Caribbean Diaspora* has been applied (Dominguez and Dominguez 1981, p. 53).

Earlier emigrations were mainly within the region, to other islands or the adjacent mainland. During and especially following World War II, mass movements to the United States, Canada and the European metropoles widened greatly the distribution of overseas West Indians. An increase in the number of women migrants in recent decades has changed somewhat the composition of the flows. As in the past, however, migration primarily involves people of working ages. The motivations remain much the same as well, with both push and pull factors being mainly economic. Involved are people in crowded countries with low wages and much unemployment attracted by job opportunities in receptive, culturally similar countries (Tidrick 1966, p. 39).

Flows of people from islands under U.S., British, French, and Dutch stewardship differed importantly from mass movements elsewhere in the Caribbean and much of the world during the same period. Political repression was not a factor. Personal liberties were protected generally throughout the various dependencies and newly independent states. Freedoms at home were little less than those available elsewhere.

Despite the major acceleration of emigration rates over the past few decades the phenomenon is not new. As early as the 1850s construction crews that completed the first railroad across Panama were drawn mainly from Jamaica (Dominguez and Dominguez 1981, p. 54). The French employed large numbers of islanders—25,000 from Jamaica alone—in the first attempt to build a canal in Panama from 1881 to 1889 (Niddrie 1971, p. 101). Successful completion of the canal by the Americans, between 1905 and 1913, was aided by at least 50,000 workers from Jamaica, Barbados, and the Lesser Antilles (West and Augelli 1971, p. 111). Over the same period perhaps an equal number of West Indians labored in sugar and banana plantations newly established along the coast in Central America (Dominguez and Dominguez 1981, p. 54). The cultural and political effects were to reinforce the Rimland character of the Central American coast. Ties remain close and tens of thousands of West Indians normally lived and worked in the Canal Zone (Niddrie 1971, p. 102).

The enormous expansion of the Cuban sugar industry following independence created a large demand for labor. The need was met in part by immigrants from Europe—Spain in particular—and from China, but large numbers of workers were imported from Haiti, Jamaica, and the Lesser Antilles as well. One source asserts that more than 200,000 Jamaicans and Haitians came to Cuba between 1912 and 1924 (West and Augelli 1971 p. 113). The flow lasted into the 1930s when a "50 percent law" was enacted. This measure, which required that at least half of the workers in any enterprise be Cuban, caused the return home of most of the Caribbean migrant workers and virtually ended that interisland seasonal connection.

Other migrations of the early twentieth century were stimulated by petroleum developments around Lake Marcaibo, Venezuela, beginning in 1916. These opportunities lasted until 1929 when political pressures caused restrictions to be applied on use of foreign workers. The shallow ocean near the oil fields contributed to the development of refineries on Curaçao (1916) and Aruba (1925). Small tankers brought crude to the deep-water islands from whence petroleum products and crude could be shipped in larger tankers to world markets. At least 20,000 émigré workers were employed in the Netherlands Antilles during this period (Niddrie 1971, p. 102).

However, in 1931 measures were adopted in the Netherlands Antilles to return home most British West Indians.

A considerable part of Trinidad's black population is a result of arrivals from the Lesser Antilles. Similarly, the more prosperous U.S. Virgin Islands have attracted blacks from other islands, the British Virgin Islands in particular. The seasonal labor needs of agriculture in the region also has sustained a continuing circulation of workers among the various islands. This last sort of movement is usually temporary and was made easier in the past when most of the islands were British. The recent increase in the number of sovereign states can be expected to raise barriers to free entry, presumably measures comparable to those taken by nearly every country in the region at some time in the past.

Flows into the United States began in the early part of the twentieth century and during the 1930s and 1940s were enhanced by immigration policies. The national origins provision of the Immigration Act—which became effective in 1929—established national quotas favorable to north-western European countries. As British subjects, West Indians were able to enter as part of the unfilled quota for that nationality. These early migrants added a distinctive ethnic element to urban black communities along the Atlantic Coast. Some of the early arrivals in New York in the 1920s and 30s sparked a burst of black cultural creativity that became known as the Harlem Renaissance (Dominguez and Dominguez 1981, p. 54). During World War II more than 100,000 West Indians were imported to alleviate labor shortages caused by that conflict. Many of this total remained to swell still further the Caribbean population component of the Middle Atlantic cities.

These flows were sharply curtailed under the provisions of the McCarren–Walter Act of 1952, which closed the immigration quota loophole for Western Hemisphere Commonwealth territories. Further labor certification requirements were added in 1965, when Western Hemisphere quotas were applied for the first time (Dominguez and Dominguez 1981, p. 56). An effect of these changes was to induce greater numbers of West Indians to by-pass the United States and take up residence in Canada where citizenship was easier to obtain.

Regardless, immigration from the West Indies has increased in numbers and as a proportion of the U.S. total. From just Barbados, Jamaica, and Trinidad and Tobago the composite official numbers were as follows: for the 1950s, about 12,000; for the 1960s, over 100,000; and for the 1970s, roughly 200,000 (U.S. Census Bureau 1981, p. 88). Inclusion of migrants from other islands as well as illegal entries would add tens of thousands more people who entered over the same period. An important recent stimulant was a policy change which applied national quotas to Western Hemisphere countries.

Favorable also was a preferred status to applicants with resident close relatives. The volume of past flows has been such that in 1980 an estimated 50,000 Barbadians, about 150,000 Trinidadians, and up to 500,000 Jamaicans lived in the United States (Dominguez and Dominguez 1981, p. 56). Living largely in the cities of the Northeast, these migrants now constitute a sizable local minority increasingly conscious of its political leverage. Electoral influence of ethnic groups in the United States has more than once affected foreign policy. Hence, these West Indian concentrations have at least potential geopolitical connotations.

Over somewhat the same period, however, the legal entrance of seasonal agricultural workers declined sharply. As late as 1970 over 15,000 such workers came from the West Indies as a whole and an equal number from the U.S. Virgin Islands. By 1980 these totals had dropped to 5,200 and 2,300, respectively (U.S. Bureau of the Census 1981, p. 91).

The influx to Canada from the islands has increased over somewhat the same period. A contributing factor was the 1967 Canadian adoption of an immigration policy that prohibited discrimination against migrants from any specific country. Current laws grant points to applicants on the basis of such qualities as a knowledge of English or French, a relative resident in Canada, the number of years of formal education, and possession of special job skills. Admission is eased for petitioners with high composite point totals. Because most West Indians qualify comparatively easily under such measures, immigration from the West Indies more than doubled just from 1966 to 1967. By 1969 Trinidad and Tobago ranked eighth as a source of immigrants into Canada, and over the decade Caribbean countries consistently were among the top ten national sources. Jamaica was fourth, both in 1976 and 1977 (Johnson and Williams 1981, p. 16–18).

To exodus to Europe was greatest following World War II. It was stimulated in part by reconstruction needs there and the upward mobility of British workers (Peach 1967, p. 289) and was eased by the citizen status of the colonials in the metropolitan country. By 1970 West Indians numbered over 300,000 in Britain, 150,000 in France, and 20,000 in the Netherlands (Dominguez and Dominguez 1981, p. 55). The volume of black West Indians was so great in Britain that in the 1960s actions were taken to reduce the ease of entry (Tidrick 1966, p. 22). Circulation between Britain and the Caribbean countries has continued but on a much reduced scale.

On the French islands both push and pull factors were operative. In 1970 unemployment on Guadeloupe and Martinique exceeded 40 percent by one estimate. The remedy of emigration was so obvious that a special bureau (the BUMIDOM) for its management was created in 1963 (Lasserre and Mabileau 1972, p. 88). The lure of the metropole influenced strongly the direction of movement. Job opportunities often existed in French Guiana, for example, yet that mainland department more experienced a population loss than an influx from the West Indies. For the Antilleans, the Paris region in particular in a mecca. The volume of flow from Guadeloupe and Marinique has been so great that a negative population growth for the islands has been estimated (U.S. Bureau of the Census 1981).

Within Latin America, only Venezuela remained an important destination for migrants from the islands. The scale of movement, however, was much smaller than to the places noted above. The main attractions were proximity and, in the 1970s, a burgeoning economy stimulated primarily by petroleum exports. Lowered world demand for petroleum and Venezuelan concern with a largely illegal flow of people from Columbia that exceeded 1.5 million (Johnson and Williams 1981, p. 155) combined to reduce opportunities in that country by the early 1980s. Trinidadian migrants were most numerous, with most of the remainder coming from the small, eastern islands. The rate of flow was inhibited by economic and cultural factors, however. Despite its rank as the richest of the Spanish–American neighbors, Venezuela offered fewer job opportunities than did Europe and North America. The Spanish culture also makes adjustment by English- and French-speaking West Indians less easy.

The increased rate of dispersal of Caribbean peoples has raised international consciousness of the region on both sides of the North Atlantic. It has also caused greater awareness among the islanders of conditions elsewhere. In the West Indies there are few inhabitants who do not have friends or relatives overseas. Two important effects of such contacts have been a reduced sense of isolation and a heightened perception of contrasts. It is the latter awareness that makes the aspirations of island peoples more difficult to satisfy even when social and economic progress is achieved. It is thus a factor that causes continuing domestic political pressures, which in turn have international repercussions.

ECONOMIC BASE

In relation to other parts of the world the Caribbean stands as a middle-income region. Comparisons based on per-capita gross national product have value but are flawed because they reveal little regarding the distribution of total income within a country. The measure is used for international evaluations, nonetheless, because the level of per-capita GNP does provide a basis for assessments of the financial resources available and the potential for development in a given state. Rankings for the Caribbean are shown in Table 5. Not all political entities are included because they were not part of the data base.

As may be expected in an area so diverse in other ways, a wide range of economic circumstances is present. Despite the range, no political entity

TABLE 5 Per-Capita Gross National Product (ranked in 1979 U.S. $)

Nation	GNP
Martinique*	4,680
Netherlands Antilles*	3,540
Trinidad and Tobago	3,390
Guadeloupe*	3,260
Puerto Rico*	2,970
The Bahamas	2,780
Barbados	2,400
Cuba	1,410
Jamaica	1,240
Dominican Republic	990
St. Lucia	780
Grenada	630
St. Vincent and the Grenadines	490
Dominica	410
Haiti	260

*political dependency
SOURCE: Adapted from Population Reference Bureau, *1981 World Population Data Sheet* (Washington, D.C., 1981), and based on 1979 World Bank data.

there is notably wealthy and, aside from Haiti, none is tragically poor. Even Haiti, although the poorest place in the Western Hemisphere, ranks higher than 22 other countries in the world. Worth remarking is the relatively high economic standing of the region's political dependencies, that is, Martinique, Puerto Rico, and so on. In addition, according to the World Bank, even the small resource-poor states of Barbados and The Bahamas had higher per-capita GNPs than did such countries as Argentina and Yugoslavia.

The accepted view of the Caribbean is as a region of developing countries. Such a status makes its independent states eligible for favorable terms with respect to international aid. The status also is relfected in perceptions of the region by its inhabitants as well as by outsiders. A less common and only selectively applicable concept of Caribbean countries is that of overdevelopment. Those who hold this view point to the severe ecological damage caused by exploitative human occupancy over several centuries. Overdevelopment is thought to have contributed to a stagnation of population totals and economic growth. As a response to overdevelopment, various peoples have of necessity sought employment away from their home islands in a series of temporary migrations. Remittances from overseas migrants are vital to the economic health of many islands and constitute a considerable, if poorly documented, segment of the regional economy (Richardson 1975, p. 390). The idea of overdevelopment offers a provocative perspective that can further understanding of conditions on a number of the small Caribbean islands.

The economies of the islands benefit importantly from three common geographical features: tropical climate, location, and small size. Continuously warm climate permits production of tropical commodities in demand in countries with colder climates. The warmth also offers attractive winter vacation environments for tourists from these same countries. In addition, the location of the island Caribbean places it closer to the wealthy countries of North America and Europe than islands with comparable climates in the Pacific and Indian oceans. The small size of the islands facilitates access to the sea for trade and tourism. It also provides a relatively large proportion of seashore, an environmental interface that is highly attractive to vacationers. The nearby ocean also moderates daytime land temperatures that otherwise can become very oppressive in the tropics.

Although remittances contribute a very important share to most island economies, in general the main sources of income generated within the Caribbean itself are connected with agriculture or tourism. The use of the conjunction *or* is precise. With few exceptions, connections between island agriculture and the tourist industry are slight. Some reasons for this circumstance are presented below but recognition of the discontinuity is important for general understanding of the region.

Both the region's agriculture and tourism require extraregional connections in order to function. Each category of activity is linked intimately by means of transfers of people or commodities with economic and political conditions elsewhere, with the consequence that changes abroad normally have effects in the Caribbean. Yet, even though the island economies cannot thrive without overseas economic partners, the islands do not hold exclusive positions regarding either their products or tropical environments.

The economic relationships thus are more dependent than interdependent. These economic circumstances have inspired several interpretations, the best known of which is termed dependency theory. Complex and polemic in tone, this concept attributes the causes for virtually all problems in a dependent country to exploitation by outside interests.[5] Regardless of how one views the causes or the conditions, the subordinate economic position of the Caribbean political entities is a basic part of the region's geopolitics.

A dimension of dependency that also has political significance is the fact that the Caribbean is less self-sufficient in basic foodstuffs than any other large world region. The relative ability of a state to feed itself is one of the most basic considerations in geopolitical analysis. A heavy dependence on food imports has important strategic implications for any country, and to an island one in particular. The reliance on food imports derives not from environmental deficiencies but mainly from historical causes. As plantations developed, a dependable source of food for the slave labor force was necessary. To raise it locally required diversion of land and labor, and planters were reluctant to do either. Fishing took even more time and, from the perspective of the slave owner, was more dangerous as it offered too many escape opportunities. The favored solution was to import the surplus grain, meat, and salt fish production of the North American colonies. Although pronounced illegal by Paris, the French colonies also participated surreptitiously in this trade with the British mainland colonies (Waddell 1967, pp. 55–56).

Following the American Revolution, London required that only English ships serve their island colonies. This mandate made imported food more expensive and stimulated schemes such as the introduction of breadfruit.[6] Greater emphasis on local food production ensued. Changes were fewer on the French islands because, lacking open access to North American suppliers, they had always relied heavily on domestic subsistence sources. A widespread practice was allotment of garden areas near slave quarters. These plots received attention from the field hands during midday breaks and on Sundays.

Both master and slave benefited. The owner lost neither productive space nor labor time. Slaves gained a sense of proprietorship, greater choice regarding food eaten, and an opportunity to earn money by marketing small surpluses. Although local food sources were subject to disruption by drought or hurricane, the advantages were considerable (Waddell 1967, pp. 56–57). But even with such local contributions, net food imports, especially of dried and salted fish and meat, remained a feature of the Caribbean economies during the slave period.

Modern conditions differ in important ways, yet several broad regional relationships continue. Commercial agriculture is concerned primarily with crops for which there is an overseas demand, whereas farming aimed at home subsistence or local markets produced crops different both from those exported and those imported for food. Most food production takes place on small holdings little different in distribution and technology from those of the early postslavery period. Although grown primarily for family subsistence, small surpluses of crops and poultry are offered in town markets, usually by women. Neither quantity nor quality is consistent, and the income derived is small and unreliable. A result, then, is that rural populations usually are sufficiently nourished from domestic sources, whereas towns and cities must rely on food imports. Redistribution of population from rural to urban settings under these circumstances tends to increase dependence on overseas food sources.

Most governments in the Caribbean have committed themselves to reduce if not to eliminate reliance on food imports. On a number of islands, however, there is little choice as thin rocky soils and/or insufficient rainfall limit agriculture at best to scattered pockets of deeper soil. Agriculture never was established to any great extent on the southern islands of the Netherlands Antilles and most of The Bahamas, or on the Caymans, Turks and Caicos, Saba, Anguilla, Barbuda, and St. Barthelemy. During the eighteenth century, sugar plantations did flourish on St. Martin/St. Maarten, on St. Eustatius (Blume 1974, p. 318), and on most of the Grenadines (Blume 1974, p. 350). Royalists from the American colonies established cotton plantations on Harbour Island, Long Island, and Abaco in The Bahamas following the Revolution. They did poorly on the permeable soils, however, and ceased operating following slave emancipation in 1834 (Macpherson 1980, p. 133). Soil depletion and erosion have reduced or nearly eliminated agriculture on these islands in recent times (Richardson 1975, p. 395).

The only commonly eaten grain that is ecologically suitable over most of the Caribbean is maize. Soil and water requirements for wet rice culture are satisfied in only a limited number of locations. Wheat, rye, or oats grow poorly in the lowland tropics, and millets and sorghums are ecologically appropriate but never have been accepted into the diet systems of the Caribbean. On the other hand, tuber crops such as sweet potatoes, manioc, yams, and taro generally thrive. The first two of these were staples for the preconquest inhabitants, whereas yams and taro reflect diffusion from Asia during colonial times. Tree crops as well as legumes and other vegetables also grow well on a variety of sites. Food tastes, however, do not always accord with ecological suitability. One of the legacies from slavery has been a common preference for rice and wheat flour over maize and starchy tubers. This partiality is particularly marked among town dwellers of all classes (Adams 1968, pp. 5–19).

Social status has a strong influence on food tastes. The more European—or white—one's diet, the greater the perception of separation from peasant status and, by implication, from the heritage of slavery. The widespread tourist trade also produces a mood for emulation that accentuates a demand for food obtained outside the Caribbean. The economic effect of these cultural manifestations is the reduce market demand for those crops ecologically most suited to the region and most familiar to island farmers, and thus those crops for which there are the fewest barriers to expanded production.

Many governments face a dilemma regarding this issue. On most islands agricultural exports constitute either *the* or *a* major source of foreign exchange, hence to divert much of the best land from production of export crops to expand food production may reduce national income. At the same time, a substantial part of national income is needed to buy food to feed the population. Superficially it would seem as if a degree of reallocation of land use would cause little net loss, but in practice complicating factors are present. Most inhibiting overall are a desire to retain existing trade structures and commitments of foreign exchange to support various development plans. The matter of maintaining employment levels also is involved.

The problem of export versus food crop emphasis is not exclusively one of capitalism. In 1980, for example, socialist Cuba was more dependent for foreign exchange on the export of sugar than was true under Batista in the 1950s. Despite possession of the most favorable ratio of fertile land per capita of any tropical country in the world, Cuba still required the importation of food, even of tropical staples such as rice.

Labor

The quality of labor is one of the most fundamental of all economic variables. Generalizations about this aspect of the Caribbean are possible but necessarily are qualified due to the complexities of place and culture. Two seemingly contradictory images are encountered. Émigré West Indians are regarded generally as excellent workers: industrious, quick to learn, and reliable. Because most are literate in English or French they have adapted particularly well to cultural conditions and employer expectations in the United States, Canada, United Kingdom, and France. In earlier decades they were in demand as labor for large-scale construction projects within the Caribbean Basin. In recent years many islanders have claimed jobs overseas as semiskilled factory workers, especially in garment industries and in service occupations such as restaurants, hotels, custodial work, and transportation (driving buses, taxis, and so on). In competition with native workers they compare well, more because of skills and reliability than any greater degree of docility.

On the islands, the image of West Indians as workers is different. There the view is of predilection for indolence and a distaste for physical labor, and especially for field labor. This image is part of literature and vocal commentary and even has been documented in limited but thorough research. For example, a 1950 study on Antigua reported that only a fifth of the unemployed would accept any sort of work offered and the rest voiced reservations about the idea. Two-thirds of those surveyed would refuse an offer to work in sugar cane fields. The expressed values were such that leisure for the present was favored over leisure in the future. The desire for leisure surpassed the desire for income (Ericksen 1962, p. 64).

For the region as a whole, workers greatly preferred to perform by the task rather than by the hour. In this way they could report at their own convenience and work at a pace set by themselves and their coworkers (Ericksen 1962, p. 70). Perceived advantages to contract arrangements were the sense of independent negotiation involved, freedom from restraint on the job, and the prospect of a postcontract period of inactivity. Such arrangements also provide opportunities to share work, and hence wages, with friends and relatives (Ericksen 1962, pp. 72–74).

As with many other cultural traits, attitudes toward work are part of the heritage of slavery and refer primarily to black and colored population elements. Because these people constitute the majority of inhabitants and those most likely to be unemployed, the generalizations are useful. Following emancipation most released slaves left the estates as soon as possible and many moved to areas as distant as each island's geography permitted. There they established villages or scattered houses and began a subsistence existence based on small fields of mixed crops, a few poultry and livestock, and fishing (Marshall 1968, pp. 254–56). Efforts to induce them to return to the cane fields as wage laborers were largely ignored. Somewhat more successful were share-cropping schemes called the *metayer* system. On Tobago, for example, the worker was allowed to take half the sugar manufactured from an agreed acreage of cane and a bottle of rum for every barrel of sugar produced (Niddrie 1961, p. 18).

These antecedents of contemporary attitudes seem clear. To be a hired field hand is "nigger work" and has low status at all social levels and especially among rural blacks. It is done, of course, out of economic necessity, but for as short a period as possible. In this sense the inherent seasonality of the sugar cane industry is advantageous. As hard and undesirable as the work may be, it will end at a recognized time and a period of leisure will follow. Thus, the physiological rhythm of cane conforms not only to the climate of the Caribbean but to the regional value system as well.

The two concepts of West Indian workers as industrious abroad and indolent at home are not as discordant as they may appear. The mere fact that a worker has migrated abroad to seek employment constitutes a selection toward adaptability. Consistent with the value system is a desire to have some choice in the conditions of employment. West Indians also work hard and skillfully in the island environments, but bargaining in advance is involved wherever possible. For migrants the choices involve where, when, and for how long. Most émigrés seek a job elsewhere to achieve a specific goal.

These ingrained Caribbean attitudes toward work do not conform well with conventional political ideology. For example, both capitalism and socialism emphasize planned outputs and regular work habits, with main power of decision in the hands of management. Neither ideology adapts comfortably to the notions of employment held by most West Indians. On the surface it would seem that the presence of acknowledged social hierarchies and an inclination toward work sharing in the Caribbean fits well with the Marxist themes of class consciousness and collectivism. Certainly political leaders and parties proclaimed as socialist have been successful.

Yet when the rhetoric is done, West Indians tend to hold to a hard core of individualism, a view that people should act with self-interest (Eriksen 1962, p. 131). Associated as well is a desire for private property. To be willing to share work and income is not quite the same as to share property (Marshall 1968, pp. 255–56). Values of this nature do not blend easily with a doctrine that demands subordination to class interests. Certainly an arrangement that involves a work contract with individually determined work schedules and periods of leisure clashes with established socialist concepts of central planning, work norms, and workers regarded as production components.

Such militant self-interest favored early formation of labor organizations. Unions flourish. On Trinidad (Samaroo 1972, p. 205) and Jamaica (Wedderburn 1977, pp. 13–14) unions provided basis for the first popular political parties. The development and political strength of unions was aided by ties with the metropolitan countries where the labor movements are strong. In addition to U.S. AFL–CIO has had a strong role. Through its international arm, the American Institute for Free Labor Development, the AFL–CIO has contributed funds and training for labor leaders from countries throughout the Caribbean Basin. It was a major sponsor of the Caribbean Congress of Labor. Neither investors from Western countries nor Marxists have been pleased with the popular strength of these free labor unions. The results of open, competitive elections on the island suggest, however, that the Marxists' ambitions for power have been most severely impaired.

Another common form of voluntary organization are growers associations. Besides regional groups concerned with marketing of commodities such as cocoa, sugar, and cotton, on nearly every island local organizations promote production and marketing of specific crops. The function of such groups is to have property owners (and renters) retain control over their individual operations, yet to furnish a means to act collectively on matters of joint interest. Members usually represent a wide range of property sizes, although often the largest operators have disproportionately greater influence. Because the orientation is primarily commercial, the small, poor farmers are little involved. The system's mix of private ownership and collective commercial identity has been resistant to proposals to install socialist forms of agricultural organization. (Stone 1974 treats this circumstance from a leftist perspective.)

Commercial Agriculture

Sugar cane is the quintessential crop of the Caribbean. It was the first and remains the most valuable single product of the region despite profound changes of many kinds over recent decades. Although production is much greater on the large Spanish islands, cane continues as the most valuable crop on Barbados, Guadeloupe, and St. Kitts and is second on Jamaica (following marijuana), Martinique, and Trinidad. However, during the 1960s production declined sharply on Antigua and St. Lucia and ceased entirely on

St. Vincents following the closing of the grinding mill. On Tobago commercial cane was phased out as early as 1923 (Niddrie 1961, p. 29). Yet even where sugar is no longer a major export, it still is grown for home consumption and to make rum.

The persistence of sugar cane as an export crop reflects cultural inertia and established economic links. Ecologic suitability is important also. Temperatures along with the amount and seasonality of rainfall generally are favorable, as are soils derived from limestone or basic lavas. Cane makes low soil demands on nitrogen and phosphorus. There is a minimal need for tillage once planted, and as a dense grass it provides an excellent ground cover against erosion. In addition, cane is less damaged by hurricanes than any other commercial crop in the Caribbean. The mills that process it are not always spared, however.

The continued importance of sugar cane can be attributed as well to the institution of the plantation. It was the original crop grown on what Carl Sauer has termed the "classical model of the factory farm" (Sauer 1954, p. 22) which had its earliest major development in the Caribbean. The plantation has been viewed as the most efficient means of producing sugar, especially when large central grinding mills are involved. The logic has been that increases in area and mechanization provide lower unit production costs. Certainly the viewpoint conforms with modern concepts regarding agricultural economics as well as the performance levels of farms in the United States and Europe. The approach has been pursued strongly in socialist Cuba as well.

Not all evidence supports the notion of the productive superiority of the plantation, however. In Jamaica the small-scale sector of agriculture was outproducing the sugar estate sector as early as 1870 (E. Paget as cited by Hills and Iton 1981, p. 3). The advantage of large scale in sugar milling also has been questioned. In Jamaica, the operating cost advantage of the largest factories was found to be neutralized by lower cane costs for most smaller units (Auty 1981, pp. 84–85). A conclusion was that despite up to a third greater revenue for large mills compared with small ones, smaller sizes offered more advantages for developing countries because despite slimmer profit margins, employment was maximized (Auty 1981, p. 88). Where jobs are too few and emigration is endemic, this latter benefit is vital, particularly in an industry that is necessarily seasonal. And since the scale advantages of large growing operations depend importantly on the assumed superior efficiency of large sugar mills, the case for retention of plantations is weakened.

Continued emphasis on sugar growing is favored also by marketing factors. For example, Guadeloupe and Martinique as departments of France benefit from sugar quotas assigned France as part of the European Economic Community. Elsewhere matters are more complicated. Exclusion of Cuban sugar imports along with a desire in Washington for cordial diplomatic relations has eased entry into the U.S. market for other Caribbean producers. Both price and production levels are volatile, however, and competition from other sources is keen. Textbook explanations of the term *inelastic market* long have cited the example of sugar. The world's producing regions simply are capable of growing more sugar than can be sold, with the consequence that prices fluctuate widely. Thus, even acceptance of the concept of the inherent suitability of cane production in the Caribbean leaves to be resolved the problem of its unreliability as a basis for financial planning. In sugar-exporting countries there is a continuing search for other, more stable sources of income.

Bananas, cocoa, coconuts, citrus, and cotton are other major crops grown on plantations in the Caribbean. With these crops, however, the advantages of large-scale production are less evident. Even where mechanized central processing prior to shipment also is necessary, the period of perishability either is much longer than that of cut cane (citrus) or nonexistent (cotton). Thus transport from field to factory can be more deliberate and a wider radius of accessibility is possible. The effect is to reduce greatly the efficiency gap between plantation and small-holder production and to encourage a greater number of growers. Under these circumstances the quality of the product tends to be less consistent. On the other hand, investment costs and the risks of loss are distributed more broadly. Perhaps more important politically, maintenance of a steady market for cash crops grown on small holdings is more compatible with regional attitudes regarding individualism and private property.

In contrast with the specialization of plantations, cash crops grown on small farms usually are planted mixed. The main exception to this practice is cotton. As perennials, commercial tree crops such as cocoa, coconuts, coffee, citrus, ginger, and nutmeg, as well as bananas can be grown on hillsides with less risk of erosion. Often the fields are carefully arranged complexes in which taller plants create shaded habitats for shorter ones and subsistence and cash crops intermingle. Bananas and cocoa especially are often interplanted. Mangos, papaya, pigeon peas, and plantains seldom are exported but are commonly consumed at home or sold locally. Ground stories of maize, legumes, vegetables, and tubers are part of the mixtures as well. The trees sometimes serve as climbing poles for yams. Plots of this sort can outrage university-trained agronomists to whom orderliness is a virtue and can frustrate economists whose obsession with yield per hectare is confounded. Mixed plots are widespread nonetheless, particularly on hill land suited for little else, and conform well with cultural and ecological conditions.

With the general exception of sugar, commercial crops in the region have periodically been damaged by outbreaks of disease. Especially affected have been bananas, cocoa, and coconuts. The usual response has been a shift in plantings to another island or part of a large island and substitution by a different export crop. Disease and hurricane devastation have caused much of the variability in crop emphasis on different islands over the past century. The most striking change was transfer to West Africa of most of the world's cocoa growing as a result of outbreaks of witches'-broom disease in the Americas. On several islands (Trinidad, Tobago, Grenada) cocoa remains an important export due in part to a processing method that produces a superior quality bean (Niddrie 1961, pp. 22–23). The barefooted trampling, called "dancing the beans," often is accompanied by music and is as much a social occasion as an economic procedure.

As a tropical crop shipped to higher latitude markets, bananas are unique. They cannot be stored. They must be picked at a precise stage of growth so that ripening will continue, transported under refrigeration at about 12°C to retard ripening, and offered to the consumer while still somewhat green. The time span rarely exceeds two weeks. Because the biological needs are so stringent, only a few of the world's hundreds of banana varieties are suited for long-distance shipment. To serve these far-off demands requires an efficient, closely coordinated marketing system. A role for large companies is virtually essential, at least for transportation. The Caribbean region, including the mainland margins, is the best located of all tropical environments to provide bananas for Europe, the United States, and Canada. A consequence of these realities is a long-established relationship between a few large enterprises and banana production in the region.

For many decades, vertical integration by large firms involved them in every aspect of bananas, from planting to wholesale distribution. For reasons both political and economic, such firms now participate less in both production and marketing. On the islands most bananas are now supplied by small operators. Distribution of production reflects both the pattern of favorable ecological sites and rapid access to a port with banana-handling facilities. The crop is favored by small growers. Harvest begins within a year following planting, and once fruit bearing begins it continues for years without need for replanting. In addition, ripening of a grove of banana plants is year-round rather than seasonal, a factor that distributes more evenly both the work load and farm income. Other advantages are that cultivation requires only simple hand tools, the bananas grow well in the sort of interplanted mixtures common in the Caribbean, and bunches rejected for export can be offered for sale locally, eaten at home, or fed to the pigs. On the other hand, bananas are highly susceptible to disease and to damage from strong winds.

Besides the main export crops of the Caribbean, on several islands minor ones are prominent. For example, pineapples are native to the region and are widely grown for subsistence, yet only on Martinique where there is a large cannery is the crop important commercially. On Grenada as much as half the foreign exchange earnings come from exports of nutmeg and mace. The island normally produces a third of the world's supply. St. Lucia also exports nutmeg and mace but in smaller amounts. The fact that both nutmeg cultivation and the processing of the mace and beans are well-suited to small growers enables more farmers to participate in the industry. Until the 1960s arrowroot was a major source of income on St. Vincents. Competition from corn starch virtually eliminated its market although a new use of the starch as a smoothing agent in computer paper has somewhat revived the industry (Macpherson 1980, p. 102).

Coffee is grown largely on interplanted small holdings on all high islands. Its lack of importance stems in part from a lack of early emphasis but is due mainly to a highly competitive world market. Only Jamaican Blue Mountain coffee has achieved a market position of any consequence outside the region. Tobacco, a native American crop, also is widely planted but principally serves local manufacturing industries.

No crop has ever had a more radical short-term economic impact within the Caribbean than has marijuana, the *ganja* of Jamaica, since about 1960. Hemp crossed the Atlantic early as a secondary component of the crop complex that long had been part of the European culture. Planted initially to supply cordage, in time it spread unaided to become an exotic member of the natural growth. Over the centuries use of the leaf as a narcotic varied in popularity but persisted as an accepted if often minor part of rural culture, especially on the larger islands. Drug use of marijuana was particularly well-established among the Maroons in the Cockpit County of West–Central Jamaica. As the legend of the Maroons grew larger in public consciousness following independence, so also did the popularity of their customs, especially among youth.

Rise of the *Ras Tafarian* sect also was influential. Use of *ganja* is part of their liturgies as well as those of the Ethiopian Zion Coptic Church, another indigenous religious group (U.S. Department of State 1981, p. 5). Unlike other *Ras Tafarian* postures such as avoidance of hair cuts, baths, and employment, smoking marijuana was a pleasurable and less conspicuous way for sympathetic young Jamaicans to express disenchantment with the status quo.

These domestic manifestations, however, were only a minor stimulus to the phenomenal escalation of marijuana to its reputed current position as the most valuable commodity in the Jamaican economy (U.S. Department of State 1981, p. 5). Rapid spread to the drug culture in the early 1960s in the United States, within a decade over much of the Western world, created enormous demand for the leaf. Illicit suppliers sought frantically to find sources comparatively secure from interruption, yet sufficiently close to the United States for convenient transport. Besides secluded sites in the United States itself, the most successful locations became the western Sierra Madre of Mexico, northern Colombia, and central Jamaica.

In Jamaica it is grown especially in the Cockpit Country where inadequate road enhance isolation, people are poor and independent in mood, and central legal authority never has been firmly established. As a crop marijuana may easily be cultivated with simple tools. It also produces superior leaf quality when grown in partial shade, a normal condition in the interplanted fields of the uplands. This practice has made detection of the growing areas even more difficult for drug law enforcement agencies.

Smuggilng into the United States is by both sea and air. An estimated 70 percent of cocaine and marijuana entering the United States crosses the Caribbean. Most comes by way of Colombia with various islands serving as way stations, particularly for light aircraft. About 10 percent of the marijuana smuggled into the United States is grown in Jamaica (U.S. Department of State 1981, p. 5). Countermeasures adopted by the United States and cooperating governments have created a hide-and-seek atmosphere reminiscent of the days of the buccaneers. Obvious differences in the modern setting are the technology employed by both factions and the fact that today it is the criminals who have the wealth. Billions of dollars are involved. Violence and corruption are features of both eras.

Food Production

A persistent regional reality is a level of food production insufficient to meet domestic demand. Yet for 350 years the Caribbean economy has been based to a major extent on agricultural exports. Despite soil depletion in many areas, export agriculture not only remains a primary activity, its potential for expansion is limited more by restricted markets than by availability of land or labor. Commercial production of foods for local markets has not developed to any great extent. Most food eaten daily is imported or is provided by small growers in open markets, a system not radically different from that present during slavery (Norton and Symanski 1975, pp. 463–64). Modern methods are in little evidence, either in the production of marketing of common foodstuffs.

As an example, rice is a favored staple throughout the Caribbean, yet is grown in quantity only in Trinidad, largely by East Indians on small holdings. Even here production rarely provides more than a third of the demand (Macpherson 1980, p. 74). Most imported rice comes from Guyana. Indeed, in 1980 Trinidad's total bill for food imports was over $400 million. Included were tomatoes flown from Florida and sold at $9 a pound (Mason 1981).

Vegetables are grown for export in the Virgin Islands and on Montserrat and sent to Puerto Rico and Trinidad, respectively. Onions grown on Barbados also are sent to Caribbean markets. In view of the climate, proximity, and close trade ties, the potential for winter exports of vegetables to North America seems strong. Expansion of such activities remains hampered, however, by U.S. competition and by legal obstacles.

Livestock and poultry are normal components of the island landscapes. The principal sources for food are small farms, although chickens, goats, milk cows, and pigs are no less visible in shantytown environs. Few grains are grown for livestock feed. Chickens and pigs often forage freely whereas the cows and goats are more likely to be tethered. In the open markets, goats and chickens tend to be sold live, whereas dried (jerked) beef and pork are common sale items. Game cocks, on the other hand, are raised for sport, not food. The training, fighting, and above all the betting of these birds is a male avocation perhaps not second even to sex, at least among many aficionados. Beef cattle keeping is widespread, although comparatively fewer people are involved. Its origins date to the earliest Spanish settlements. On several islands—Anguilla, Barbuda, and the Grenadines—cattle keeping is the main activity. The role of cattle on the islands named is as much social as economic, and the meat qulaity is mediocre at best.

Efforts at modernization of the livestock industry have focused on dairying. Fresh milk is very expensive to import and the sanitary properties of the product from small farmers too often is unsuitable for the urban markets. Controlled breeding programs have greatly improved the quality of both beef and dairy herds, although not yet widely at the level of small farmers. The crossing of breeds from Europe, Africa, and India has produced animals well-suited to Caribbean environments. Best known of these cross-breeds are the Jamaica Hope (dairy) and Jamaica Red (beef), types of increasing prominence in the region's commercial herds (Niddrie 1971, p. 113).

Efforts to redress the imbalance between domestic food production and consumption have caused misunderstandings between government planners and small farmers. Officials with university training and experience in developed countries generally insist that improved production requires modernization. Implied in the term is the adoption of mechanized cultivation, monocropping in straight rows, crop specialization, use of improved seeds, and greater use of chemicals (fertilizers, pesticides, herbicides). A corollary is expanded scale of operation, an increase necessitated as much by a need to support the investment required to modernize as by the benefit of greater efficiency. The small farmers' reluctance to accept the prescriptions has too often been decried as ignorance (Marshall 1968, p. 261), conservatism, and unreasonable resistance to economic betterment. Farmers in turn tend to regard what is perceived to be inappropriate advice with bewilderment and some suspicion.

As with most issues, truth probably lies somewhere between, but from the perspective of geographers with extensive field experience, the farmers make a better case. Carl Sauer long ago called attention to the merits of the *conuco* system that supported native peoples prior to conquest and which later has been practiced in modified forms by transplanted Africans. The *conuco* was, Sauer pointed out, "an imitation by man of tropical nature, a many-storied cultural vegetation producing at all levels, from tubers underground through understory of pigeon peas and coffee, a second story of cocoa and bananas, to a canopy of fruit trees and palms" (Sauer 1954, p. 21). As constructed, these complexes fill all ecological niches and make full use of light, moisture, and soil nutrients. They are resistant to soil depletion and accelerated erosion even on sloping land. As a source of subsistence they provide a diversity of nutritional needs and a nearly continuous harvest. The system can be maintained with simple hand tools and the work load is distributed over long periods rather than being concentrated in peak seasons.

To critics ignorant of their character and long-term stability, such plantings are primitive, haphazard, disorganized, or "higgledy-piggledy" (Hills and Iton 1982, p. 3). One of the objections to mixed plantings is that of low productivity. Part of the difference of opinion stems from different concepts of what productivity means. Measured in terms of single-crop yields, mixed plantings have low outputs. In terms of *total* yield of all crops, on the other hand, mixed-planted fields consistently outproduce mono-cropped fields at comparable levels of fertilization (Innis 1976, p. 3). Where no fertilizer is available, a circumstance common on small isolated farms, mixed plantings especially outyield monocropping.

Small farmers' reluctance to accept outside advice they consider ill-informed is backed by a growing body of scientific evidence. Controlled studies have indicated that applications of chemical fertilizers in the Caribbean increase at best only slightly the yields of common varieties of staples such as white potatoes, sweet potatoes, yams, manioc, and maize. Fertilized fields of other common food crops (tannia, dasheen, and eddoes) showed virtually no yield increases when compared with average peasant yields on unfertilized land in Trinidad. Fertilized pigeon peas even had lower yields (Davis 1975, p. 135–37). Of greater promise has been a maize variety developed on Jamaica by an American seed company specifically for Caribbean environments. When heavily fertilized this variety had yields up to five times native varieties (Davis 1975, p. 138). To exploit such potential, however, would require major changes in established food preferences. Research aimed at comparable varietal advances in other favored foods has been inadequate (Hills and Iton 1981, p. 4).

A strong argument in favor of mixed plantings—called "food forests" by Hills and Iton (1982)—is their demonstrated ecologic and cultural stability. Often singled out as destructive of vegetation and conducive to soil erosion (Niddrie 1961, pp. 52–53; Marshall 1968, p. 261), they have endured on hilly surfaces at least since the end of slavery. Operated with little dependence on outside resources they continue to provide subsistence for the farmers, surplus for local markets, and major proportions of the export crops. The extent to which such farming is more destructive of the environment than large-scale modern farms is not proven. More important, one can ask, what substitute offered for hillside farmers is superior? Certainly mechanization induces even greater erosion. Indeed, mechanization is not possible in many fields now planted to food crops, and if the hills are to be reserved for forest regrowth, where else can poor people make a living? Even more basic, where else and how else will an equivalent amount of food be grown on many small islands?

To some extent it seems as if the deficit food production that concerns many governments is a self-inflicted wound. A tendency on the part of bureaucrats to dictate rather than to listen to small farmers has created unnecessary tensions and has hampered development of market-oriented food production (Hills and Iton 1981, pp. 12–15). That the current practices of small farmers could be improved by judicious infusions of agronomic science seems obvious. That successful modifications require better understanding of both the ecological merits of the indigenous sytems and the value sets of the farmers appears equally obvious. Approaches that enlist cooperation on the basis of mutual respect offer greater chances for success, if only because attempts at mandates and coercion have produced dismal results.

Increased domestic food production in the Caribbean appears feasible, particularly on Jamaica, on Trinidad and Tobago, and on the high volcanic islands of the Lesser Antilles. The prospects are favorable because there are no serious ecological obstacles. Rather, the degree of success appears to depend more upon the soundness of the management strategies adopted. Lessened reliance upon food imports in turn would have stragegic implications. Complete food self-sufficiency seems neither possible nor desirable. Opportunities for consumer choice are a mark of an open society, and all evidence suggests that West Indians value highly their liberties. On the other hand, there is a clear difference in national self-esteem between a condition wherein food imports are an option and one in which they are necessary for survival.

Tourism

Unlike plantation agriculture, the other current mainstay of Caribbean island economies—tourism—has recent origins. Expansion began following World War II as an outgrowth of the established winter tourist trade of South Florida, particularly by way of cruise ships to Cuba and The Bahamas. By the 1950s visits by U.S. tourists included Antigua and Barbados, an extension that in effect opened the entire eastern Caribbean to the industry by the early 1960s. The main stimulus came from managers of hotel chains.

For example, Montego Bay, Jamaica, was fashioned and promoted as an overseas version of Miami Beach (Carrington and Blake 1975, p. 34).

Of particular importance also was the increased use of jet airliners. Such craft made short period—even weekend—visits a comfortable option for the affluent in the eastern United States and Canada. Promotions by hotel chains, airlines, and travel agents also helped create greater tourist interest in the region. Cruise ships, with their itinerary of multiple-port visits, constituted a separate and expanded dimension of the industry as well. A wider development of tourist facilities on the smaller islands was spurred also by the U.S. economic boycott of Cuba that began in 1960.

The attractions to North Americans are obvious. The islands have year-round sunny weather with a nearby ocean at nearly every hotel. The accommodations, food, and entertainment are generally excellent and comfortably familiar. Familiar also are the languages spoken. For most Americans and Canadians the locations are more convenient than any other tropical area, including Hawaii.

Promoted initially among the affluent, a Caribbean vacation early acquired the image of a luxurious experience. The effect was to heighten its allure and to narrow its market. The greater capabilities of jet aircraft motivated marketing strategies aimed at a wider clientele. The subsequent increase in number of tourists was impressive, especially in view of the small populations on most islands. By the mid-1970s both Antigua and Barbados had more visitors annually than their national population totals (Carrington and Blake 1975, p. 17). On major winter holidays, as many as 80,000 tourists from cruise ships alone might be in St. Thomas, Virgin Islands (McElroy 1975, p. 53). The greatest numbers visit The Bahamas, which by the mid-1970s received over 2.5 million tourists annually (Maynard 1975, iv). Contributing to increases in numbers were adjustments such as provision of lower cost hotels and guest houses and the option of package tours. The latter arrangement appealed particularly to price-conscious travelers.

The economic impacts of tourism are distributed unevenly. Tourism is weakly developed on many very small islands such as the Grenadines, Turks and Caicos, Barbuda, Anguilla, and Saba, as well as the larger areas of Grenada, Dominica, and St. Vincent. And although Jamaica is more involved in the industry than is Trinidad and Tobago, due to greater size and complexity, in neither country is tourism the leading sector of the economy. Similarly, earnings from large numbers of vacationers on Aruba and Curaçao do not supplant the economic primacy of petroleum-related industries. At the other extremes are the aforementioned Bahamas, Barbados, U.S. Virgin Islands, and Antigua, where income from tourism is dominant. In this category as well are St. Lucia and St. Martin/St. Maarten. The remainder of the islands fall somewhere between. Provision of major new facilities or changes in preference can produce dramatic changes in popularity, however.

Despite the primary role of outside interests in the growth of Caribbean tourism, the investments initially were welcomed on the various islands. The appeal was understandable. Money spent on construction provided jobs and aided infrastructure development, particularly in the matters of utilities, roads, and airports. Visitors with money to spend were expected to stimulate expansion of related service industries. Accepted also was the premise that tourism was a cheaply acquired tool of development. That is, capital, infrastructure, employment, and worker skills could be obtained with little national sacrifice and through planning be used to accelerate comprehensive national development (Doxey 1975). Such expectations are now rare. In their place is the growing realization that economic development is different and more complex than economic growth, and that the two are not necessarily related (Carrington and Blake 1975, p. 1).

Indeed, large-scale tourism is widely criticized, as much on social and ecological grounds as on economic ones. Prime Minister Lynden O. Pindling of The Bahamas has expressed reservations regarding the impact of massive tourism on the morals, attitudes, consumption patterns and cultural forms of island young people (Maynard 1975, ii). Also present is resentment regarding the revival of the social forms of slavery, that is, the constantly renewed circumstance of white affluence and leisure in a setting of poor black servants. The fact that tourists the world over can be intoxicated and demanding intensifies the contrasts. Consequently, tourism is more and more regarded by island residents as an exploitative activity that generates tensions and hostility (Carrington and Blake 1975, p. 4).

Awareness of the ecological ramifications of massive tourism is less common. Most basic is the matter of waste disposal. Involved for the most part are small islands with high visitor concentrations along the coasts. Modern-style showers and flush toilets are prerequisite for commercial success in the industry. Provision of sufficient water and sanitary disposal of sewage is particularly difficult. Inordinate consumption of scarce water is an issue on some islands. One expensive solution is sea-water desalination, an alternative currently employed in the Netherlands Antilles and U.S. Virgin Islands. Just how to prevent tourist-generated sewage from polluting the very waters they traveled far to enjoy is a more difficult problem. At far too many beach resorts the problem has not been solved and the danger of water-borne disease has increased. Construction of roads and trails along with high human densities have adversely affected vegetation and accelerated erosion as well.

Cost/benefit analyses also highlight inherent defects of economies based on tourism. Even though tourism can generate considerable gross income—as much as 77 percent of the foreign income of The Bahamas, for example (Maynard 1975, iii)—only part of that income directly benefits the host country. Income associated with Caribbean tourism normally has a high import content. This term refers to that proportion of the income expended elsewhere to bring in goods and services needed to sustain the industry (Jefferson 1975, p. 59). According to one estimate only 40 cents of every tourist dollar remained in the region (Caribbean Community Secretariat 1973, p. 8). Much of this financial leakage was used to buy foods needed to please tourists. When away from home, North American tourists in particular are not adventuresome in the matter of diet. Local growers generally cannot supply many of the types of food demanded.

Better hotel services often include European chefs, imported for their ability to prepare European recipes. This practice reduces still further the demands for local commodities, and the wages paid such expatriates constitute another form of leakage. Also part of the appeal of the Caribbean region for tourists has been duty-free shopping. As the name itself states, comparatively little of such expenditures for imported goods remains in the country of purchase.

Insufficient linkage with other components of the island economies has been another weakness of tourism. Most commonly recognized is poor integration with local agriculture. Solutions are not easy. Purchasing agents for large hotels, for example, require assured quantity and quality of specific foods in order to maintain efficient operations. Caribbean small farmers are ill-equipped and organized to meet such expectations on a sustained basis. And where tropical fruits are grown commercially, their destination is as likely to be canning or processing plants as tourist centers. Local fishing is even more poorly developed than small farming. Thus, tourists and their future meals may at times arrive on the same flight from the United States.

Linkages with manufacturing are little better, although the reasons are less obvious. Often purchase of domestic rum drinks offers little price advantage over imported Scotches, to the detriment of the local economy (Doxey 1975, p. 83). Despite manufacture in the Caribbean of items such as sheets, towels, mattresses, and furniture, many hotels rely on imports for their needs. Regional trade patterns show a number of such inconsistencies.

Tourism does create service and maintenance jobs. Just how beneficial such employment is to current economies and national development is questioned, nonetheless. On small islands with major facilities the proportions are high. Estimates for Barbados, for example, were that as much as 11 percent of the total employment was related to tourism. On the other hand, for Jamaica the contribution was less than 3 percent of the work force (Carrington and Blake 1975, p. 25). Reservations are expressed, however, about the fact that most such work is at best semiskilled, that a degree of servility is expected, and that few skills acquired are applicable to other sorts of employment. In addition, work is not only seasonal (December to May) but it coincides with the peak demand for labor in the sugar industry. The two activities are not at all complementary in terms of timing. Indeed, there is concern that work in tourist centers diverts labor away from more arduous agricultural jobs. In addition, unionization of service workers has increased wage levels considerably, a factor that has been construed as hampering development of other activities such as agriculture and manufacturing (Carrington and Blake 1975, pp. 18–19).

No issue related to tourism, however, is more politically potent—domestically and internationally—than that of foreign ownership and the unavoidable dependence of the industry on conditions elsewhere. Many hotels are foreign-owned, three-fourths of the large hotels on Barbados, for example (Carrington and Blake 1975, p. 28). So also are most associated travel agencies, banks, advertising, and airlines. Only Air Jamaica of the five regional airlines has important extraregional connections. Even where majority ownership is domestic, large tourist hotels often have expatriate managers (Carrington and Blake 1975, p. 32). Compounding the lack of control over their economies is awareness in the Caribbean that tourist flows are fickle. Economic recession, air-fare adjustments, modified currency regulations, or emergence of alternative vacation regions can reduce the number of visitors drastically. As was demonstrated in 1960 in Cuba, international political animosity can have negative effects as well.

Thus despite its status as one of the world's most favored vacation areas and tourism's great contributions to various national economies, governments in the Caribbean are not content with the industry as it is presently constituted. The tendency of tourist facilities to function as enclaves, located on the islands but tied culturally and economically elsewhere, is a matter of wide concern. Proposed remedies are many (see Carrington and Blake 1975, pp. 36–52) but the impediments to unilateral management of an immutably international activity are great. Prospects are slim for basic modifications over the next few decades. Hence the tourist industry can be expected to contribute to diplomatic friction and even political instability over the next few decades.

Minerals and Energy

Fundamental to regional economic analysis is assessment of available energy sources. By this measure, the island Caribbean is poorly endowed. Only Trinidad, a geologic extension of the Venezuelan mainland, has significant production of petroleum and natural gas. Trinidad and Tobago is, in fact, a member of OPEC. It is, however, one of that cartel's smallest members, producing less than .5 percent of world production (Macpherson 1980, p. 66). The deposits lie under the southern plains and offshore to both the east and west (Blume 1974, p. 365). During the period of high prices in the late 1970s, petroleum accounted for about 90 percent of the country's exports, a proportion that reflects as much the small economy as the volume of production. However, employment totals in the petroleum industry are relatively small, perhaps only 5 percent of the labor force (Macpherson 1980, p. 68). A related resource is the world's largest deposit of natural asphalt.

The remainder of the island Caribbean has almost no known fossil-fuel resources aside from small deposits of oil and natural gas exploited on and offshore Barbados. The search has been active, despite little expectation of more than modest finds. Prospects seem greatest under waters southwest of Jamaica, and optimism has been expressed regarding the area surrounding Antigua as well. Explorations intensified in 1981, with involvement by both U.S. and Canadian companies (Paul 1981). No coal is present and except for Jamaica the islands are too small, too low, too dry, or all three to possess useful hydroelectric potential. Centuries of deforestation has seriously depleted even wood resources other than on Jamaica, Tobago, and The Bahamas. The potential use of sugar for ethanol and bagasse for fuel has nowhere been effectively exploited (Orfila 1982).

With the exception of Trinidad, the Caribbean islands supply almost none of their own modern energy needs, 95 percent of which are supplied by imported oil. Yet collectively the 22 political entities had a petroleum consumption level half that of Mexico and twice that of Venezuela. Roughly half that total was consumed in Cuba and Puerto Rico, and the Netherlands Antilles and U.S. Virgin Islands together took over a fourth, mainly to supply petrochemical industries (Drewry 1981, p. 13). The needs of the other islands were small, the volume being commensurate with the relative population of each. Because of the necessity for imports, the surge in world oil prices that began in 1973 produced economic distress nearly everywhere. For example, Jamaica's oil import bill rose from $44 million in 1972 to over $800 million in 1980 (Huey 1981).

The world glut of petroleum supplies in the early 1980s eased pressures on the region only slightly and in ways even exacerbated the situation. Under the San Jose Pact, Venezuela and Mexico acted to mitigate the distress caused by the price rises through subsidized petroleum sales to energy-deficient states in the region. The fall in world demand beginning in 1980, however, greatly reduced the income of these two exporters, leading to economic crisis in Mexico and recession in Venezuela. The future of these subsidized supplies was unclear at the time of writing, but optimism was muted as Venezuela had already reduced its subsidy.

The dearth of fossil-energy sources in the Caribbean may yet be counterbalanced by the potential for development of unconventional sources. Most obvious of these are solar- and wind-power conversion devices. Sunshine and the tropical easterlies are two of the most reliable aspects of the environment. Both sources were utilized in colonial times. The wind powered sugar cane grinders, and solar pans were used to evaporate salt from sea water. The latter technique, in fact, is still employed. In advanced countries the technology to utilize both sources for electrical generation advanced greatly during the 1970s. Current stages of development suggest that applications at commercially feasible scales to Caribbean conditions will soon be possible. The greatest reservations are expressed regarding wind-powered generators. Facilities capable of withstanding the region's hurricane winds are difficult to design.

The volcanic islands also offer prospects for geothermal development. Use of underground heat to produce steam, or natural steam itself for generation of electricity, has been accomplished in a number of places in the world. Islands with potential in this regard include: Dominica, Grenada, Guadeloupe, Martinique, Montserrat, St. Kitts, St. Lucia, and St. Vincent. The concept attracts planners in the region and a number of feasibility studies are under way. The appeal of a pollution-free, inexhaustible domestic source of power is considerable.

Somewhat more exotic is the technique of ocean thermal energy conversion. The idea is old; it was first proposed in 1881. Yet not until the 1970s had research developed the technology to make such installations practical. The concept is simple. In the tropics and subtropics there is a sharp temperature contrast between surface water (around 25°C) and deep water (about 5°C). Both open- and closed-cycle systems have been studied, with each employing a heat exchanger to convert the contrasting water temperatures into heat sufficient to produce steam. Many technical details remain to be solved, but ocean conditions in the Caribbean are well-suited to the operation of such systems. Indeed, the first ocean thermal conversion plant was built in 1930 in Matanzas Bay, Cuba. Although operated successfully, the installation was destroyed by heavy seas after two weeks. (A thorough account of contemporary ocean thermal energy conversion technology can be found in Sheets 1981.)

The technology needed to exploit each of these unconventional energy sources was yet incomplete in 1983. Installation of any one of the systems would require considerable investment. The potential returns from such facilities are also great. The resources of sun, wind, and ocean temperature contrasts are available on all islands, and eight islands have geothermal possibilities in addition. Despite high capital investment costs, once installed each system would utilize inexhaustible and virtually free natural energy sources. Over the long term it is not irrational to envision these currently energy-deficient islands as places with adequate to abundant electrical capacities. Even transportation needs could then be met through use of battery-powered vehicles, an option well-suited to the small size of most islands. As the history of petroleum has demonstrated over the past century, advances in technology can drastically alter geopolitical circumstances in the world. Such a prospect exists for the Caribbean.

Mineral resources likewise are generally deficient with the major exception of Jamaica. Bauxite reserves there are among the world's largest and are found generally above 1,000-feet elevation in a doughnut-shaped area surrounding the central highlands (Macpherson 1980, p. 44). Their presence was known for decades before exploitation began in 1952. From that point the pace of development was so rapid that production reached 8.5 million tons in 1955 (Blume 1974, p. 201) and soon held first rank in the world, attaining a maximum of 15 million tons in 1974 (Macpherson 1980, p. 45). Development was accomplished initially by one Canadian and four U.S. corporations and was stimulated in part by geopolitical considerations. North America has no major deposits of this strategic ore, and World War II had demonstrated the vulnerability to attack of shipping connections from more distant sources such as the Guianas. Both dried ore and alumina from Jamaican processing plants are shipped to the United States and Canada for refining, a process that requires abundant cheap electricity which in turn is not now available in the Caribbean.

Jamaica's position in the early 1970s as the world's leading producer caused then-Prime Minister Michael Manley to attempt to create an International Bauxite Association modeled after OPEC. In an effort aimed at achieving more "justice" between producing and consuming countries, Jamaica and six other members of an 11-member group raised bauxite export levies 600 percent (Nag 1981). Despite the move, enough alternative sources remained to cause a sharp drop in export income, a severe economic blow at a time when bauxite and alumina sales earned two-thirds of the country's foreign exchange (Huey 1981). By 1976, Jamaica's share of the world market dropped to 18 percent to rank third behind Australia and Guiana (Macpherson 1980, p. 45). Adjustments in these levies had been negotiated even before the 1980 election of Edward Seaga, and since that event relations between the companies and the Jamaican government are marked by cooperation rather than confrontation. Indeed, new investments in the industry could reach $1 billion by the late 1980s (Huey 1980).

Other than bauxite, petroleum, natural gas, and asphalt, mining within the area of study is confined to rock minerals. Gypsum is extracted on Jamaica and massive deposits of aragonite (similar to calcite) are exploited on Sandy Cay in The Bahamas. Limestone is quarried widely for domestic use, mainly for construction and to supply cement factories. Evaporation of sea water in solar pans to supply salt is not precisely a mining operation but is carried out at a number of sites. Salt from The Bahamas is sent to the U.S. East Coast for use in snow clearance.

Manufacturing

By a wide margin, petroleum refining is the leading industrial activity in the Caribbean. Taken as a whole, the Caribbean islands in 1980 accounted for 12 percent of the entire refinery capacity in a contiguous area that included the United States. Of this proportion, the Netherlands Antilles, U.S. Virgin Islands, The Bahamas, and Trinidad and Tobago held 10 percent of the capacity. Production for that year was at two-thirds capacity, a level consistent with worldwide operational levels (Drewry 1981, p. 16). All refineries but those on Trinidad process imported oil and 90 percent of output is exported. It is an activity that takes considerable advantage from the intermediate location and island nature of the region.

Refining is done at six places of unusual significance. The Amerada Hess refinery at St. Croix, V.I. (728,000 barrel/per day capacity) is the largest single operation outside the socialist bloc. The other five are at Freeport, Bahamas (500,000 barrels per day); Aruba (440,000 barrels per day) and Curacao (360,000 barrels per day), Netherlands Antilles; and Pointe-a-Pierre (356,000 barrels per day) and Point Fortin (100,000 barrels per day), Trinidad and Tobago (Drewry 1981, p. 19). Under construction at Cul de Sac Bay, St. Lucia, is a 150,000 barrel per day capacity refinery sited in conjunction with the transshipment facility that opened in 1981 (Drewry 1981, p. 68). A much smaller export-oriented refinery on Antigua has operated since 1981 and provides the most valuable export on the island (*Caribbean Year Book* 1978, p. 368). The remaining refineries convert imported crude for domestic needs. The largest of these (34,000 barrels per day) is a government-owned facility at Kingston, Jamaica (Drewry 1981, p. 20). Smaller refineries operate on Barbados and Martinique.

Diverse manufacturing activities are present only in the larger, more populous countries of Jamaica and Trinidad and Tobago. In addition to their concerns with the processing of bauxite and petroleum, respectively, each fully qualifies for the category of more developed country rather than lesser developed country. Each produces a wide range of consumer goods for both domestic and external markets.

Food processing is especially important, with textiles, clothing, shoes, containers, furniture, pharmaceuticals, and appliances other common categories of goods. The export industries in these countries and throughout the region are usually of an assembly nature, with imported components being transformed into finished items. In such "screwdriver" industries (Macpherson 1980, p. 75), the main locational advantages are location, a receptive investment climate for multinational companies, and an abundant supplying of willing, moderately priced workers. As with tourism and agriculture, the foreign ownership of such enterprises produces resentment and has political repercussions.

Aside from petrochemical industries associated with the main refinery centers, the smaller islands' main industries are procesing local agricultural commodities and manufacture of consumer goods for a domestic market. Thus sugar, rum, beer, footwear, foods, garments, and cement are produced widely, sometimes in very small factories. Several islands have acquired specific industries out of the ordinary. Martinique has a dry dock and ship repair facilities, precision tools are made in the Caymans, and on Antigua the Arawak Hustler is assembled from parts imported from Britain. The Hustler is a small, open-top vehicle designed for sport, hotel transport, and light commercial uses. Assembly industries linked with multinational companies also are expanding on the smaller islands. Most common thus far are clothing, containers, and electrical components.

Finance

The Bahamas and Cayman Islands occupy special places in the fields of finance and business. Both have adopted extremely generous tax laws that make it advantageous for companies to register and operate. The number of banks and investments enterprises is particularly notale. In the late 1970s, for example, the Caymans alone were the licensed headquarters of over 200 banks as well as more than 8,000 companies (Macpherson 1980, p. 61) and by 1983 the number of banks exceeded 400 (Goodale 1983). Concentrated in these two otherwise obscure political units is an extraordinarily large share of all capital transfers in the Western Hemisphere. The economic activity is unusual in that it requires little infrastructure beyond a comprehensive and dependable communications network. A receptive and stable political atmosphere also is prerequisite.

Tax treaties with the United States in 1955 created financial havens of a somewhat different sort in the Netherlands Antilles and, until June 1982, in the British Virgin Islands. The effect of the treaties was to enable corporations registered there to borrow investment capital through London banks in the form of Eurobonds. Not only were the interest rates often favorable but a U.S. corporation operating through an Antilles subsidiary was exempt from payment of a 30 percent federal withholding tax on interest payments to foreigners. The process, known as "going through the Antillean window," was basically a tax dodge. Its potential attracted an estimated 15,000 registered corporations to the islands, although only about 200 Eurobond loans were on record in 1982. Losses to the U.S. Treasury were estimated to be as high as $25 billion. On the other hand, the $50 million a year revenues and employment opportunities for politically restive college graduates have aided greatly the economies and political stability of the resource-poor islands. Congressional efforts to close the loophole in 1983 were expected to remove this unique economic aspect of the Caribbean. (Details were taken from Fialka 1982.)

The sites where these enormous volumes of financial transactions take place are not necessarily fixed. Most businesses could relocate their legal centers of operations in a matter of days, perhaps in hours if pressed. Nonetheless, several geopolitical considerations are involved. The small size of each makes maintenance of a favorable investment climate less complex and also reduces international pressures to conform. Ministates are perceived less as major economic competitors. More important perhaps is their location within a few hours distance by air in time zones little different from those of major financial centers on two continents. Such proximity permits convenient personal and electronic contacts between mainland and island offices during normal working hours at each place.

The Bahamas also recently have become involved in another sort of international financial activity, that of a center for registry of foreign shipping. Although ship owners were slow to use the Bahamian register after the enabling legislation was passed in 1977, the tonnage under the flag of The Bahamas increased rapidly after 1981 and was expected to exceed a million tons by 1984. Use of open registries, or flags of convenience as they are called, grew rapidly after World War II, mainly because of the tax advantages to owners.

The surge of interest in Bahamian registry by ship owners was sparked by a military coup in Liberia, the world's leading flag of convenience. Also, the fact that the British lease of the Crown Colony of Hong Kong from China expires in 1997 has raised doubts concerning the future there among Hong Kong ship owners who now control about 20 percent of all open-registered tonnage. The opportunity for registration in The Bahamas was enhanced by its political stability, established reputation as a tax haven and banking center, and its proximity to the United States.

In an effort not to be stigmatized by the poor safety record often attributed to ships of foreign registry, the Bahamian government has imposed strict construction and operating standards on the ships it accepts for registration.

As of mid-1983 comparatively fewer U.S. ship owners had availed themselves of Bahamian registry, even though The Bahamas Merchant Shipping Act was amended in 1982 to allow foreign owners to commit their ships registered in The Bahamas to effective control of their home governments in time of war or national emergency. In December 1982 the Federation of American Controlled Shipping added The Bahamas to the list of three open-registry countries approved by the federation. It joined Liberia and Panama and replaced Honduras. The decision was based in part on a declined in tonnage registered in Honduras and in part because of the high standards required for Bahamian registry.

In addition to the financial benefits to The Bahamas from the practice, there are military implications for the United States as well. The number of ships owned by American companies is far greater than the number registered in the United States. The right to use that foreign-registered fleet for transport during a national emergency is a major consideration for strategic planners (adapted loosely from Kelly 1983).

Communications

The electronic communications system of the Caribbean was improved greatly during the late 1970s. Virtually every island is now linked into an efficient modern network that not only serves intraregional needs but is tied to the rest of the world as well. The eastern Caribbean microwave scheme can carry 960 high-grade voice channels on many thousands of telegraph, telex, and data channels. The stations are sited as follows: United States, St. Thomas, Tortola, Saba, Antigua, Guadeloupe, Maria Galante, Dominica, Martinique, St. Lucia, St. Vincent, Carriacou, Grenada, Trinidad, Guyana. The spur between Barbados retains an over-the-horizon wideband radio system because distance and the low elevations on Barbados prevent direct-line contact. Otherwise line-of-sight hops of up to 100 miles are employed. Connections also tie in Jamaica and the Caymans as well as Grand Turk, North Caicos, and Providencials Islands (*Caribbean Year Book* 1978, ix–x).

This microwave system is joined to the global telecommunication networks through cable and microwave links from Tortola in the north and by a satellite earth station on Trinidad. Connections also are present on Martinique and Barbados (*Caribbean Year Book*, 1978, x). The high standard of telecommunication is of great benefit to the tourist industry. Visitors, especially those in business, expect and may require communication facilities similar to those at home. Airlines, banks, and travel agencies have comparable needs. Successful integration of the Caribbean islands into the regional and worldwide networks is a development resource of considerable worth. The effect is to remove the onus of isolation, at least in terms of communication, from small maritime states and dependencies.

REFERENCES

Abbott, George C. 1981. "The Associated States and Independence." *Journal of Inter-American Studies and World Affairs*, 23, pp. 69–93.

Adams, Nassau A. 1968. "An Analysis of Food Consumption and Food Import Trends in Jamaica, 1950–1963." *Social and Economic Studies*, 17, pp. 1–22.

Alvarez, Fernando Bueno. 1982. Personal correspondence. July, SMT, Mexico City, Mexico.

Augelli, John P. 1962. "The Rimland–Mainland Concept of Culture Areas in Middle America." *Annals of the Association of American Geographers*, 52, June, pp. 119–29.

Auty, Richard M. 1981. "Caribbean Sugar Factory Size and Survival." *Annals of the Association of American Geographers*, 66, May, pp. 76–88.

Ballard, O. N. 1971. "Literacy in a Rural Area of Jamaica." *Social and Economic Studies*, 20, pp. 28–51.

Banks, Arthur S. and Overstreet, William (eds.). 1981. *Political Handbook of the World: 1981*. New York: McGraw-Hill.

Bartlett, Paul. 1982. "World Tanker Fleet—Future Prospects." *Seatrade*, April, p. 47.

Blume, Helmut. 1974. *The Caribbean Lands*. London: Longman Group.

Britannica Yearbook. 1960. "Cuba," pp. 189–91. Chicago: Encyclopedia Britannica.

Caribbean Community Secretariat. 1973. *The Caribbean Community: A Guide*. Georgetown, Guyana: Author.

Caribbean Year Book, The, 49th Edition, 1978–79. 1978. Toronto: Caribook Limited.

Carrington, Edwin W. and Blake, Byron W. 1975. "Tourism as a Vehicle for Caribbean Development." In *The Economic Impact of Tourism*, edited by C. T. Maynard, pp. 1–52. Nassau: Caribbean Tourism Research Center.

Central Intelligence Agency. 1980. *National Basic Intelligence Factbook* (GC BIF 79-001). Washington, DC: Government Printing Office.

Clarke, Colin G. 1975. *Kingston, Jamica: Urban Growth and Social Change, 1692–1962*. The American Geographical Society Research Series Number 27. Berkeley: University of California Press.

_____. 1976. "Insularity and Identity in the Caribbean." *Geography*, 61, January, pp. 8–16.

Davis, Carlton G. 1975. "Agricultural Research and Agricultural Development in Small Plantation Economies: The Case of the West Indies." *Social and Economic Studies*, 24, March, pp. 117–49.

Dominguez, Virginia R. and Dominguez, Jorge. 1981. *The Caribbean: Its Implications for the United States*. Headline Series 253, February. New York: Foreign Policy Association.

Doxey, George V. 1975. "Tourism as a Tool of Development." In *The Economic Impact of Tourism*, edited by C. T. Maynard, pp. 79–89, Nassau: Caribbean Tourism Research Center.

Drewry, H. P. 1981. *Caribbean Oil Trades* (Number One Hundred in a Series). London: HPD Shipping Publications.

Emery, K. O. and Uchupi, Elazar. 1975. "The Oil Potential of the Caribbean." In *The Tides of Change*, edited by Elizabeth Ann Borgese and David Krieger. New York: Mason/Charter.

Eriksen, E. Gordon. 1962. *The West Indies Population Problems*. Lawrence: University of Kansas Publications.

Eyre, L. Alan. 1972. "The Shantytowns of Montego Bay, Jamaica." *Geographical Review*, 62, pp. 394–413.

Fialka, John J. 1982. "Corporate Tax Haven in Netherlands Antilles is Bracing for a Disaster." *Wall Street Journal*, October 10, pp. 1, 14.

Frank, Andre Gunder. 1967. *Capitalism and Underdevelopment in Latin America*. New York: Monthly Press Review.

Girvan, Norman. 1973. "The Development of Dependence Economics in the Caribbean: Review and Comparison." *Social and Economic Studies*, 22, March, pp. 1–33.

Goodale, Gloria. 1983. "Why Cayman Islanders in the Caribbean Prefer Living Under the Union Jack." *Christian Science Monitor*, January 11, p. 11.

Goode's World Atlas. 1982. 16th Edition, pp. 237–41. Skokie, IL: Rand McNally.

Gullick, C. J. M. R. 1982. "Confused Identity in the Caribbean." *Geographical Magazine*, 54, pp. 522–23.

Hall, Douglas. 1972. "The Ex-Colonial Society of Jamaica. In *Patterns of Foreign Influence in the Caribbean*, edited by Emanuel de Kadt, pp. 23–48. London: Oxford University Press.

Harris, R. N. and Steer, E. S. 1968. "Demographic–Resources Push in Rural Migration: A Jamaican Case Study." *Social and Economic Studies*, 17, pp. 398–406.

Hills, Theo. L. and Iton, Stanley. 1981. "Let's Reassess the 'Traditional' in Caribbean Small-Scale Agriculture (horticulture)." May. Montreal: McGill University Geography Department. Mimeographed.

_____. 1982. "The 'Food Forest' a Type of Intensive Tropical Mixed Garden Agriculture—Its Contemporary Ecological Significance." May. Montreal: McGill University Geography Department. Mimeographed.

Hoetink, Harry. 1972. "The Dutch Caribbean and its Metropolis." In *Patterns of Foreign Influence in the Caribbean*, edited by Emanuel de Kadt, pp. 103–20. London: Oxford University Press.

Huey, John. 1980. "For Socialist Jamaica, Big Capital Infusion may be only Solution." *Wall Street Journal*, February 25, pp. 1, 33.

_____. 1981. "Money Returns to Troubled Jamaica." *Wall Street Journal*, April 27, p. 30.

Innis, Donald Q. 1976. "Traditional Versus Modern Methods of Increasing Tropical Food Production (in India and Jamaica)." General Economic Geography, *Proceedings* of the 23rd International Geographical Union, 6, pp. 203–08. Moscow.

Jackson, Steven, et al. 1979. "An Assessment of Empirical Research on Dependencia." *Latin American Research Review*, 14, pp. 7–28.

Jefferson, Owen. 1975. "Some Economic Aspects of Tourism." In *The Economic Impact of Tourism*, edited by C. T. Maynard, pp. 53–69. Nassau: Caribbean Tourism Research Center.

Johnson, Kenneth F. and Williams, Mile W. 1981. *Illegal Aliens in the Western Hemisphere*. New York: Praeger Publishers.

Keagy, Thomas J. 1975. "The Redlegs of Barbados." *Americas*, 24, January, pp. 14–21.

Kelly, Nicki. 1983. "Bahamas Makes Waves as a Shipping Registry." *Christian Science Monitor*, May 11, p. 10.

Lasserre, Guy and Mabileau, Albert. 1972. "The French Antilles and Status as Overseas Departments." In *Patterns of Foreign Influence in the Caribbean*, edited by Emanuel de Kadt, pp. 82–102. London: Oxford University Press.

Lenoir, J. D. 1975. "Surinam National Development and Maroon Cultural Autonomy." *Social and Economic Studies*, 24, pp. 308–19.

Lewis, Vaughn A. 1974. "The Bahamas in International Affairs: Issues Arising from an Archipelagic State." *Journal of Inter-American Studies and World Affairs*, 16, pp. 131–52.

Macpherson, John. 1973. *Caribbean Lands: A Geography of the West Indies* (3rd edition). Trinidad: Longman Caribbean.

_____. 1980. *Caribbean Lands: A Geography of the West Indies* (4th edition). Trinidad: Longman Caribbean.

Mahan, A. T. 1898. *The Interest of America in Sea Power, Present and Future.* Boston: Little, Brown.

Marshall, Woodville K. 1968. "Peasant Development in the West Indies Since 1838." *Social and Economic Studies*, 17, pp. 252–63.

Mason, Clifford. 1981. "Trinidad: A Rich Land That Doesn't Work." *Wall Street Journal*, November 2, pp. 26.

Mathews, Thomas. 1975. "Historical Patterns of Caribbean Communication." In *The Tides of Change*, edited by Elizabeth Ann Borgese and David Krieger, pp. 222–38. New York: Mason/Charter.

Maynard, C. T. 1975. "Remarks." In *The Economic Impact of Tourism*, edited by C. T. Maynard, pp.ii–vi. Nassau: Caribbean Tourism Research Center.

McElroy, Jerome L. 1975. "Tourist Economy and Island Environment: An Overview of Structural Disequilibrium." *Caribbean Educational Bulletin* (The Association of Caribbean Universities) 2, pp. 40–58.

McGinnis, Charles I. 1974. "A New Look at the Panama Canal." *Military Engineer*, 66: 432, July-August, pp. 219–22.

Nag, Amal. 1981. "Jamaica and Aluminum Firms Seen Close to Accord on Reduction in Aluminum Levy." *Wall Street Journal*, March 20, p. 29.

Naipaul, V. S. 1963. *The Middle Passage*. New York: Macmillan.

Niddrie, David L. 1961. *Land Use and Population in Tobago*. Bude, England: Geographical Publications.

_____. 1971. "The Caribbean." In *Latin America: Geographical Perspectives*, edited by Harold Blakemore and Clifford Smith, pp. 73–120. London: Methuen.

Norton, Ann and Symanski, Richard. 1975. "The Internal Marketing Systems of Jamaica." *Geographical Review*, 65, pp. 461–75.

Orfila, Alejandre. 1982. "Reagan's Caribbean Plan is Coated with Sugar Quotas." *Wall Street Journal*, July 20, p. 30.

Padelford, Norman S. and Gibbs, Stephen R. 1975. *Maritime Commerce and the Future of the Panama Canal*. Cambridge, MD: Cornell Maritime Press.

Paul, Bill. 1981. "Caribbean Nations Intensify Oil Search." *Wall Street Journal*, June 19, p. 29.

Peach, G. C. K. 1967. "West Indians as a Replacement Population in England and Wales." *Social and Economic Studies*, 16, pp. 289–94.

Pearcy, G. Etzel. 1965. *The West Indian Scene*. Princeton, NJ: D. Van Nostrand.

Population Reference Bureau. 1978. *World's Children Data Sheet 1978*. Washington, DC: Government Printing Office.

_____. 1982. *World's Children Data Sheet 1982*. Washington, DC: Government Printing Office.

_____. 1979. *World Population Data Sheet 1979*. Washington, DC: Government Printing Office.

_____. 1980. *World Population Data Sheet 1980*. Washington, DC: Government Printing Office.

_____. 1981. *World Population Data Sheet 1981*. Washington, DC: Government Printing Office.

Price, E. (ed.). 1973. *Maroon Societies—Rebel Slave Communities in the Americas*. New York: Doubleday.

Reid, George L. 1974. *The Impact of Very Small Size on the International Behavior of Microstates* (International Studies Series, No. 02-027). Beverly Hills, CA: Sage Publications.

Richardson, Bonham C. 1975. "The Overdevelopment of Carriacou." *Geographical Review*, 65, pp. 390–99.

Samaroo, Brindley. 1972. "The Trinidad Workingman's Association and the Origins of Popular Protest in a Crown Colony." *Social and Economic Studies*, 21, pp. 205–22.

Sauer, Carl O. 1954. "Economic Prospects in the Caribbean." In *The Caribbean: Its Economy*, edited by A. Curtis Wilgus, pp. 15–27. Gainesville: University of Florida Press.

———. 1966. *The Early Spanish Main*. Berkeley: University of California Press.

———. 1981. "The Indian Food Production in the Caribbean." *Geographical Review*, 71, pp. 272–80.

Sheets, Herman E. 1981. Ocean Thermal Energy Conversion—An Overview." In *Ecology and Environmental Protection in the Pacific Region*, edited by N. A. Shilo and A. V. Lozkin, pp. 237–49. Moscow: Publishing Office Nauka.

Sheridan, Richard. 1970. *The Development of the Plantations to 1750: An Era of West Indian Prosperity, 1750–1775*. Barbados: Caribbean Universities Press.

Shryock, Henry S., et al. 1973. *The Methods and Materials of Demography* (Vol. 1). Washington, DC: Government Printing Office.

Stone, Carl. 1974. "Political Aspects of Postwar Agricultural Policies in Jamaica." *Social and Economic Studies*, 23, pp. 145–75.

Tidrick, Gene. 1966. "Some Aspects of Jamaican Emigration to the United Kingdom, 1953–1962." *Social and Economic Studies*, 15, pp. 22–39.

U.S. Bureau of the Census. 1981. *Statistical Abstract of the United States, 1981* (102nd Edition). Washington, DC: Government Printing Office.

U.S. Department of State. 1981. *International Narcotics Control Strategy* (Current Policy No. 345). Washington, DC: Government Printing Office.

Waddell, D. A. G. 1967. *The West Indies and the Guianas*. Englewood Cliffs, NJ: Prentice-Hall.

Wedderburn, Earl Clive. 1977. "The Labor Movement in Jamaica." Term Paper, Harvard Trade Union Program. Cambridge: Harvard University. Mimeographed.

West, Robert C. and Augelli, John P. 1971. *Middle America: Its Lands and Peoples* (2nd edition). Englewood Cliffs, NJ: Prentice-Hall.

EXPLANATORY NOTES

1. Those with socialist leanings maintain that independence did not truly begin in Cuba until Fidel Castro took power in January 1959.

2. By definition a hurricane-force wind exceeds 75 miles per hour.

3. Adapted from Table 2.

4. The Atlantic crossing from Africa to the Caribbean.

5. A fuller explanation of this analysis is found in Andre Gunder Frank (1967). More balanced and comprehensive later summations are part of Girvan (1973) and of Jackson et al. (1979).

6. A decision that thrust into the history books the voyage of the H.M.S. *Bounty* and Captain Bligh.

3

HISTORICAL BACKGROUND

EARLY HISTORY

Secure knowledge about the inhabitants of the Caribbean prior to the Columbian discoveries is lacking. Archeological sources are fragmentary, and written sources depend upon the writing and observational skills as well as the personal experience of the early Spanish visitors. These accounts understandably reflect the biases, backgrounds, and purposes of each writer. Subsequent scholarly reconstruction is itself rarely completely objective, to the extent that different schools of thought regarding preconquest conditions have developed. Two opposing interpretations have come to dominate the literature.

One view is that the region was inhabited sparsely by peoples who had achieved only a very primitive level of technology and social organization. These aborigines then had little to offer the conquerors from civilized Europe, and their rapid extermination in subsequent decades was unfortunate but a consequence of little significance. (See Waddell 1967, 35. This source is cited merely as an example of comparable views expressed by other writers, especially Latin American ones.)

At the other extreme are those scholars who maintain that although none of the Caribbean island societies merited the title of civilization, the peoples were numerous, well-organized, and occupied their habitats in rational and productive ways. This latter group of writers gives greater credence to early Spanish accounts. The controversy has a contemporary pertinence beyond that of ordinary scholarly discourse.

As Denevan has observed, acceptance of either view has implications in the sense of understanding more fully not only the destructive impact of the Europeans but also the potential food productivity of environments currently thought to have low human carrying capacities (Denevan 1976, xvii–xviii). Acceptance of the view that the island of Hispañola had 100,000 people at the time of conquest (Rosenblat 1976, p. 45) results in assumptions very different from those based on an interpretation of up to eight million inhabitants (Cook and Borah 1971, p. 407). If the latter number is even approximately true, one must not only be stunned at a scale of extermination that challenges those of Hitler and Stalin but also become curious about how such population numbers were sustained.

Without either accepting the largest population estimates or contributing to the debate, it does seem that the evidence of a very numerous native population in 1492 is more persuasive. The work of Carl Sauer is particularly influential in this regard (Sauer 1954, 1966, 1981). Sauer's studies of the ecology and purposes of traditional food systems in the Americas were unsurpassed. In addition, his earlier speculations regarding prehistory (Sauer 1952, pp. 19–61, passim) have been supported by an increasing body of evidence. The brief account that follows derives from the assumption that native peoples successfully and in rational ecologic ways lived in large numbers in Middle America at the time of European contacts. That the subsequent annihilation was nearly complete on the islands is indisputable, only the numbers are in question. Greater awareness of how local resources could feed sufficiently large numbers of people has pertinence for current governments and hence a geopolitical dimension.

On the basis of linguistics, the native peoples were classed mainly as Arawaks and Caribs. A map prepared by Cestmir Lautka suggests that Arawak speakers inhabited most of the western islands, including The Bahamas (Lautka 1967). Caribs were present in the eastern extremities of Cuba, Hispañola, and Puerto Rico as well as being dominant in the Lesser Antilles. Lautka suggests that both groups shared the northern small islands in the east. Arawak speakers also occupied the coastal Guianas, whereas Caribs lived in northeastern Venezuela.

Several assumptions are generally accepted. The Arawaks were more numerous, had more complex social structures, were primarily farmers, and although armed were not aggressive peoples in comparison with Caribs. Conversely, Caribs made warfare a special avocation, were skilled long-distance sailors, and had cannibalistic rites (Pearcy 1965, pp. 40–41). As an apparent result of these cultural differences, at the time of Columbus the Caribs were in the process of advancing into Arawak islands, and Arawak defensive measures were inspired principally by that menace.

Sauer added the assessment that native society on Hispañola, at least, had developed an aristocratic character, with class structure and distinct territorial organization (Sauer 1966, pp. 45–50). The character of earlier peoples is even less clear. Sauer does emphasize, however, that the wind and ocean currents as well as linguistic traces support the idea that Arawaks, like the Caribs, advanced onto the islands by way of northeastern South America (Sauer 1962, pp. 196–98).

Interpretations of food systems show less agreement. Those who argue for smaller numbers assume that crude tools and weapons aided scattered shifting agriculture, hunting, fishing, and gathering, systems similar to some observed elsewhere in the Americas. Sauer and others postulate much more productive systems, especially with regard to agriculture. Without question a wide variety of cultigens were available to Middle American peoples. Cook and Borah point out that "In general, American Indians had available food plants of far greater yield than any cultivated in the Old World other than yams" (1971, p. 408). Maize was and is the world's highest yielding grain, and manioc yields even more in weight. Both crops store well. Other food crops of varying distribution were sweet potatoes, arrowroot, beans, peppers, avocados, papayas, peanuts, and pineapples. The list is not complete.

The main agricultural system on the islands bore the Arawak name of *conuco*. The emphasis was on root crops reproduced vegetatively, with manioc (*yuca*) and sweet potatoes the main staples. Besides having an unexcelled level of yield, the flat sheets of unleavened bread made from ground manioc remain tasty and nutritious for months following baking, even in warm humid weather. Sweet potatoes producer a lesser yield but mature in less time. With a growth form of a spreading vine, sweet potatoes also inhibit soil erosion during rains and soil moisture loss during drought. Seed plant complexes of maize, beans, and squash are believed to have diffused later from the mainland and were incorporated only partly into the *conuco* systems (Sauer 1966, pp. 53–54).

Tree crops added fruit, fiber, dyes, and implements. Tree gourds were used for containers, for example, and anatto for red body dye, the use of which established the enduring appellation of Red Men for Native Americans. Tobacco and other recreational drugs were grown, as was cotton for cordage, nets, and fabric. Among Caribs but not among Arawaks, Sauer insists, pineapples were grown principally to produce alcohol for ceremonies that were believed to be lengthy and frequent (Sauer 1981, p. 278).

Conuco cultivation consisted primarily of crops planted mixed on raised mounds. The main staple occupied a central placement whereas the others were selected for growth form, root depth, nutritional contribution, and timing of maturation. The principles evidently were exceedingly sound. Once raised, the mounds remained productive, with constant changes in the crop complex serving to reduce fertility loss. Slope was only a slight deterrent as hand tools were used, and the constant cover of plants provided protection from erosion. It was, and in parts of Latin America still is, a stable and productive agricultural system. Personal field observations in Venezuela attest to this fact. Yields of no single crop are unusually high but the combined food harvest from such mixed plantings is quite high on a sustained basis. The assumption can be made that yields were high for preconquest peoples also. Certainly early Spanish accounts suggest so.

The sea also was regularly exploited for food, not only for fish but for shallow-water crustaceans, manatees, and turtles as well. Manatees and turtles were present in the Caribbean in numbers greater than those anywhere else in the world. Nets as well as hooked lines and spears were employed. Another technique was to herd fish by means of torches into underwater corrals to be taken as needed. Fish were preserved by means of salting and drying.

Birds provided food. Migratory waterfowl wintered in the region and were taken in fresh and salt water. The only domesticated birds were the turkeys and the Muscovy duck, a roosting duck that nests high in trees near tropical rivers. Other land birds were hunted as well. Eggs were commonly gathered and eaten, including turtle eggs. Land animals suitable for food on the islands were limited to iguanas and rodents, the latter fairly abundant (Sauer 1981, pp. 275–76). There were reports also of the eating of dogs, some reportedly kept for that purpose.

The evidence that food resources and the skills to exploit them were available does not, of course, prove the contention that pre-Columbian peoples were numerous. It does, however, weaken the position of those who maintain that the numbers must have been small because primitive cultures could not support more people. The extent to which accounts by early observers can be believed and extrapolated for the region likewise is controversial. Those who present the thesis of large numbers view the accounts as supportive evidence. (Cook and Borah, Sauer, and Denevan can be cited here.) An abundant professional literature on traditional tropical agriculture as well as personal field experience also contribute to acceptance of the interpretation that millions of people lived in the Caribbean at the time of European contacts. (For a review of various positions on the subject, see Woodrow Borah 1976, pp. 13–33.)

Regardless of the uncertainties regarding actual pre-Columbian numbers, the subsequent human extermination was real. By 1518, written evidence supports the presence of a remaining native population on Hispañola of fewer than 20,000 people (Cook and Borah 1971, p. 401). Sauer noted that a number of reasons for the dying off of the Indians has been offered and believed that all were true to some extent. Brutality by masters of newly enslaved peoples combined with official callousness toward the treatment were documented. The requirement of forced labor and a Spanish obsession with the production of gold on Hispañola caused forced dislocations, destruction of family structures, and crowded, unsanitary living conditions.

Sauer also has speculated that although cassava bread was provided to workers in abundance, cessation of hunting and fishing habits is likely to have induced widespread malnutrition, especially protein deficiencies. Disease exacerbated by poor sanitation presumably was a factor, yet the early accounts did not stress its early ravages. Smallpox was reported first in 1518, a date by which the Indian population on Hispaniola was already nearly destroyed. Sauer speculated that enforced and radical changes in the society, unaccustomed hard labor, and a loss of hope weakened the will to live and reproduce (Sauer 1966, pp. 203–04).

Whatever the causes, the deed was done. The effect was to essentially depopulate a large and productive world region. Its subsequent human components and cultural forms were accomplished by Western Europeans over a span of several centuries. It is from this span of history that current human conditions in the Caribbean are derived.

EARLY COLONIAL PERIOD

Following discovery of the Caribbean by Columbus, the region's geopolitics were greatly affected by the Papal Donation of 1493. As modified a year later by the Treaty of Tordesillas, it divided claims to land and sea between Spain and Portugal at about the present 50th Meridian (Menon 1979, p. 344). Its effect was to reserve for the Spanish Crown exclusive rights for exploitation and trade in the Caribbean. This legal monopoly freed Spain to act as it wished and guaranteed conflict with ships from any other nation that appeared in the restricted waters.

The interests of Spain were primarily conquest in search of treasure—gold in particular—and the spread of Catholicism, and not always in that order. It was the former, however, that was a major cause of the destruction of the native inhabitants on Hispaniola and nearby islands. Their labor was exploited mercilessly. Islands where the prospects of finding gold were slight or where its search proved fruitless were ignored as *islas inutiles*, unless strategic location was deemed worthy of a garrison. The meager gold ores of Hispaniola and Puerto Rico were soon exhausted and attention shifted to the mainland. Conquest of the Aztecs in Mexico in 1519 and of the empire of the Inca in Peru a little over a decade later provided treasures of gold, silver, and precious stones on a scale unprecedented in world history. The islands became little more than way stations for incoming ships. Outgoing fleets were loaded with treasure and followed the winds and currents north of Cuba. Only Havana was a regular stopping point for European-bound craft, and not all stopped even there.

Spain's monopoly and the policy that the colonies existed primarily to benefit the Crown led to centralized control supervised by the Council of the Indies and implemented by restrictive regulations. Trade with the colonies was limited to Spanish ships which were obliged to travel in convoys. The colonies were prohibited from producing items that competed with those of Spain. Making wine, for example, was forbidden. Colonies were not allowed even to trade with one another, necessitating at times slow and costly transshipment through Spain (West and Augelli 1976, p. 63). Such inhibitions hampered economic development, especially where precious metals were not produced. These restrictions also produced resentment among the colonists and provided incentive for smugglers, who of necessity were rarely Spanish.

Entrance of Northern European ships in the Spanish sea was motivated by prospects of trade and loot and was encouraged covertly by competition among monarchs at home. The earliest reported intruder was an English captain who called "in distress" at Santo Domingo in 1527. Within a decade French pirates had successfully attacked a treasure ship and raided elsewhere, a menace that increased over time as irregulars from other countries joined in harrying the forbidden lands and sea. The Spanish response was to gather treasure at Vera Cruz and the Isthmus for twice-yearly convoys to Spain (Roberts 1940, p. 99). Hence was born the legendary Silver Fleet, a practice that continued from 1561 to 1748 (West and Augelli 1976, p. 63). Begun in the 1550s were massive fortifications at key harbors around the seas. The earliest were at Santo Domingo, Havana, Verz Cruz, Cartegena, and Nombre de Rios and Puerto Belo on the isthmus (Roberts 1940, p. 100). Eventually all large Spanish ports were fortified, with those at Santiago de Cuba and San Juan, Puerto Rico, most notable.

The English and Dutch became especially active by the late sixteenth century. The English came as privateers, most successfully under Drake and Hawkins, and as slave traders. Destruction of the Indians and the lure of fortunes on the mainland had created labor shortages on the islands. This new aggressive policy adopted by Queen Elizabeth has been cited as the beginning of the British Empire (Roberts 1940, p. 102). The Dutch were motivated by plunder as well but especially were in search of salt. The union of Spain and Portugal in 1580 denied Holland access to salt from Portugal. The needs of their salted herring industry were such that other sources were sought; a general hostility to the Spanish was not a minor factor. Before the end of the century, Dutch salt carriers were exploiting on a large scale natural pans on Puna del Rey a short distance north of Cumana on the coast of Venezuela (Goslinga 1971, p. 117) and were the basis of later occupations of St. Maarten and Curacao.

The activities of the interlopers into what Spain regarded as private domain led to increasing levels of violence. A contributing factor was an article of the 1598 Treaty of Vervins between France and Spain. It provided for no end to hostilities south of the Tropic of Cancer and west of the Azores. Other countries joined in and a state of war was continuous (Roberts 1940, p. 128). For over two centuries the Caribbean was one of the most bloody regions in the world, a cockpit. It was during this era that the colonial affiliations of the region were fixed.

By 1600 the Spanish had occupied at differing densities those lands for which they perceived strategic or economic value. The others lay empty of European presence. These latter areas included the Gulf Coast of the present United States and most of the western Caribbean coastline between Yucatan and Cartegena. The vital exceptions along the Caribbean were the treasure ports on the isthmus and Trujillo in Honduras from where Central American gold was shipped. The Atlantic coast south from Trinidad to Brazil also was unclaimed, so much so it was termed the Wild Coast. In terms of contemporary development, however, the uncolonized condition of the small islands, from the Virgin Islands to Aruba, was most significant. In the Atlantic, The Bahamas, Turks, and Caicos were similarly free of the Spanish presence. It was into these political vacuums that the Northern Europeans came.

In 1605 the English claimed but did not attempt to settle Barbados, then strangely empty even of Caribs (Roberts 1940, p. 128). It was the first non-Spanish territorial assertion and endured without change until independence was granted in 1966, a continuity of ownership rare in the region. English, French, and Dutch all contested for settlements in the Guianas early in the century, with the Dutch settling first in 1616. By the 1620s these same countries spread their efforts to the Lesser Antilles. Spanish power had slackened following the depredations of Hawkins and Drake and Dutch ships dominated the eastern Caribbean, changes that eased dangers for the tiny new settlements (Waddell 1967, p. 39). The English landed on St. Kitts in 1623. Two years later French settlers took part of the same island. The English spread to nearby Nevis, and the English and Dutch separately occupied St. Croix. Despite opposition by the native Caribs, the land grab by Northern Europeans in the Caribbean was under way.

Over almost two centuries, control of various islands changed a number of times, most frequently on Tobago which experienced 20 such shifts. Besides the English, French, and Dutch who vied with each other and the Spanish for ownership of the islands, other European entities held claims of varying duration. Included were Denmark and the Knights of Malta in the Virgin Islands, Sweden for a century on St. Barthelemy, and even the Duchy of Courland on the Baltic which established a colony briefly on Tobago (Roberts 1940, pp. 180, 222). Transfer between contending countries resulted from battle and treaty until the present affiliations were stabilized in 1805. Later changes came about with U.S. entrance into the region and with independence.

Several switches of colonial dominance had effects of particular influence on the modern character of this region. In 1648 Spain conceded ownership of Dutch holdings, the first concession to an outside power in the West Indies (Waddell 1967, p. 46). England seized Jamaica in 1655, and 15 years later Spain accepted British sovereignty over that island and all others held by her (Roberts 1940, p. 154). Spain conceded authority over the western half of Hispañola to France in 1697. Subsequently known as Saint Domingue, this territory became the richest of all tropical colonies and received enduring elements of French culture. A slave revolt a century later led to establishment of the first independent country in the Caribbean in 1802. Its black elite, however, retained their French affinities. A few years earlier, in 1797, Britain took Trinidad from a weakened Spain. Several of The Bahamas were occupied by the British in the 1640s, and the archipelago was recognized as a colonial unit in 1671 (Roberts 1940, p. 179).

Of contemporary geopolitical significance were English actions in the western Caribbean. Beginning in the 1660s timber cutters from Jamaica worked illicitly on unoccupied coastal areas south of Yucatan. As Spanish power declined, permanent occupation developed the colony of British Honduras, now Belize. Offshore the Bay Islands were used as stopping points on the way to Jamaica, and over time their inhabitants acquired British culture, language in particular.

The culture diffused in somewhat of a reverse process to the south. An English colony was established on Providence Island (Isla de Providencia) in 1625, and it prospered until crushed by the Spanish 16 years later (Roberts 1940, p. 131). Subsequently the Spanish and English exchanged control of the island several times. Regardless of the political turmoil, the first and several subsequent occupations established an English presence and a cultural residue on the adjacent mainland fringe. These English influences were increased when the Moskito Coast and Bay Islands were used in the late eighteenth century as dumping grounds for recalcitrant Maroons from Jamaica and Black Caribs from the Windward Islands. Although the British finally relinquished claims on the Nicaraguan coast in 1860, history and cultural links combine to maintain ties between this rimland and the eastern islands (Gullick 1982, pp. 522–23). The area received world-wide notoriety in 1981 due to Sandinista repressions of the Moskito Indian inhabitants. Although there were political dimensions to the tensions, a major factor was cultural differences between the inland and coastal peoples.

THE PLANTATION ERA

Development of the new colonies was rapid following introduction of sugar as a plantation crop. The process of development was complex involving technology, as well as economic and political maneuvering. Earlier in Iberia, Portuguese and Shephardic Jews had greatly advanced sugar manufacture and had contributed greatly to plantation develop.. first in the Cape Verde Islands and later in northeastern Brazil. The Dutch acquired these skills during several decades of occupation of the Brazilian sites, and when driven out in the 1650s, they and Shephardic Jews transferred the technology to the Guianas and West Indies (Sheridan 1970, p. 12). By this time the slave trade was long established, and demand in Europe for sugar and rum had increased. Once all these factors were assembled into a functioning system, the region became the most valuable part of the hemisphere.

The era of sugar plantation dominance began in the mid-1600s when sugar was found to be more profitable than tobacco (Waddell 1967, p. 41), reached its peak roughly from 1750 to 1775, and continued until about 1870. The last date coincided with the end of the last vestiges of slavery and the rise of larger scale and more modern sugar operations in Cuba, Puerto Rico, and the Dominican Republic. Major competition came as well from Indian Ocean producers in Mauritius and India. Most damaging of all was development of the beet sugar industry of Europe. Beet production on the continent developed in the early 1800s and was subsidized heavily until 1902 (Waddell 1967, p. 95). The growers' bounty reflected both the political pressures of farmers and the strategic advantages of a domestic supply.

During the era of prosperity, the region was celebrated for its wealth and significance. The North American colonies were meager in comparison, an evaluation illustrated vividly by the Dutch exchange in 1667 of New York City and most of New York State for the sugar-producing territory of Surinam (Roberts 1940, p. 179). The wealth generated from the trade associated with the industry (sugar, molasses, rum, slaves, salted fish and meat, plus grain) accumulated in North America and northwestern Europe. It is this capital that contributed importantly to industrialization, and in Europe to imperial expansion in Africa and Asia (Williams 1944, p. 210). The impact on British politics also was considerable. Absentee owners in England commonly either served in House of Commons—70 did so between 1730 and 1775 alone—or bribed those who did (Sheridan 1970, p. 107). British domestic and foreign policies for over a century were heavily influenced by the interests of this planter class.

During this period local government in the British West Indies was remarkably liberal for the age. The basic form was of an assembly with members elected by property holders and an upper house appointed by the governor, who in turn was appointed by the Crown. Deadlocks on issues were frequent, but as the assembly held the power of the purse, its views frequently prevailed. This format in time became known as the Old Representative System and lasted for over 200 years (Roberts 1940, p. 180). Emancipation of the slaves and deterioration of the established order led to changes. A protest by blacks at Morant Bay, Jamaica, in 1865 was put down with unnecessary violence. The event so alarmed the planters that the assembly voted itself out of existence and asked establishment of a Crown Colony, a form of rule like the one that had prevailed on Trinidad. In short order similar changes occurred throughout the colonies (Roberts 1940, p. 295). Despite the transfer of local powers to the colonial office in London, the legacy of limited self-rule provided a precedent for the loosening of metropolitan supervision in the mid-twentieth century. Indeed, the current form of government on British dependencies differs mainly from the old system in that suffrage now is universal.

THE EARLY ROLE OF THE UNITED STATES

Decline of the plantation era coincided roughly with the increasing presence of the United States. Enunciation of the Monroe Doctrine in 1823 and its subsequent interpretations has had geopolitical effects comparable in many ways to those of the Papal Donation. Monroe declared, "We should consider any attempt on their part [European powers] to extend their system to any portion of this hemisphere as dangerous to our peace and safety" (Perkins 1966, p. 91). Presented and perhaps even conceived as a gesture of protection for the newly independent Latin American states, the doctrine has been interpreted at home and abroad as a declaration of a sphere of influence in which the interests of the United States were to become preeminent. The incorporation of California followed by the Gold Rush of 1850 increased greatly U.S. interests in Middle America as an interocean route.

The Spanish–American War of 1898 began the era of direct U.S. involvement in the Caribbean. Not only was territory acquired in Puerto Rico and a naval base at Guantanamo Bay in Cuba, but in the Platt Amendment the United States claimed the right to interfere in newly independent Cuba in the event of unstable political conditions. Panama's declaration of independence in 1903 was accompanied by transparent interference by the United States. The motivation was a desire to contract an interocean canal for which a strategic need had been demonstrated during the recent war with Spain. Purchase of the Virgin Islands from Denmark in 1917 secured control over the Anegada Passage and also provided a convenient coaling station for the fleets and commerce of that period.

In 1904 President Theodore Roosevelt enunciated what became known as the Roosevelt Corollary of the Monroe Doctrine. In essence it claimed for the United States the right and duty to exercise international police power in any state in the hemisphere when it disapproved of internal conditions there, under the pretext, of course, of providing protection from nonhemispheric powers. Subsequently, United States armed forces intervened for varying periods of time in Cuba, Mexico, Haiti, Panama, Nicaragua, and the Dominican Republic. This "right" was renounced in 1933 as part of the Good Neighbor Policy of President Franklin Roosevelt. Since that time the United States has interfered in different ways in a number of countries. It backed the successful overthrow of a leftist-oriented government in Guatemala in 1954 and encouraged the overthrow by the army of the Marxist Allendé government in Chile in 1973. On the other hand, the U.S.-supported exile forces that landed at the Bay of Pigs in 1961 failed spectacularly in their effort to topple Fidel Castro in Cuba. The landing of Marines during political turmoil in the Dominican Republic in 1965 was the last direct U.S. intervention in the island Caribbean.

With the outbreak of war in Europe in 1939, the status of the colonial holdings in the Caribbean became a matter of concern for the United States. In a "consultation" of Foreign Offices held in Panama in October 1939, 21 American republics warned the belligerents to commit no warlike acts within a 300-mile zone of the hemisphere, excluding Canada. Although unenforceable, the Declaration of Panama demonstrated the unity of the various American countries on this issue.

On the day that German forces invaded The Netherlands in May 1940, British and French marines occupied Curaçao and Aruba. Washington was notified in advance of this action by the British and French and received Dutch acknowledgment that its forces were too weak to protect the oil installations on the islands. The occupation was motivated by a fear of Nazi claims on the various Caribbean territories based on a right of conquest in Europe. It was the first such shift of European control in the Americas since enunciation of the Monroe Doctrine (Roberts 1940, pp. 336–37).

In the same year the United States obtained from Britain 99-year leases on bases in Newfoundland, Bermuda, The Bahamas, Jamaica, St. Lucia, Antigua, Trinidad, and British Guiana (Rippy 1940, p. 264) in exchange for 50 destroyers (Lend-lease Act). Combined with existing facilities in Florida, Guantanamo Bay, Puerto Rico, as well as the Canal Zone, the effect was to tighten the outer line of protection for the canal and navigation on Gulf–Caribbean waters. Development of ballistic missile testing in Florida led to agreements in the 1950s to establish tracking stations in The Bahamas and the Turks and Caicos Islands.

With the advent of independence the new governments have reserved the right to reassess individually the various treaties arranged earlier by the British. The effect has been to abrogate most of the agreements regarding military bases. In 1983, the closest relations on defense matters were those between the United States and The Bahamas, with provisions not only for missle tracking but also air and naval facilities (U.S. Department of State 1982, p. 8). However, in 1983 the provisions of the U.S.–U.K. Mutual Defense Assistance Act of 1950 was still in effect in Barbados, Jamaica,

St. Lucia, and Trinidad and Tobago, as well as in the British dependencies. A U.S. space tracking and communications facility on Antigua also was in place. The combined effect of these understandings and installations was to maintain U.S. access to the most strategically located islands in the event of a protracted emergency.

The geopolitics of the Caribbean were affected most profoundly in modern times by Castro's coming to power in Cuba in January 1959. Subsequent relations with the United States deteriorated rapidly, hastened by the abortive attempt to overthrow Castro by means of a landing by Cuban exiles at the Bay of Pigs in 1961. On May Day 1962, Castro pronounced himself a Marxist–Leninist and began to create a Soviet-style state in close cooperation with the USSR. An effort by the Soviets in October 1962 to install ballistic missiles in Cuba caused a major crisis. This event was the first bonafide threat to the security of the U.S. mainland in modern history and was the closest so far that the world has come to nuclear conflict. The confrontation ended with the agreement that the Soviets would remove the missiles and install no more offensive weapons in Cuba. In return the United States would not actively interfere in Cuban internal affairs.

Offensive actions can be political as well as military, however, and an early policy adopted by Castro was export of his revolution through the undermining of other governments in the Western Hemisphere. Until the late 1960s Cuban men and arms entered many Latin countries, and Cuban sympathizers were prominent in the region's political life. Particular trouble was caused in Venezuela in the early 1960s where the Social Democrats under Romulo Betencourt were regarded as especially serious rivals. The effect was to create fears in Washington of "another Cuba," a mood that has colored U.S. views of hemisphere events to varying degrees ever since. The actions also served to isolate Cuba diplomatically from nearly all other Latin American countries with the notable exception of Mexico. Relaxation of Cuban efforts for about a decade until the late 1970s eased tensions and resulted in a restoration of relations by most OAS members. Along with the distraction of Vietnam they also served to put concerns with Castro on the back burner in Washington.

DEVELOPMENT OF MODERN CARIBBEAN POLITICS

Internal political developments leading toward greater self-rule were manifested most importantly on the large islands of Jamaica and Trinidad. Political parties in both places grew out of labor movements. Trinidad's first political party, the Trinidad Labour Party, was formed in 1932 following 35 years of increasing worker agitation. Indeed, the early decades of the century were marked by political pressure from worker groups in British Guiana,

Jamaica, and Barbados as well. But the Trinidad Workingman's Association, formed in 1897, was the first of its sort in the West Indies (Samaroo 1972, pp. 205–06). The first union-led strike in the Caribbean was by the oil and asphalt workers of Trinidad in 1917. Increase in strength of the movement was enhanced in 1919 by the leadership of men who returned from war service incensed by the racial humiliations endured by West Indian volunteer forces overseas.

The first clear-cut demand for self-government in the Caribbean colonies was made in 1936 when Jamaican expatriates in New York City founded the Jamaican Progressive League (Roberts 1940, p. 338). The action was related to a growing atmosphere of labor unrest throughout the British West Indies in the mid-1930s, especially in Barbados, Trinidad and Tobago, and Jamaica. The discontent reached crisis proportions in Jamaica in 1938 (Post 1969, p. 375). On all islands both rural and industrial workers were involved. It was in that way that the Industrial Trades Union was formed by Alexander Bustamante. The union grew to become for several decades the largest and most powerful labor organization in the Caribbean (Wedderburn 1977, p. 4). At about the same time Jamaica's first political party, the Peoples National party, was formed under the leadership of Norman Manley (Roberts 1940, p. 338).

Political development both in Jamaica and in Trinidad and Tobago followed somewhat parallel lines in the sense of close ties with labor and affinities with the British Labour Party. Socialist and Communist elements were active throughout the region, although only the former ever achieved significant influence. A key difference between the two main islands was that on Trinidad traditional white–black–colored and economic differences were complicated further by the presence of a polygot East Indian population component. Elections for legislative seats under conditions of full adult suffrage were held for the first time in Jamaica in 1944 and in Trinidad and Tobago in 1946. Bustamante was the main winner in Jamaica under the banner of his Jamaica Labour Party (JLP), formed only a year earlier and based importantly on his labor union (Wedderburn 1977, p. 11). Other parties were involved but the main loser was the Peoples National Party (PNP). The more complex circumstances in Trinidad were reflected in the competition of five principal parties, three of which captured eight of the nine seats decided (La Guerre 1972, p. 195).

Contempoary political forms in Jamaica were forged mainly during a period of factional struggle and some violence from 1945 to 1951. The product was a two-party, two-union system, with the labor and political elements intertwined but still distinguishable. The pairings are the JLP and the Bustamante Industrial Trades Union arrayed against the PNP and the National Workers Union formed in 1952. The unions are similar in many ways. The leaders of both normally serve in Parliament and both unions are blanket types in that a wide cross-section of worker categories is represented. Significant in 1952 was expulsion of a Marxist bloc of leaders from the PNP, an event which increased further the resemblance of the unions (Wedderburn 1977, pp. 11–13). External forces have been influential in the development of the union–political structure. Most important have been the American, British, Canadian, German, and Norwegian governments and labor movements, the International Confederation of Free Trade Unions, and the International Labor Organization. A model of special significance is the Scandinavian concept of worker participation in control of an industry rather than its ownership. Concern for a complementary relationship of industrial and political democracy has provided widely accepted models for government (Wedderburn 1977, pp. 24–25).

Jamaica's modern politics have involved essentially two parties and four main personalities. Bustamante and Norman Manley were the formative and dominant leaders over most of that time. With the death of Bustamante, Edward Seaga succeeded as head of the JLP. After Norman Manley's death his son Michael assumed leadership of the PNP. Michael N. Manley was elected Prime Minister in 1972 and soon embarked on efforts to alter the structure of the society in ways that caused distress in Jamaica and alarm within the Caribbean and United States. Combining fiery rhetoric with restrictions on free enterprise he achieved a seven-year record of negative economic growth, the first such period in Jamaica's history. Sharp oil price rises and a declining world economy were factors in the downturn but Manley's raising of the bauxite export levy and a demagoguery that frightened tourists were more damaging, as was the development of increasingly close relations with Cuba. These actions and the plunging economy fostered a steady flight of capital and professionals that harmed the country in a number of ways. The political effects were to strengthen support for Seaga's JLP, which won the election of October 1980 after a violence-marked preelection period that cost over 600 lives.

Control of government in Trinidad and Tobago since 1956 has been by the black-dominated People's National Movement (PNM) led by Dr. Eric Williams until his death in 1981. Up to 1971 the opposition was the largely Indian Democratic Labour Party (DLP). Gerrymandering placed the mainly rural Indian minority of 40 percent in control of only a third of the electoral districts and served to keep the PNM in such continuous political power that the DLP dissolved as a party in 1971. For several years following the PNM held all 36 seats in Parliament.

In 1976, however, unprecedented cooperation between black oil worker and Indian sugar worker unions led to formation of the United Labor Front (ULF) headed by Basdeo Panday. This first ever racially plural political force regained most of the opposition seats vacated by the defunct DLP. Superficially the union–ULF relationship resembles circumstances in

Jamaica, with important differences. Ideologically its leaders are more to the left, it represents a narrower cross-section of workers, and it functions within a society where preoccupation with racial power is paramount. This latter mood had been manipulated skillfully by Williams, and presumably his successors in the PNM will attempt the same tactics (Panday 1978, pp. 32–34). Up to nine other political parties existed as well, with the Organization of National Reconstruction of Karl Hudson-Phillips most competitive. The election of November 1981 retained power for Williams's successor, George Chambers, although the mood of the electorate was restive in an atmosphere of economic mismanagement (Goolrick 1981).

Political developments on several small islands have been equally complex and flamboyant, but generally were less regionally significant than those of the more populous Jamaica and Trinidad and Tobago. The third most influential of these Caribbean states is Barbados, which gained independence in 1966. The early guiding force of its move toward sovereignty was Sir Grantley Adams. Along with Bustamante, Manley, and Williams, Adams was a major figure in the region's politics; he was the Prime Minister of the West Indies Federation from 1958 to 1962. Despite civil disturbances in the 1930s, progress toward statehood was relatively calm. Universal adult suffrage came in 1951 and autonomy in domestic affairs in 1961. The two major parties are the Barbados Labour Party, headed by J.M.G.M. (Tom) Adams, son of Grantley, and the Democratic Labour Party of Errol Barrow. Barrow is relatively more to the left and help power until upset by Adams in the 1976 election. Adams won reelection in June 1981 by a close margin in a campaign that stressed economic issues. Labor unions are strong and both parties emphasize social concerns. Barbados has become one of the most politically stable and open societies in the world and ranks with Costa Rica as the two most successful democracies in Latin America.

In The Bahamas, self-rule was implemented in 1967 with the electoral victory of the Progressive Liberal Party headed by Lynden O. Pindling. Independence was granted in 1973 at the urging of the Progressive Liberal Party, and contrary to the position of the Free National Movement. Because of its nature as an archipelago, population distribution and local government are more diffused than is the case for the other independent states. Decentralized political institutions are strongest on those Bahamian islands with the greatest populations. Pindling has remained head of government, a fact that reflects political stability, but which also is rumored to have increased the level of corruption. Of the island states, The Bahamas are closest to the United States, a fact that makes them both more strategic and more accessible. Close diplomatic and economic relations have served the best interests of each country. As a consequence, the United States is perhaps most sensitive of all to the prospect of radical political change there.

The newest of the small island states, Antigua–Barbuda, attained independence in November 1981. Vere C. Bird, who had been premier of the associated state, became prime minister. Bird was expected to continue a policy of close relations with the West and to maintain an open, orderly government. Despite the tiny size of Antigua–Barbuda, which also includes the nearly uninhabited island of Redonda, the country faced some pressure for devolution. The fewer than 2,000 inhabitants of Barbuda long have been suspicious of domination from Antigua and sought ways to maintain a degree of political distinctiveness. Few circumstances in the Caribbean highlight more vividly this aspect of the governance problems of the island ministates.

Independence in November 1978 brought turbulent times to Dominica. Patrick John was designated prime minister but a period of demonstrations and strikes caused his resignation in June 1979. Changes of scandal against his successor continued the turmoil until July 1980 when Mary Eugenia Charles of the Dominican Freedom Party was elected prime minister. Charles is pro-Western and conservative, whereas John as prime minister had initially proclaimed, but made no steps to implement, a socialist society. In 1981 two coup attempts by John were unsuccessful. A measure of the atmosphere of legality prevailing was the court-ordered release of John after a period of custody.

Following independence in February 1979 political changes in St. Lucia were also hectic. An election six months later saw the St. Lucia Labour Party of Allan Louisy oust former premier John G.M. Compton of the previously dominant United Workers Party. The left-leaning Louisy moved away from Western ties toward Cuba and the Nonaligned Movement. However, personality conflicts and public discontent caused several changes in national leadership. In April 1982 Compton was returned to power in a landslide for the United Workers Party, an outcome highly satisfying in Washington and London.

Robert Cato became prime minister of St. Vincent two months after independence in October 1979. The day following, a black power revolt instigated by Ras Tafarian elements erupted on Union Island in the Grenadines. The scale was such that only 20 policemen were required to put down the attempt and only one life was lost. Two aspects of geopolitical significance were the obvious determination of Cato to oppose fragmentation of the state and the speedy assistance granted by the government of Barbados. As head of the St. Vincent Labour Party, Cato is a moderate strongly oriented toward the West.

Geopolitically, conditions in Grenada were the most unsettling in the eastern Caribbean. Independence in February 1974 brought to power Eric Gairy, a man once removed as premier in 1962 by the British for malfeasance. As prime minister Gairy became an autocrat and employed strong-arm methods in an atmosphere of graft and corruption. A coalition of opposition parties was intimidated and ineffective. In March 1979 a coup led by Maurice Bishop of the New Jewel Movement took over the government while Gairy was visiting the United Nations. The coup was the first in the Commonwealth Caribbean. Bishop immediately announced formation of a Peoples Revolutionary Government and suspended the constitution. Early free elections were promised. Rhetoric of the new government was Marxist–Leninist and Cuba sent technicians, doctors, and military advisors within days of the takeover.

Greeted at first with relief, popular enthusiasm for the revolution has waned with growing realization that the political effect was to replace a rightist dictator with a leftist one. Rule was through a series of Peoples Laws, interpreted personally by Bishop. Measures pressed by the government included a wide campaign to increase literacy and health care, especially in rural areas and among women. The main export industry of mace and nutmeg was nationalized, although most cropland remained in the hands of small farmers. At the same time the never large flow of tourists had diminished and small businesses suffered badly. Nongovernment newspapers were closed, editors were detained, and a severe law banning unauthorized publications was imposed. Political prisoners were held, although reports varied regarding the actual number. The political repressions have drawn increasing criticism from neighbors, especially Barbados, and from initial supporters in the Socialist International in the Western Hemisphere and in Europe (Freedman and McColm 1981).

An increased Cuban presence and expansion of the airport runaway to over 9,000 feet had greatest geopolitical implications. Billed as an aid to the tourist industry, the actual purpose of the airport improvement was questioned by those who noted that neither the highway to town nor other parts of the tourist infrastructure were even scheduled for repair (McColm 1981, p. 15). Situated in a position to command the main oil tanker passages into the eastern Caribbean, Grenada also lies fewer than 300 miles from the oil fields of Trinidad and eastern Venezuela. The close ideological relations between the governments of Cuba, Grenada, and Nicaragua raise the prospect of military aircraft hostile to U.S. interests based at three points of a triangle that includes most of the Caribbean region. Assuming the basing of Mig-23s with a 600-mile (520 nautical mile) combat radius at Santiago de Cuba, Puerto Cabezas in Nicaragua, and Grenada, the only strategic facilities in the region outside that range are the oil fields near Maracaibo, Venezuela.

Aside from the special case of Grenada, political conditions on the island states bore many similarities in early 1983. The rule of law stemming from Commonwealth tradition was firmly established. In the most recent general elections voters given a choice had rejected the left by chosing pro-

Western candidates or turned to the right, depending upon one's ideological perspective. Whatever the phrasing, leaders friendly to the United States were in office. Professed fears of U.S.-sponsored intervention caused Bishop to create a 1,500- to 2,000-member people's militia (Greiff 1981 and also McColm 1981). Anxieties about the United States notwithstanding, the most serious challenge to the government as of mid-1983 was an attempted coup by ultraleftists early in 1980. Political conditions in Grenada were the most unsettling in the eastern Caribbean for strategy planners in Washington, a mood intensified by establishment of a Soviet diplomatic mission there in September 1982 (Banks and Overstreet 1981, pp. 213–14). Despite the dominance of freely elected governments in the region, the ease with which the leftist coup in Grenada was accomplished raised concern in the United States. Bishop's forces numbered fewer than two score and only two deaths resulted. Yet the action placed a dictatorial regime unfriendly to the United States in control of a strategically located island. Admittedly, the corrupt and authoritarian Eric Gairy was more unpopular than are the elected leaders elsewhere, but the size of the strike force required to seize power raises questions about the susceptibility of ministates to small-scale subversions. Not enough yet seems known about the geopolitical ramifications of very small size, and this issue is one of the most important uncertainties.

REFERENCES

Banks, Arthur S. and William Overstreet (eds.). 1981. *Political Handbook of the World: 1981*. New York: McGraw-Hill.

Borah, Woodrow. 1976. "A Historical Demography of Aboriginal and Colonial America: An Attempt at Perspective." In *The Native Population of the Americas in 1492*, edited by William M. Denevan, pp. 13–33. Madison: University of Wisconsin Press.

Cook, Sherbune F. and Woodrow Borah. 1971. *Essays in Population History: Mexico and the Caribbean*. Berkeley: University of California Press.

Denevan, William M. (ed.). 1976. *The Native Population of the Americas in 1492*. Madison: University of Wisconsin Press.

Freedman, Rita and R. Bruce McColm. 1981. "Grenada Stirs Discontent Among Socialists." *Wall Street Journal*, August 24, p. 12.

Goolrick, Chester. 1981. "Election in Trinidad Comes Amid Signs the Ruling Party is Losing its Grip." *Wall Street Journal*, November 9, p. 32.

Goslinga, Cornelis C. 1971. *The Dutch in the Caribbean and the Wild Coast, 1580–1680*. Gainesville: University of Florida Press.

Greiff, Peter, 1981. "Grenada Still Waiting for Elections." *Wall Street Journal*, June 2, p. 35.

Gullick, C.J.M.R. 1982. "Confused Identity in the Caribbean." *Geographical Magazine*, 54, pp. 522–23.

La Guerre, John Gaffar. 1972. "The General Elections of 1946 in Trinidad and Tobago." *Social and Economic Studies*, 21, pp. 184–204.

Lautka, Cestmir. 1967. "Ethno–Linguistic Distribution of South American Indians." *Annals of the Association of American Geographers*, Map Supplement 8, 57, June, insert.

McColm, R. Bruce. 1981. "The Grenada Experiment." *Freedom at Issue*, 62, September–October, pp. 15–16.

Menon, P. K. 1979. "The Anglo–Guatemalan Dispute over the Colony of Belize (British Honduras)." *Journal of Latin American Studies*, 11, Part 2, pp. 343–71.

Panday, Baseo. 1978. "The Role of the Opposition in Trinidad and Tobago." *Caribbean Review*, 7, Summer, pp. 31–36.

Pearcy, G. Edzel. 1965. *The West Indian Scene*. Princeton, NJ: D. Van Nostrand.

Perkins, Dexter. 1966. *The United States and the Caribbean*. Cambridge, MA: Harvard University Press.

Post, K.W.J. 1969. "The Politics of Protest in Jamaica, 1938: Some Problems of Analysis and Conceptualization." *Social and Economic Studies*, 18, pp. 374–90.

Rippy, J. Fred. 1940. *The Caribbean Danger Zone*. New York: J.P. Putnam & Son.

Roberts, W. Adolphe. 1940. *The Caribbean: The Story of Our Sea of Destiny*. Indianapolis: Bobbs-Merrill.

Rosenblat, Angel. 1976. "The Population of Hispanola at the Time of Columbus." In *The Native Population of the Americas in 1492*, edited by William M. Denevan, pp. 43–66. Madison: University of Wisconsin Press.

Samaroo, Brindley. 1972. "The Trinidad Workingman's Association and the Origins of Popular Protest in a Crown Colony." *Social and Economic Studies*, 21, pp. 205–22.

Sauer, Carl O. 1981. "The Indian Food Production in the Caribbean." *Geographical Review*, 71, pp. 272–80.

———— 1966. *The Early Spanish Main*. Berkeley: University of California Press.

———— 1962. "Middle America as a Cultural Historical Location." In *Readings in Cultural Geography*, edited by Philip L. Wagner and Marvin W. Mikesell, pp. 195–201. Chicago: University of Chicago Press.

———— 1954. "Economic Prospects in the Caribbean." In *The Caribbean: Its Economy*, edited by A. Curtis Wilgus, pp. 15–27. Gainesville: University of Florida Press.

———— 1952. *Agricultural Origins and Dispersals*. New York: American Geographical Society.

Sheridan, Richard. 1970. *The Development of the Plantations to 1750: An Era of West Indian Prosperity, 1750–1775*. Barbados: Caribbean Universities Press.

U.S. Department of State. 1982. *Treaties in Force: January 1, 1982* (Publication 9285). Washington, DC: Government Printing Office.

Waddell, D.A.G. 1967. *The West Indies and the Guianas*. Englewood Cliffs, NJ: Prentice-Hall.

Wedderburn, Earl Clive. 1977. "*The Labor Movement in Jamaica*." Term Paper,

Harvard Trade Union Program. Cambridge, MA: Harvard University. Mimeo-graphed.

West, Robert C. and John P. Augelli. 1976. *Middle America: Its Lands and Peoples* (2nd edition). Englewood Cliffs, NJ: Prentice-Hall.

Williams, Eric. 1944. *Capitalism and Slavery*. Chapel Hill: University of North Carolina Press.

4

CONTEMPORARY GEOPOLITICAL ISSUES

This chapter treats in brief detail six issues that currently receive diplomatic attention in the Caribbean basin. In order of presentation the issues are: marine boundaries, the shipment of petroleum and petroleum products, the predominance of democratic governments, the roles of nonstate actors, the emergence of new regional power centers, and recent U.S. policies toward the Caribbean. Despite their variety, these issues have several qualities in common.

Each is comparatively new in the sense that the issue was not always of specific concern in the past. Rather, they reflect conditions that have become important in the context of modern events. Extended national jurisdiction over the adjacent ocean and wide acceptance of a single law of the sea are historically recent developments, as is the increased economic and strategic significance of the long-distance movement of petroleum. Growing international interest in the relative representativeness of national governments stems from a greater popular awareness of political conditions around the world. Contributing factors are the technical revolution in communications and a public desire for wider adherence to the provisions of the 1948 United Nations Universal Declaration of Human Rights. To an extent never known before, there is a world opinion on such matters. In addition, political devolution since 1945 has produced a far greater number of countries, and hence more governments to be concerned about.

Nonstate actors have greater geopolitical roles than previously for somewhat the same reasons. Not only are there more countries in the world, many of them are very small. The sense of powerlessness of these new ministates provides most with an incentive for a greater degree of collective identification and group action. These perceived national needs have in turn contributed to the growth in number and influence of various nonstate actors. Somewhat similar sentiments favoring a diffusion of influence have caused small states to seek alternatives to regional dominance by great powers. In the Caribbean this mood has reduced somewhat the past level of hegemony by the United States and has given greater international weight to the concerns of several other countries in the region.

Despite a diminution of the past preeminence of the United States, its attitudes and actions remain the single most powerful element affecting international relations in the Caribbean. Thus the recent policies emanating from Washington are examined individually as an issue that affects the contemporary geopolitics of the region, and especially the political and economic circumstances in the island ministates. This power may be used well or unwisely in terms of the interests of the United States and the other Caribbean states, but it cannot be ignored. The policies of the United States not only influence conditions there but also to some extent create conditions, which in turn may induce reactions and adjustments in a number of other countries.

The issues identified here do not all conform with traditional concepts of geopolitical analysis. This fact notwithstanding, they appear pertinent to an effort to understand more fully current international relations in the geographic setting of the Caribbean. A consideration of most of the issues can be discerned to some degree in the diplomatic discourse and strategies adopted by the various countries of the region. To what degree their significance will persist into the future is unclear. As noted earlier, the Caribbean is a region of change. As its political and economic components evolve, so also do those factors that affect its geopolitics. It is this theme, implicitly if not always explicitly, that sustains the thrust of this book.

MARINE BOUNDARIES

For the world as a whole and for island states in particular, few issues have altered geopolitical circumstances more than changes in the law of the sea. Historically, Western Hemisphere countries have long been leaders in the extension of national jurisdiction over adjacent ocean. It was, for example, the United States in 1793 that unilaterally became the first country to proclaim a three-mile-wide neutrality zone (Bath 1974, p. 85). This distance, based importantly upon the range capabilities of the shore batteries of the period, was widely adopted and remained a legal standard for many countries into recent years.

Until the 1930s only two categories of national authority were applied to the seas. Internal waters were partially enclosed arms of the ocean treated legally as if they were land areas in terms of international access. Territorial waters were offshore margins over which national sovereignty was claimed and enforced but through which innocent passage by foreign vessels was a navigation right. All else was considered high seas, a principle taken seriously by all maritime powers and the basis for naval action when infringed. Blockades associated with warfare were accepted practices but were expected to be confined to vessels serving the official enemy. Much of the neutral-state animosity against Germany in World War I, for example, developed because its submarine fleet too often did not observe this distinction.

A precedent for more extensive national claims dates from 1878. In that year Britain announced that "the legitimate jurisdiction of her majesty extends and always has extended over the open seas adjacent to the coasts of the United Kingdom and all other parts of her Dominion to a distance necessary for her defense and security" (Bath 1974, p. 61). In itself the position constituted a remarkably open-ended and self-defined legal concept. And considering the extent of the British Empire in 1878, an enormous area of ocean was at least potentially included. This affirmation notwithstanding, Britain was an is a firm proponent of narrow national sovereignty over the seas and a maximum extent of open ocean. This attitude befits its insular character and need for free movement of ocean commerce. Its former territories, especially the island ones, tend to maintain comparable positions even during the recent era of expanded claims.

A more significant legal opening was the failure of the 1930 Hague Conference to agree upon standards for a law of the sea. Thus national inhibitions with respect to departures from the accepted three-mile limit were removed indirectly (Suman 1981, p. 132). The United States was the first to take advantage of this opportunity. The Anti-Smuggling Act passed by Congress in 1935 authorized the President to proclaim an area with a radius of 62 miles from the coast as a zone where a ship suspected of smuggling was subject to U.S. customs jurisdiction. Following the start of World War II, President Roosevelt in 1939 decreed the formation of a "neutrality" patrol that would monitor warship movement up to 200 miles offshore (Bath 1974, pp. 61–62).

In response to U.S. diplomatic urging, Latin American states in the 1939 Declaration of Panama established a defense zone 300 miles wide around the hemisphere. This declaration proclaimed the "inherent right" to keep the zone free of hostile actions by non-American powers. Following World War II, the Inter-American Treaty of Reciprocol Assistance of 1947 made permanent a hemispheric security zone and extended it from pole to pole (Bath 1974, p. 62).

Broader extension of national claims to the continental shelf and its resources began in modern times within the Gulf/Caribbean region. In the 1942 Treaty of Paria, Venezuela and Britain (on behalf of Trinidad) divided the continental shelf of the intervening Gulf of Paria into national marine zones (Hodgson and Smith 1979, p. 424). Then the Truman Proclamation of September 1945 laid U.S. claim to mineral resources of the continental shelf beyond territorial waters off Texas. The proclamation also urged establishment of coastal conservation zones (Smith 1980, p. 217). A month later Mexico issued a Presidential Declaration on the continental shelf which advanced Mexico's right to adopt unilateral steps to protect living resources on high seas off her shores (Sunman 1981, p. 132). Yet that same year Britain made similar claims on behalf of Trinidad (Payne 1980, p. 328).

By 1950, comparable extension of economic jurisdiction had been made by Panama (1946), Costa Rica, Guatemala, Nicaragua, Honduras (1947; Bath 1974, p. 64), and by Britain for Jamaica (1948) and The Bahamas (1949; Payne 1980, p. 328). Over the same period Argentina developed the idea of an "epicontinental sea" that would make the *continual* shelf and adjacent waters subject to sovereign power (Suman 1981, p. 133). The concept was a precursor of a new stage of maritime claims within the hemisphere.

In a series of actions beginning in 1947, the South Pacific American countries gradually asserted national authority over resources to a distance of 200 nautical miles regardless of ocean depth. These attitudes were codified for Chile, Peru, and Ecuador in the Declaration of the Maritime Zone signed in Santiago in August 1952 (Suman 1981, p. 133). It was this action that first firmly established the standard distance now applied worldwide. Important also was an insistence that this ocean zone be regarded as territorial waters, not solely an area of national economic rights.

Caribbean countries in general adopted positions different from those states on the Atlantic and Pacific margins of the continent. A regional conference limited to Caribbean basin countries was held in Santo Domingo in 1972. General sentiment was to continue the custom of relatively narrow zones of territorial waters but to propose a new concept, that of the "Patrimonial Sea." The idea was for a zone adjacent to the territorial sea in which a state exercises sovereign rights over living and mineral resources. These sovereign rights were offered as less than territorial rights and would offer no interference with freedom of navigation or overflight (Suman 1981, p. 136). Presumably the insular nature of many participating states and their close proximity on a nearly confined sea made wider claims impractical. The territorial sea claims of Gulf/Caribbean countries are presented on Table 6. Note that only Nicaragua and Panama, which also have Pacific coasts, claimed 200 miles.

TABLE 6 Territorial Sea Claims of Gulf/Caribbean Countries

Distance	Nation
Three nautical miles	Bahamas
	Dominica
	Netherlands
	St. Lucia
	St. Vincent & the Grenadines
	United States
	United Kingdom
Six nautical miles	Dominican Republic
Twelve nautical miles	Barbados
	Colombia
	Costa Rica
	Cuba
	France
	Grenada
	Guatemala
	Guyana
	Mexico
	Suriname
	Trinidad & Tobago
	Venezuela
	Jamaica
	Honduras
	Haiti
Two hundred nautical miles	Nicaragua
	Panama

SOURCE: Office of the Geographier, *National Claims to Maritime Jurisdictions.* No. 36, 4th Revision, Limits of the Seas Series, U.S. Department of State (Washington, DC: May 1, 1980), pp. 9–10.

Map 4 was designed to illustrate the affects extended marine boundary claims could have on the semienclosed waters of the Gulf/Caribbean. The location of negotiated boundaries is based upon published sources. Hypothetical boundaries were placed according to the principle of equidistance between facing countries. One can only speculate the extent to which future bilateral negotiations will produce agreements resembling those shown.[1]

Two points of geopolitical significance seem obvious from the patterns shown. One is that even apart from the narrow passages connecting to the Atlantic, no waters in the region remain unclaimed by a coastal state. The

Map 4

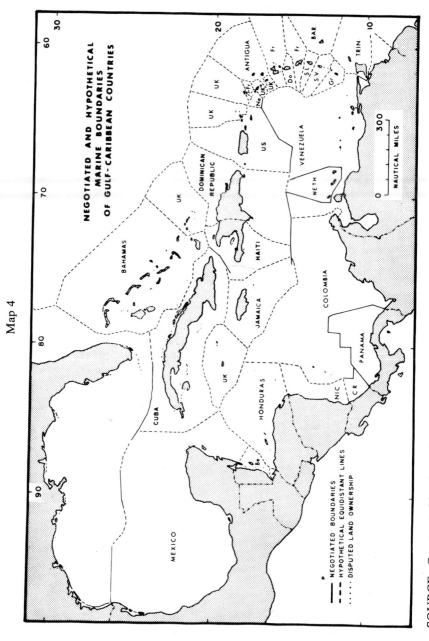

NEGOTIATED AND HYPOTHETICAL
MARINE BOUNDARIES
OF GULF-CARIBBEAN COUNTRIES

SOURCE: Constructed by the author.

other point is that the large number of Caribbean political units produces a very complex pattern of marine claims. The contrast between the waters of the Gulf of Mexico with only three large coastal states and the Caribbean is striking. Although most notable in the eastern Caribbean, complicated boundaries are a feature of the entire sea. Diplomatic settlements of current uncertainties can be expected to be tedious, but once established are likely to endure. Enforcement of the multitude of sovereignties in ocean beyond sight of land can be expected to be a continuing source of international friction, however.

The problems associated with the observance of marine boundaries by small craft was anticipated during the Santo Domingo Conference. It was recognized that not only do many of the region's fishing boats lack modern navigation equipment but also that the living resources of the sea are neither equally distributed nor fixed in location. Hence Colombia, Mexico, and Venezuela proposed that legitimate use of the patrimonial sea by third states be permitted in circumstances in which such uses do not interfere with coastal-state rights (Suman 1981, p. 137).

Perhaps in no other area of the ocean are the needs of coastal states for innocent passage and overflight more obvious. The region and the islands in particular have always depended primarily on free movement by ocean commerce. Such mutual self-interest has produced diplomatic cooperation between states otherwise in sharp disagreement. For example, two of the earliest successful boundary negotiations completed were those between the United States and Cuba and between Haiti and Cuba. It would seem that similar needs took precedence over ideology in both instances.

The only disputed boundary shown on the map involves Navassa Island, which lies off the southwest tip of Haiti. The island, which is only about five square kilometers in area, was claimed by the United States in 1916 and currently is only used as a site for an unmanned Coast Guard lighthouse (Banks and Overstreet 1981, p. 523). Claimed also by Haiti, negotiations regarding sovereignty of the island continue at a low key, and diplomatic wisdom suggests a settlement in favor of that poor third world state. On the other hand, Navassa Island does have strategic significance as its location permits the monitoring of sea traffic in the lanes between Cuba, Jamaica, and Haiti. Presumably, pressures from the Pentagon will influence the eventual settlement.

Other marine boundaries also have been in dispute. Venezuela and Colombia had not yet officially resolved conflicting claims over the Gulf of Venezuela. Venezuela held the position that the entire gulf was internal waters. Colombia claimed the part of the gulf that is seaward of its share of the Guajira Peninsula as well as Los Monjes Islands off the tip (Banks and Overstreet 1981, p. 26). If published sources are correct, the boundaries shown on Map 4 are very close to those likely to emerge from the negotiations.[2]

Late in 1979 the Sandinista government of Nicaragua renounced existing marine boundary treaties with Colombia. Specifically involved were San Andrés and Providencia islands. Several factors motivated this action. The revolutionary government on general principles rejected agreements made during rule by the Somozas. More basic is the geographic reality that a continental shelf extends eastward into the Caribbean. The treaty concluded in 1928 was not in accordance with currently accepted principles regarding coastal-state sovereignty over adjacent continental shelf, although neither country has a clear claim in this respect.

Nicaraguan desires for control over the resources of the entire adjacent continental shelf also contributed to rejection of a 1972 agreement in which the United States relinquished to Colombia its claims over the banks and cays of Roncador, Quito Sueño, and Serrana (see Map 5). This settlement, which entered into force in September 1981, was ratified by the Senate with the understanding that it does not affect the position of third countries regarding territorial claims on the entities (U.S. Department of State, T.I.A.S., No. 10120, 1981). Colombia, on the other hand, regards the territories as part of its own continental shelf, although its case is strengthened most by the precedent of long historical occupation and recognition of its status by the United States, Costa Rica, and Panama. It is widely believed that Colombia's unwillingness to join in the general Latin American condemnation of Britain during the recent Falklands/Malvinas conflict was the geological and historical similarity of the two separate disputes.

By mid-1983 the issue had produced little more than angry words and increased Colombian naval and air patrols. Potential for more serious confrontation exists, however, given the modern armaments the Sandinistas are stockpiling. The fact that the disputed area lies along the main sea routes between the Panama Canal and both the Yucatan Channel and Windward Passage makes the matter one of concern to more countries than just the two involved. Certainly a settlement in favor of Nicaragua would increase its claims over Caribbean waters by a factor of three or four and make its marine area one of the largest in the region.

Another diplomatic issue concerned the Corn Islands. Nicaragua holds undisputed sovereignty over Great and Little Corn islands, which lie near its shore. However, as part of the Bryan-Chamorro Treaty of 1914 designed to permit possible construction of an interocean canal across Nicaragua, the United States was granted a 99-year lease to use the islands. Such use was limited and consisted of radio and navigation facilities for several decades during and following World War II. The United States relinquished all its rights under that treaty in a convention signed in 1971 (U.S. Department of State, T.I.A.S., No. 7120, 1971).

Venezuela's claim to Isla Aves, a tiny speck of land about 75 nautical

Map 5

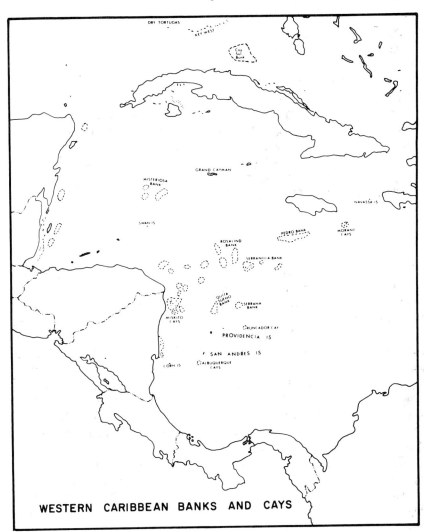

WESTERN CARIBBEAN BANKS AND CAYS

SOURCE: Constructed by the author.

miles west of Guadeloupe, also has been challenged by several of the new ministates, Dominica in particular. Acceptance of Venezuelan sovereignty there by the United States contributed to settlement of the marine boundary between the two countries. A future judicial decision in favor of another country would necessitate the reopening of U.S.–Venezuelan negotiations. There seems little likelihood that the dispute over Isla Aves will create a threat to peace.

The mood for independence on Aruba has opened an issue with possibly more serious consequences. The political faction on the island that has been most insistent on gaining a status independent of the Netherlands Antilles had made known its dissatisfaction with the present treaty boundary with Venezuela. Aruba lies north of the Paraguana Peninsula, an area where undersea rock strata have a high potential for substantial petroleum deposits. As of mid-1983, all the principal factors—Aruban independence, boundary challenge, and petroleum discovery—remained latent. The circumstances, however, offer evidence of the complexities involved in the orderly settlement of marine boundaries in the Caribbean.

PETROLEUM TRADE

The Gulf/Caribbean has unusually great significance with respect to the movement of petroleum and its products, which in turn are the most valuable commodities traded in the world. One recent authoritative source maintains that of total world trade in petroleum, about 25 percent of the crude oil and nearly 50 percent of refined products are loaded or discharged within the Gulf/Caribbean region (Drewry 1981, Introduction). Several factors help to account for this preeminence. Most important is the status of the United States as the world's leading consumer of petroleum products. Collectively, total consumption is also very large in the other fringing countries. In addition, the United States, Mexico, and Venezuela are among the world's largest producers of crude. On a much smaller scale, Trinidad and Tobago also produces and exports petroleum.

One consequence of this proximity of high levels of both consumption and production is a concentration of petroleum refining centers in the region. In addition to major refining activity along the Gulf/Caribbean coasts of the United States, Mexico, and Venezuela, important export-oriented refining centers are located on the islands as well. Largest are those in the Netherlands Antilles, The Bahamas, the U.S. Virgin Islands, Trinidad–Tobago, and Puerto Rico, but other islands also have refineries. These refineries have a total capacity approaching 3 million barrels per day, whereas transshipment facilities often linked to the refineries have a total throughput capacity of 3.5 million barrels per day. Capacities of such a scale provide the potential for the shipment of enormous volumes of petroleum materials.

Although the semienclosed seas have a number of connections with the Atlantic, tanker movements are greatest through only a few channels. As noted above, tankers of only relatively small size (no more than 65,000 deadweight tons) can transit the Panama Canal. Petroleum movement across the isthmus is greatest from the Pacific, with the main sources being Alaska, Ecuador, and Bolivia. Comparatively little moves toward the Pacific. Crude movements into the Caribbean from the Pacific can be expected to increase greatly in 1983 with completion of a transshipment system across Panama. Intended mainly for Alaskan oil, port facilities, a pipeline, and storage facilities are being completed. The Pacific unloading terminal at Puerto Amuelles, Panama, can handle tankers of up to 265,000 deadweight tons (DWT) and the storage tanks had a capacity of nearly 2.5 million barrels. Initially, the off-loaded oil is to be transferred to smaller tankers for canal transit. Eventually a 125-kilometer pipeline near the border with Costa Rica will connect to off-shore loading facilities in the Caribbean. The pipeline system is expected to lower transit costs greatly (Drewry 1981, p. 68).

Long-distance transport of crude oil is accomplished mainly by means of very large ships. Those of 175,000 to 400,000 DWT are termed VLCC (Very Large Crude Carriers), whereas still larger ones are called ULCCs (Ultra Large Crude Carriers). The largest ships now afloat are about 540,000 DWT. Because there has been a surplus of tanker capacity since the early 1970s, larger craft are not likely to be constructed. Ships of such enormous tonnages were built because their use lessened the ton–mile cost of transporting petroleum over long distances. The dimensions of VLCCs and ULCCs are unprecedented in all respects, but it is their great drafts when loaded that most restricts the movement and docking of the tankers. In general such deep-draft ships draw at least 60 feet of water when loaded, and the largest have a draft of 93 feet (Exxon 1975). Assuming that a minimal under-keel clearance of a fathom is required for safe operation, ocean depths ranging from 66 to 99 feet are needed for their operations.

Map 6 is designed to show the patterns of three depth categories related to deep-draft tanker operations in the Gulf/Caribbean. As defined, negative ocean is too shallow for loaded deep-draft ships and open ocean is deep enough for any ship afloat. Conditional ocean refers to areas where depths permit deep-draft tankers of various sizes to move safely depending on sea conditions.

Several relationships are evident. The main basins of the gulf and Caribbean contain no depth restrictions, nor do the main connecting channels. Islands, cays, and reefs between Jamaica and Central America complicate but do not preclude deep-draft tanker movements. Even the Old Bahama Channel between Cuba and The Bahamas is sufficiently deep despite its narrowness. More significant for the oil trade are the shallow waters that fringe the Atlantic Coast and the Gulf Coast of the United States and Mexico. It is ironic that the only part of the U.S. coast south of Maine where water is sufficiently deep for deep-draft ships to reach land lies

Map 6

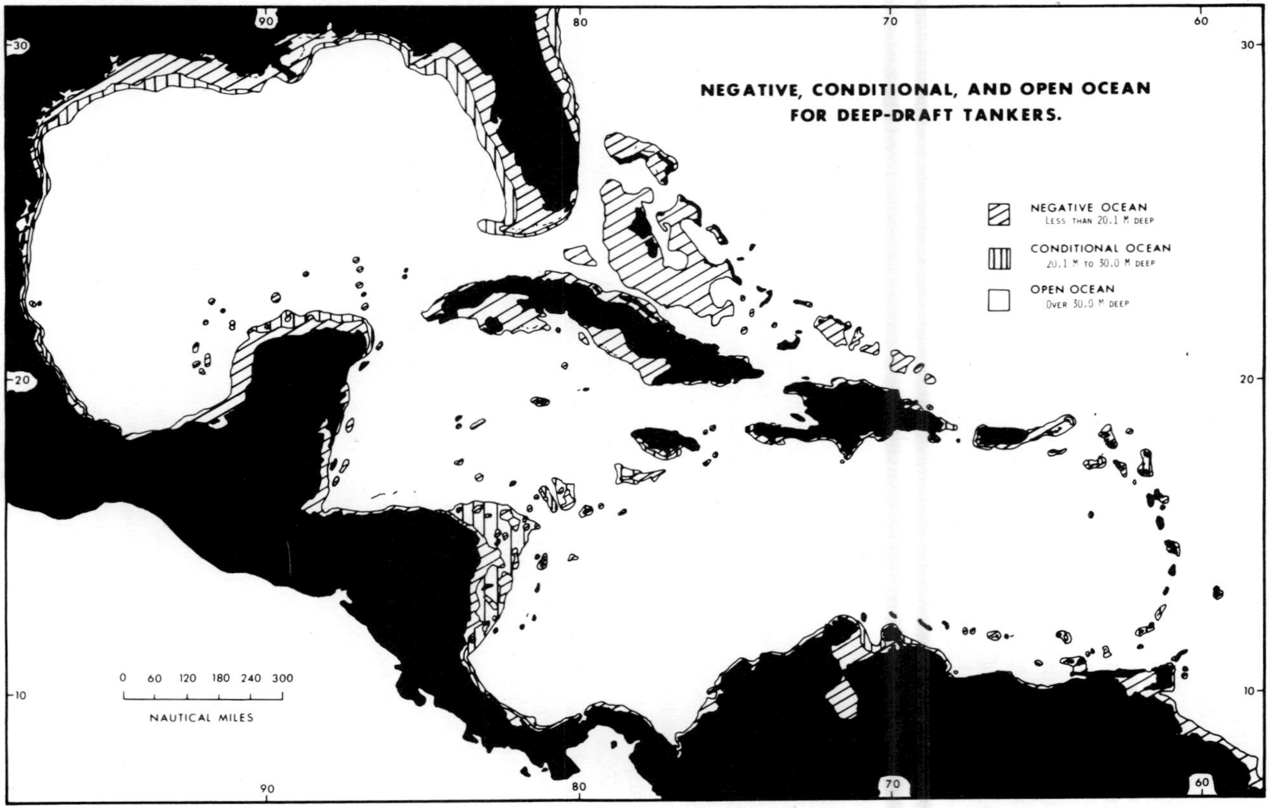
NEGATIVE, CONDITIONAL, AND OPEN OCEAN
FOR DEEP-DRAFT TANKERS.
NEGATIVE OCEAN
LESS THAN 20.1 M DEEP
CONDITIONAL OCEAN
20.1 M TO 30.0 M DEEP
OPEN OCEAN
OVER 30.0 M DEEP
0 60 120 180 240 300
NAUTICAL MILES
90
80
70
60
30
20
10

SOURCE: Constructed by the author.

between Miami and Palm Beach. Considering the value of the current recreational uses, it is unthinkable that an oil unloading port would be constructed in that area. In fact, deep-water coasts hardly exist anywhere on the mainland and are not common even on the larger islands of the Gulf/ Caribbean region.

A number of deep-water ports are present, however. On Map 7 are drawn places where the handling of petroleum is particularly important. Shown on the map in full capital letters are the names of unloading facilities capable to serving ships of up to 500,000 DWT. A major function of Caribbean and Bahamian deep-water ports is the transshipment of crude from deep-draft tankers to smaller (50,000–70,000 DWT) craft. The crude comes from the Middle East, West and North Africa, and the North Sea, for the most part. The smaller tankers are capable of entering ports on the U.S. coast. Transshipment sites generally require large storage capacities for which user fees are charged. Most also lie near refinery operations. The three that serve only a transshipment function are: South Riding Point, Bahamas; Cul de Sac Bay, St. Lucia (completed in 1981); and the offshore ship-to-ship transfer facility off Grand Cayman Islands. The Netherlands Antilles are most significant in this transfer function, with Curaçao by far the leading such center in the Caribbean (Drewry 1981, pp. 65–67).

Lightering is a common alternative to transshipment for deep-draft tankers carrying crude oil to U.S. Gulf and Atlantic ports. Lightering involves the transfer at sea of petroleum from large to smaller tankers. Some large tankers are completely unloaded at sea and return from that point for another cargo. Others are partially lightened until their draft is reduced sufficiently to permit them to enter a U.S. harbor. An estimated 11 million DWT of oil were lightered or lightened off the U.S. East Coast in 1980 (Drewry 1981, p. 62). In general, tankers over 60,000 DWT cannot enter U.S. harbors without lightening, although Corpus Christi harbor is being deepened to accommodate fully loaded craft of up to 90,000 DWT.

It is assumed that for U.S. Gulf Coast ports, full operation of the off-shore unloading facilities termed LOOP (Louisiana Offshore Oil Port) and TOP (Texas Offshore Port) will reduce greatly the ship-to-ship transfers that now are necessary. Completed in 1981 and capable of serving tankers up to 500,000 DWT, crude from LOOP is transferred inland by underwater pipeline (Drewry 1981, p. 57). TOP is scheduled for completion in the mid-1980s and will accommodate tankers of up to 200,000 DWT (Drewry 1981, p. 60). The combined impact of both ports on transshipment activities in the Caribbean is uncertain. It is estimated that direct shipment of Mideast oil via LOOP would reduce transport cost by up to 30 percent (Drewry 1981, p. 57). Assuming a high volume of by-pass routing in a period of reduced world oil demand, the impact on the economies of the Caribbean island trans-shipment centers could be severe.

Map 7

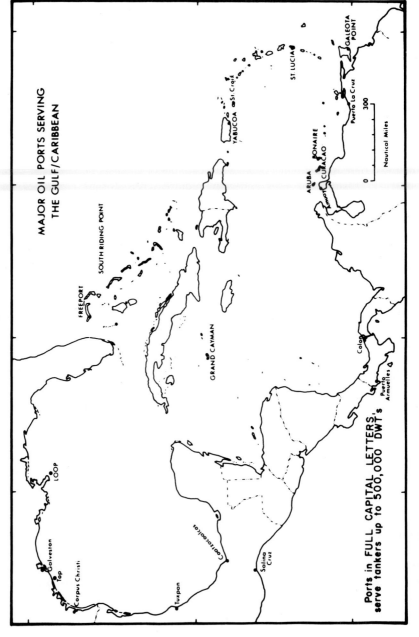

MAJOR OIL PORTS SERVING
THE GULF/CARIBBEAN

Ports in FULL CAPITAL LETTERS,
serve tankers up to 500,000 DWT's

SOURCE: Constructed by the author.

Tankers entering the Caribbean from the Persian Gulf and West Africa mainly use three passages. Those intending to transship oil in the Netherlands Antilles mainly pass south of Grenada through Galleons Passage. Most others pass on either side of St. Lucia. From there they head for other transshipment or refining centers in the Caribbean or reach the U.S. Gulf Coast by way of Yucatan Channel. The alternative route through the Old Bahama Channel and Florida Strait is no farther but is little used due to the strong eastward flow of the Gulf Stream south of Florida. Tankers bound for ports in The Bahamas normally use the Providence Channel. These choke points thus are of unusual strategic significance to the economies of not just the United States but also to island states involved directly in the oil trade.

DEMOCRACY AS A GEOPOLITICAL ELEMENT

The relative amount of freedom in other countries has long been important to U.S. citizens. As a people that takes pride in its own individual liberties, their restriction or absence elsewhere attracts attention and approbation, particularly in the media. These public concerns in turn influence U.S. foreign policies. Although the open concern with human rights around the world under President Carter was an unusual foreign policy emphasis, the position that the nation favors representative governments over dictatorship has long existed. Admittedly, that attitude is not always reflected in governmental policies, but such departures must endure public examination and criticism that tend to restrain if not actually change unpopular policies. The position that any professed anti-Communist leader, regardless of his excesses, merits U.S. backing faces continuous popular opposition.

It is in this context that the comparative level of democracy of various governments becomes part of geopolitcial analysis. With its status as a superpower, the extent to which the United States supports or opposes another government is of itself a geopolitical condition. It is particularly a factor for countries near our borders. Hence, U.S. affinity with a friendly democratic Canada contrasts sharply with its attitude toward an unfriendly dictatorship in Cuba. The policies toward friendly dictatorships such as those now in power in Guatemala and Haiti have been hedged and variable, reflecting the ambivalence of the country as a whole. The small island Caribbean, with one exception, poses few problems in this last regard.

The Caribbean Basin is one of the most democratically governed regions in the world. There are 24 countries and 12 self-governed dependencies that lie between the United States and Brazil. Unelected regimes hold power only in Guatemala, Nicaragua, Panama, Cuba, Haiti, Grenada, and Suriname. In addition, suspected voting fraud in Guyana, civil strife in El Salvador, and corruption in Honduras made the democratic nature of those governments suspect. Regardless, of 36 governments, no more than ten habitually repressed political rights. Measured on the basis of population, out of a regional total estimated in 1982 at 206 million, no more than 38 million, or 18 percent, suffered arbitrary leadership (Population Reference Bureau 1982). The effect is to rank the region fourth in the world in this regard, after Anglo–America, Western Europe, and the southwestern Pacific. Actually, in number of elected governments it is second only to Western Europe.

The most consistent and generally most accurate published measure of political rights and civil liberties around the world is compiled by Freedom House in New York. Directed by Raymond D. Gastil, the Comparative Survey of Freedom has rated conditions in every state and dependency annually since 1974. In a broad sense, the survey employs three categories: Free, Partly-Free, and Non-Free. Each government, however, is first compared on a seven-point scale for both political rights and civil liberties. Places most free are ranked as 1 and the least free as 7. In the absence of absolute standards, the comparative conditions serve as a guide under the logic that in no state are inhabitants absolutely either free or unfree. Listed in Table 7 are the countries and dependencies of the Caribbean Basin and their ratings as of December 1982.

Ratings of 1 and 2 on political rights reflect either a fully competitive electoral process or one that works less well due to economic inequality, illiteracy, or violence. At the other extreme, a 6 designates individual or small-group rule tempered by public opinion or tradition, whereas at 7 political despots are hindered neither by public opinion nor tradition. In terms of civil liberties, the scale is more continuous, with 1 signifying general freedom to speak, print, and move as one wishes under full protection of law. A rating of 7 means an atmosphere of pervading fear where little independent expression takes place even in private. In general, ratings of 1–2 are classed as Free; 3–4–5 as Partly-Free; 6–7 as Non-Free. Where the number on each scale differs, the rating represents a rough but not strictly numerical averaging (Gastil 1983, p. 7).

According to the evaluation, political conditions within the area of focus were especially good. All the independent states were ranked as Free, save Grenada which was Non-Free. Of the dependencies, the lowest ranked were the British Virgin Islands, Guadeloupe, and Martinique. In each case conditions were viewed as only slightly below a Free rating. The remaining four countries of the island Caribbean were split evenly. The Dominican Republic and Puerto Rich were ranked as Free, whereas Cuba and Haiti were ranked Non-Free. Within the latter two countries, however, were more than half the population of the island region.

Four Caribbean Basin countries were judged to be unusually successful democracies. They are Barbados, Costa Rica, Dominican Republic, and Venezuela. The U.S. Commonwealth of Puerto Rico also was ranked very high, more so in civil liberties than in political rights. This assignment reflects the coexistence of U.S. civil codes in a political dependency.

The lowest ranked states were Haiti, Suriname, Cuba, Guatemala, Grenada, and Nicaragua, with Haiti being least free. There are a variety of governments. Cuba is officially a Marxist–Leninist state with a ruling Communist Party. Revolutionary leaders in Grenada and Nicaragua espouse Marxist–Leninism but as of early 1983 had made neither formal declarations nor adjustments to institutionalize the position. In Suriname a military group seized power from an elected government in February 1980. After a period of ideological floundering they have become increasingly violent and appeared to be aligning diplomatically with Cuba (Martin 1983, pp. 1, 20).

Guatemala, on the other hand, was the only remaining right-wing military dictatorship in the Americas north of Paraguay. A series of coups there placed in power General Efraín Ríos Montt who, although more moderate than his predecessors, had neither restored democracy nor ended widespread killing in the countryside. In Haiti the personal feifdom of President-for-Life Jean Claude Duvalier did not seem to have a political ideology. Power simply has been held and frequently exercised arbitrarily. Despite the Freedom House rating and frequent brutality, it is probable that personal repression was less pervasive in Haiti than in Cuba. Such a circumstance, if true, would result less from government benevolence than from ineptitude and terrain. Haiti is mountainous and the inefficient government apparatus was less a part of daily life than was the case in Cuba.

A particularly important measure of the level of democracy in a country is the degree of freedom enjoyed by the media. A recent study of conditions in the Caribbean Basin employed a five-category scale arrayed from most to least free (Hufford 1982, pp. 34–36 and Appendix I). The press and broadcast media in the various countries were ranked as follows:

Category 1: Costa Rica, Dominican Republic
Category 2: Bahamas, Barbados, Belize, Jamaica, Mexico, St. Lucia, St. Vincent and the Grenadines, Trinidad and Tobago, United States (for comparison), Venezuela
Category 3: Columbia, Dominica, Guyana, Honduras, Panama, Suriname
Category 4: El Salvador, Grenada, Guatemala, Haiti, Nicaragua
Category 5: Cuba.

TABLE 7 Comparative Survey of Freedom—January 1983

Independent	Political Rights	Civil Rights	Combined Rating	Dependencies	Political Rights	Civil Rights	Combined Rating
Antigua–Barbuda	2	3	F	Anguilla	2	2	F
The Bahamas	2	2	F	British Virgin Islands	3	2	PF
Barbados	1	1	F	Cayman Islands	2	2	F
Dominica	2	2	F	Guadeloupe	3	2	PF
Grenada	6	5	NF	Martinique	3	2	PF
Jamaica	2	3	F	Montserrat	2	2	F
St. Lucia	2	2	F	Netherlards Antilles	2	2	F
St. Vincent and Grenadines	2	2	F	St. Kitts–Nevis	2	3	F
Trinidad and Tobago	1	2	F	Turks and Caicos Islands	2	2	F
				U.S. Virgin Islands	2	3	F
*Other Independent Entities**				*Other Dependencies**			
Belize	1	2	F	French Guiana	3	2	PF
Colombia	2	3	F	Puerto Rico	2	1	F

Costa Rica	1	1	F
Cuba	6	6	NF
Dominican Republic	1	2	F
El Salvador	4	5	PF
Guatemala	6	6	NF
Guyana	5	4	PF
Haiti	7	6	NF
Honduras	2	3	F
Mexico	3	4	PF
Nicaragua	6	5	PF
Panama	5	5	PF
Suriname	7	6	NF
Venezuela	1	2	F

*Indicates countries not within the author's study focus.

Note: F = Free; PF = Partly-Free; NF = Non-Free.

SOURCE: Adapted from Raymond D. Gastil, "The Comparative Survey of Freedom," *Freedom-at-Issue*, No. 70 (January/February 1983), pp. 8–10.

Although specific criteria were employed, any ranking of this sort necessarily involves subjective judgments. It also can be quickly outdated as is illustrated by subsequent worsening of conditions in Panama and Suriname. Nonetheless, the attempt does call attention to the most significant single measure of the relative openness of a society. It also adds perspective to claims of universal literacy under a dictator. If publications print only the views of the government, what are the political advantages of literacy?

Despite minor differences in detail, small independent states and dependencies share a number of the conditions of democracy. Universal adult suffrage is a right in the political context of multiple parties and scheduled elections. Basic civil liberties to speak, write, and move freely are protected. The rule of law with a procedure for appeals is a functioning part of society. Although sovereignty is recent, popular experience with legal equality, political participation, and open government is not. Part of the colonial heritage, these components of democracy were neither imposed nor grafted onto a native tradition of a different sort. Rather they evolved in the overseas holdings as a consequence of the growth of liberalism in the metropolitan centers through the mechanism of the planter class. Their diffusion through the population at large was more recent but was as much a domestic expansion as a foreign intrusion. A result is that many of the various populations regard government as "us" rather than "them."

A political effect is to provide continuity in form despite changes in personality. The policies adopted by Seaga in Jamaica have differed sharply from those of Manley. The democratic structure of the government lies intact, however, and constitutional mechanisms for future changes in leadership are open to all the political forces. The orderly selection of a new head of government in Trinidad and Tobago following the death of Eric Williams was an illustration of a different dimension of the same democratic process. Recent leadership changes in Barbados, Dominica, and St. Lucia were likewise demonstrations of popular will expressed by means of established procedures. Political stability is difficult to predict in any society, much less in small countries with short histories of sovereignty, but the record of the small-island Caribbean is encouraging.

The precedent of peaceful change by means of contested elections becomes of increasing importance in the Caribbean as those persons who led the former colonies into independence reach death or retirement. The transition to a new generation of leaders has been smooth thus far in Barbados, in Jamaica, and in Trinidad and Tobago. Presumably the next challenge will be to replace Lynden O. Pindling in The Bahamas.

Evidence of wide support for radical programs or leaders is scant, despite a tolerance for dissent that allows extremists to compete openly. The lone radical success by Bishop in Grenada was accomplished not through the ballot but rather by stealth against an undemocratic tyrant. Popular backing for this deed was genuine. The extent of approval for the programs imposed was difficult to assess in the atmosphere of intimidation and suppression of opinion that followed. The fact that the new revolutionary leadership in Grenada immediately sought to muzzle the press, other political parties, and free labor unions did suggest that despite early public acclaim, a degree of insecurity existed at top levels of government. On the other islands the majority appears to favor change within the context of existing institutions, or reform rather than revolution if one prefers that phrasing.

The growth of democracy notwithstanding, the economic power of traditional business interests and foreign investors remains preeminent. This power in turn brings influence in political matters. The influence, however, is directed at elected officials who have commitments to an electorate which has its own claims on the government. These voters generally are well-informed, as there are few secrets on a small island with a free press. For those in office the political arts of persuasion and compromise are necessary skills. A common aim is to provide various factions with enough of what they want to keep each sullen but not mutinous. The problems of government are complex. In place are leaders linked politically with organized labor who have simultaneous commitments to expand social services and to induce greater investment by free enterprise. The extent to which such broad programs succeed, or perhaps do not fail badly, will affect greatly the future political stability of the various governments.

Some critics have alleged that unless the elected leaders of the Caribbean soon demonstrate that the current close ties with the West will improve economic conditions, popular pressure will demand more radical approaches. Such pressures may indeed develop, although why anyone should expect radical approaches to do better economically is unclear. The record elsewhere of avowedly Marxist governments in economic management is not at all impressive. Only in military matters have such governments done consistently well. So far the various Marxist–Leninist governments of the world have demonstrated that they can do effective but not superior jobs in the exploitation of natural resources (minerals, fisheries, forests), in transportation, and in expansion of heavy industry. As a group they have mediocre achievements in areas of technology development and production of consumer goods, are poor in agricultural output and management, and are patently inferior in commercial enterprises. It is precisely the last four categories of economic activity that offer the best prospects for expanded development in the island Caribbean.

Consider the following statistics. Measured on the basis of per-capita gross national product (GNP) and excluding the three richest oil exporters, of the 22 most wealthy countries of the world, 13 were resource-poor countries with industrial market economies. Only one of the richest 22, East

Germany, was a Communist state and its per-capital GNP was little more than half that of West Germany. The next highest ranking Communist states were Poland and Hungary, both of which had economic performances roughly comparable to those in Singapore and Hong Kong (World Bank 1981, p. 135). Poland's economy has declined sharply since those figures were compiled. Evidence suggests that small, resource-poor states can thrive economically, but not under a Socialist economic system.

Pressures from the left continue, nonetheless, based upon the ideology of the historical inevitability of socialism and professed desires for what is termed greater social justice. At the same time, the likelihood for the emergence of strong right-wing political factions on the small Caribbean islands is slight. Unlike nearby Latin American states, neither a tradition of authoritarianism nor an entrenched military caste is part of the societies. The middle holds power with the sanction of popular elections. The threat of repressive government in the island Caribbean lies primarily on the left, not the right. It is this situation that properly concerns the region's governments as well as policy planners in Washington.

The inhabitants of the microstates and self-governing dependencies then, with the exception of Grenada, enjoy democratic rule in a region comprised for the most part of governments with similar values. Foreign governments, and the United States in particular, deal with leaders with constituencies, not despots with whims. In the Caribbean, stability refers to the way leaders are chosen and laws formulated, not necessarily to a perpetuation of personality. Because continuation in office requires satisfaction of the expectations of a majority of the electorate, positions taken by such heads of state are likely to reflect genuine national interests rather than ideology. Press freedoms ensure that no false images of total agreement on vital issues obscure reality. At best, leaders can muster a consensus, never unaminity. Such officials may be persuaded with respect to diplomatic or business matters but rarely are they in a position personally to strike a deal. These qualities contribute to the geopolitical personality of the region and distinguish it from most of the rest of the third world.

NONSTATE ACTORS

The emergence in modern times of a multitude of nonstate actors on the world scene has made geopolitics more complex. Two broad categories of such actors can be distinguished. One is comprised of sovereign states and has an administrative body that functions internationally as a separate entity. Examples are the UN on a world scale and NATO on a regional one. The other category includes private citizens or groups from different countries who have united for a common purpose. The International Red Cross is an example. Both types can be regional or global in scope and the influence of each can range from ineffectual to powerful. (See Manspach et al. 1976 for fuller treatment of the concept.)

As a region filled with ministates, the role of nonstate actors has been especially large in the Caribbean. The power and resources of these states are limited by size or, put differently, smallness makes each more vulnerable. This vulnerability increases their dependence on others and decreases their ability to respond individually in international matters. Because at least some degree of dependency seems inescapable, a way to retain greater autonomy of action is to divide dependence among a number of sources. Ministates thus often become heavily involved in international affairs as members of nonstate actors (Reid 1974, pp. 38–39).

Over time the most important nonstate actor in the Caribbean has been the British Commonwealth of Nations. Of the 23 political units on the islands, 15 are Commonwealth members. Nine of these are independent states, as are Belize and Guyana on the mainland. Ties with the Empire are strongest, of course, in the remaining Crown colonies and Associated States. Relationships with the independent states tend to weaken with time but has been retained for a variety of reasons. Involved is a sense of tradition and identification, but there are political and economic advantages as well. Until adoption by Britain in January 1983 of a new and qualified citizenship status for Caribbean peoples, migration access to Britain had been a benefit of considerable importance. A certain amount of intra-Commonwealth economic aid was available although most agreements were bilateral. Official British aid to the Commonwealth as a whole in 1981 exceeded a billion pounds for the first time.

The sense of identification by Commonwealth members is suggested by the participation of 41 of 45 members at a meeting of Commonwealth Heads in 1981. Officially independent, Commonwealth members can be subject to peer pressures to alter individual policies. For ministates, fraternal and legal ties to militarily more powerful friends greatly enhance national security. British, and even Canadian, military forces can be asked to respond in times of emergency. Access to educational, publishing, technological, and professional services also can be beneficial. Even though the role of the Commonwealth is diminishing and may eventually become only ceremonial, it has served a vital role in the path toward independence in the Caribbean, a role that probably will continue. Geopolitically, the continued association has eased the anxieties of weak states at the same time that it has maintained a wide official British presence in the region. In 1983, Britain, as head of the Commonwealth, was still one of the most important powers in the Caribbean.

The affiliation with the British Empire produced a common regional identity among the Caribbean states. It was at the instigation of Britain that the postwar aspirations of greater freedom were translated into the West Indies Federation in 1958. Members were Antigua, Barbados, Dominica, Grenada, Jamaica, Montserrat, St. Kitts–Nevis–Anguilla, St. Lucia, St. Vincent, and Trinidad and Tobago. It was a political union with a federal government and a parliament directly elected by people from all member islands. Economic integration never was implemented. The federation could not survive interisland rivalries and collapsed in 1962, followed shortly by separate independence for Jamaica and for Trinidad and Tobago and later by six others.

Demise of the federation did not end desires for greater interisland cooperation. The failure did provide experience useful for further efforts at stronger ties. Subsequent years produced a number of proposals and several attempts at closer union. The latter involved primarily the eastern Caribbean islands. One was the West Indies Associated States Council of Ministers (WISA) formed in 1967 among the seven small islands (Antigua, Dominica, Grenada, Montserrat, St. Kitts–Nevis, St. Lucia, St. Vincent) minus Barbados. Most significant of the regional groupings was the Caribbean Free Trade Association (CARIFTA) formed officially in May 1968 after three years of negotiations. Members of WISA became members after first establishing an East Caribbean Common Market. CARIFTA came to include the original ten members of the West Indies Federation, plus Belize and Guyana. The Bahamas did not choose to join. Unlike the original federation, CARIFTA was devoted mainly to mutual economic matters rather than political ones.

In August 1973 CARIFTA was transformed into the Caribbean Community (CARICOM). The intention was to have three areas of activity: economic cooperation through the Caribbean Common Market, common services and functional cooperation, and coordination of foreign policy among the independent countries. A distinction was made between the roles of CARICOM and the economic integration reserved for the Caribbean Common Market. Despite a political role CARICOM was not a federation, since taxes, laws, and policy formulation remained the province of each state (Caribbean Secretariat 1973, pp. 18–27).

An indication of the concern among the smaller islands at the prospect of having their interests submerged into a regional whole were the efforts toward development of an organization of their own. Although still members of CARICOM, in July 1981 they agreed to change WISA, the oldest association of states in the Caribbean, into the Organization of Eastern Caribbean States (OECS). Its members were Antigua–Barbuda, Dominica, Grenada, Montserrat, St. Kitts–Nevis, St. Lucia, and St. Vincent and the Grenadines. The Central Secretariat of the organization was located at St. Lucia, with the Economic Affairs Division at Antigua. Within the framework of CARICOM, OECS was designed to strengthen subregional ties and address issues of more specific concern to its members. Objectives of high priority were economic integration and foreign policy harmonization (WISA Secretariat 1981).

The Caribbean states are affiliated also at hemispheric and global scales as members of the Organization of American States and United Nations, respectively. Membership in the UN conveys status and a sense of participation at the world level. The diplomatic impact of the ministates on the General Assembly usually is slight, however, and most issues there deal with places far away. On the other hand, the rush to independence in the Caribbean has given the island states a third of the membership of the OAS. The newly independent Caribbean states number ten of the 30-member OAS. Belize and Guyana are not a part, having been denied membership because of unsettled boundary disputes with Guatemala and Venezuela, respectively. When acting collectively there, they form a powerful voting bloc. More important, the concerns of the OAS are hemispheric. Situated geographically in the middle, few issues are not of direct interest to the ministates. Unlike the UN, however, the OAS is subject to disproportionate influence by a single huge member, the United States. At the UN other great powers and associations provide counterbalance. Membership in both organizations gives the ministates access to the services of a diversity of agencies and alternative avenues for adjudication of disputes. It also averts a need for reliance upon either one.

The conflict between Argentina and the United Kingdom over control of the Falklands/Malvinas put a sharp focus on the differences between the Caribbean ministates and the Latin members of the OAS. The Latin countries supported at least Argentina's claims to the islands and many vigorously backed its military occupation as well. Only Colombia openly criticized the Argentine invasion, using that exact description, and also abstained from voting on OAS resolutions related to the issue. On the other hand, ministers from the English-speaking states from the beginning of the debates refused to back any resolution that did not mention the initial use of force by the Argentines. Collectively it was the first OAS issue that divided the Anglo–Afro countries, which were called derisively "anglofonos" by the Latins, from the Spanish-speaking majority. To what extent this divergent position by the island states represents a different legal heritage or merely a rebirth of the English–Spanish animosity that bloodied the Americans for centuries is unclear. Regardless, the cultural and historical differences between the two groups of countries can be expected to surface again with regard to other issues before the OAS (Crossette 1982).

A number of financial nonstate actors have major roles in the region. Most important of these institutions are the International Monetary Fund, the World Bank, and Inter-American Development Bank. Politics cannot be separated from economic development and social welfare under either dictatorial or democratic rule. Access to credit has become a geopolitical element of increasing significance in the third world, and as with so much else the problem is more severe in the case of ministates. The financial troubles that led to the electoral defeat of Michael Manley in Jamaica were not caused by the International Monetary Fund but the political repercussions were certainly exacerbated by the conditions imposed by it for extension of future credits. A major part of the sense of powerlessness present among poor small countries is their dependence on such international agencies for assistance. The fact that the main sources of credit and leadership of the agencies are located in the major Western countries contributes to continuing suspicion regarding motives and to resentment at the dependent relationship.

The Falkland/Malvinas crisis also provided an illustration of the modern geopolitical significance of the need for access to credit by third world countries. Although members of the OAS debated seriously the action of economic sanctions on Britain following its landing of troops on the islands, no resolution to that effect was passed. Reports suggested that many countries were restrained by a fear of possible adverse economic counter moves by Britain or its European allies at a time of economic distress in the Western Hemisphere (Riding 1982).

A mixed lot of nonstate actors affect the region in various ways. The greatest impact was caused by the huge increases in petroleum prices imposed by OPEC beginning in the mid-1970s. As a member the decisions brought to Trinidad and Tobago a period of unprecedented prosperity. Because the other islands are oil importers, the affects were negative and contributed importantly to their economic tribulations over the past ten years. It is well to recognize that despite blatant efforts by media in the United States to depict OPEC as an Arab entity, in reality its members are worldwide. Besides Trinidad and Tobago, Ecuador and Venezuela are other hemispheric members. Indeed, Venezuela was one of the founders and consistently has been an advocate of high prices and strong member discipline.

The organization known as the Nonaligned Nations also has influence in the region. Comprised in 1983 of 108 members, the group is a loosely structured amalgamation of countries presumably not allied with the USSR or the United States. In the Caribbean, Cuba has been most closely involved with the movement and in 1979 hosted the sixth conference of Nonaligned Nations at which Fidel Castro was elected head. Guyana and Jamaica under Manley also have been active in the movement. The remainder of the ministates have tended to maintain more distant relaions, due in part to the mainly anti-Western stances of the organization. Denounced at a recent Nonaligned Nations conference was the "imperialist intervention" by the United States as well as its use of economic sanctions against Argentina, Cuba, Grenada, Nicaragua, and Suriname. In comparison with the democracies in the Caribbean, the countries named are a notable cluster of repressive governments.

Active at unofficial levels in the region were the Socialist International (SI) and Amnesty International. Representing Social Democratic parties around the world, the SI acts mainly as a link between Western European countries and those of the Caribbean. It also is a bridge between the Spanish- and English-speaking countries of the Caribbean as well as between the islands and the mainland. Especially influential are the Social Democratic parties in Barbados, Costa Rica, the Dominican Republic, and Venezuela. Dedicated to social and labor gains in the framework of plural democracy, the SI has been an active and often effective opponent of Marxist–Leninist factions. Although the SI initially was a supporter of the revolutions in Grenada and Nicaragua, it gradually became a critic. The change in attitude was motivated by increased governmental restrictions on organized labor, that segment of society with which the SI identifies most strongly (Freedman and McColm 1981). Politically and economically, in the view of one commentator, the ultimate purpose of the SI is to act as a "third force" between capitalist and communist worlds (Rabkin 1980/81, p. 347).

Amnesty International operates as a moral force of growing world repute. Composed of private citizens in many countries, it is concerned with prisoners of conscience. As such it finds little business in the democratic ministates but it does provide a mechanism by means of which their citizens can join in the pressures exerted on the governments of their more repressive neighbors. In the recent past it has successfully focused world attention on injustices in Cuba, Grenada, Guatemala, Guyana, Haiti, El Salvador, Nicaragua, and Suriname.

This treatment of nonstate actors in the Caribbean is meant to be instructive, not comprehensive. Other actors are present, including service clubs such as Rotary and Kiwanis, trade and industrial associations of many sorts, as well as religious organizations. In reference to the last, it is well to note that a crucial difference between Latin American states and those ministates with British and Dutch affiliations is the role of organized religion. The Roman Catholic hierarchy in particular has comparatively minor influence on the islands in contrast with Nicaragua, El Salvador, and Guatemala where the church is a major nonstate actor.

THE ROLE OF CUBA AND OTHER POWER CENTERS

Cuba

Under the leadership of Fidel Castro, Cuba has become a country with worldwide influence. Castro assumed power on January 1, 1959, following popular overthrow of the dictatorship of Fulgencio Batista. Worsening relations with the United States soon followed, highlighted by the U.S.-backed Bay of Pigs attempt at overthrow in 1961. A break of diplomatic relations occurred in 1962 and on May Day of that year Casro proclaimed a socialist (communist) state. Cuba's open alliance with the Soviet Union not only altered Cold War strategic relationships but also represented the first dangerous foreign presence in the Western Hemisphere since enunciation of the Monroe Doctrine in 1823.

Secret introduction by the Soviets of missiles into Cuba in October 1962 nearly provoked world war and greatly increased U.S. sensitivity to the vocally hostile Castro regime. The episode produced tacit U.S. acceptance of Castro's rule in exchange for a Soviet pledge not to introduce offensive military capabilities into Cuba. This superpower understanding, however, did not restrain Fidel Castro from interfering against established governments, first in Latin America, then in Africa, and by the late 1970s somewhat more cautiously in both at the same time.

A great deal more can and has been written about modern Cuba. Most to the point, however, has been its status for over two decades and for the first time in its history as an acknowledged power center in the hemisphere. The geopolitical significance of this reality is heightened by several factors. Cuba is close to the United States and occupies the most strategic location in the Gulf/Caribbean. It is linked ideologically and economically with America's most dangerous adversary and has consistently sought to export its system throughout the region. Although few in Washington regard Cuba as an actual military threat to the U.S. homeland, it has become a major competitor for influence in countries long thought to be within a zone of U.S. hegemony.

To a degree greater than in any other country in the world, except perhaps Libya, the nature of Cuba's government and its actions reflect the dominance of a single individual. As Carlos Rangel has observed, Fidel Castro is the most powerful *caudillo* in the history of Latin America (Rangel 1971, p. 284). Despite progress toward institutionalizing the Revolution, its form and especially its function reflect in many ways the personality of Castro. He views himself as the embodiment of the nation and acts accordingly. His title, the Maximum Leader, is not exaggeration. Thus, more so than is usual, examination of Cuba as a power center requires assessment of its ruler. The policies of Cuba, and to a considerable extent its international interests, are those decided personally by Castro.

Castro's influence derives both from events and his charisma, a quality acknowledged even by his enemies. Other leaders in the forces opposed to Batista braved more danger and accomplished more militarily, but none had Castro's ambition, supreme egotism, and talent for publicity. Once in power he quickly purged possible contenders. The event that most established his position as a counterforce in world affairs was the crushing of the CIA-sponsored landing by Cuban exile forces at the Bay of Pigs. In Latin America and elsewhere in the world the failure of the United States to overturn an unfriendly leader in the hemisphere was greeted with glee and a certain astonishment. Castro's macho stance and unsurpassed ability to heap public scorn and ridicule on his frustrated opponents created a heroic image that endured into the 1980s despite the accumulation of considerable tarnish. Castro standing defiant against the Yankee giant became a propaganda theme that won massive approval at home, supporters abroad, and grudging respect even from nonadmirers.

Once fully in power, Castro resolved to transform Cuba into a modern nation through the mechanism of communism. The country was to become the ideological beacon of the third world and serve as a new model for economic development. In the march toward improvement of the Cuban people's well-being, authoritarian measures were justified by the goals sought. It was a symbolic position accepted by many Cubans and enthusiasts elsewhere and which maintained Castro and Cuba as a factor in international affairs. The success of Cuban forces in Angola and Ethiopia furthered their reputation for prowess achieved earlier against Batista and at the Bay of Pigs. By the 1970s the Cubans ranked with the Viet Cong as the vanguard of the third world against imperialism in the eyes of the left around the world.

The military achievements contrasted with the failure of central planning and a regimented society to produce sustained economic growth, causing Castro to assume new objectives. His inability to bring into being the rich Cuba of his rhetoric could only be the fault of someone else, so he blamed the failure on unfair competition from a largely capitalist world and the U.S. economic blockade. Hence the collapse of capitalism was accepted as a precondition of economic success. Thus the Cuban people were to be deployed as the catalyst of revolution wherever the power of the United States and Western Europe seemed incapable of warding it off. The premises were familiar if not terribly convincing to the uncommitted: Communism inevitably will be imposed on a worldwide scale, but until a time when communist leaders are able to dictate a just commercial order, third world countries will not be able to develop. Because of Castro's views on the evils of capitalism and his stated desire for its elimination, it is ironic that one of the duties of the Cuban troops sent to support a Marxist government in Angola is to protect Western-owned petroleum facilities there from attacks by UNITA, a rebel force backed in part by the People's Republic of China. (Much of the preceding commentary is adapted loosely from Montaner 1979, pp. 6–7.).

With massive Soviet aid, especially since 1975, Cuba has developed a potent military force second in size in Latin America only to that of Brazil, a country much larger in area and with a population 12 times larger. Regular units, including army, air, navy, state security, and border guards, approach 140,000 personnel (*The Almanac of World Military Power* 1980, pp. 118–119). Ready reservists, consisting mainly of discharged regulars who, because they train 45 days a year, can be mobilized within days, roughly double the total force availabe for rapid deployment. A people's militia that includes women and youth numbers roughly a half million more. This militia has only a defensive capability but does serve to secure the homeland in the event regular forces are engaged elsewhere. Troops trained and equipped for airborne operations numbered about 4,000 in 1982, with an airlift capability to transport at least 3,000 such troops in a single operation. This offensive capability is now enhanced by modern assault helicopters.

The airforce consists of some 200 Soviet-made Migs, including two squadrons of Mig 23s which, with greater range, have increased offensive capabilities. Map 8 is used to illustrate the amount of the Caribbean potentially within operating range of Mig 23s based at each end of Cuba or deployed from bases in other countries friendly to Cuba: Puerto Cabeza, Nicaragua, and Point Salines, Grenada. The navy is equipped primarily for coastal defense by means of small craft armed with surface-to-surface missiles. Two diesel-powered submarines and a modern frigate, however, provide the means for a limited extension of national power. (Adopted largely from U.S. Department of State 1982a.)

As of 1983, the Cuban military establishment was neither strong enough nor equipped well enough logistically to perform large-scale offensive missions. Soviet sea and air transport assistance could quickly correct the latter deficit, however. The force is sufficient, on the other hand, to deter all but a massive outside assault and to maintain internal security. Also stationed in Cuba is a 4,600-man Soviet military contingent. This force consists of a military advisory group of 2,000 and a 2,600-strong brigade, with a tank battalion and three motorized rifle battalions (Ibid. 5). Its purpose appears to be two-fold. One is to serve as a trigger for a Soviet response in the event of an external attack, much like the mission of NATO troops stationed in West Berlin. It also has been viewed as a sort of Praetorian Guard to assist against a domestic uprising. The latter circumstance is unlikely under Fidel Castro, but his sudden death would create a very unpredictable situation.

As constituted, Cuba's forces could intervene rapidly to aid a regional ally—Grenada or Nicaragua, for example—and to interdict regional sea and air lanes. The Straits of Florida and the Yucatan Channel are the most obvious surface routes that could be challenged. A diplomatic effect of this strong military posture is to make credible Havana's expressions of deep concern on various regional issues. Internally as well it must be recognized that after Castro, the army is the most influential political faction in the Cuban Communist Party (Leiken 1981, p. 100).

Map 8

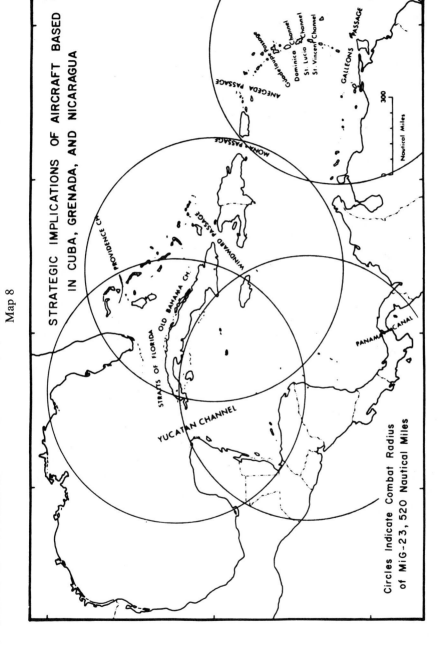

STRATEGIC IMPLICATIONS OF AIRCRAFT BASED IN CUBA, GRENADA, AND NICARAGUA

Circles Indicate Combat Radius of MiG-23, 520 Nautical Miles

SOURCE: Constructed by the author.

Cuba's strategy for extension of its influence has mechanisms other than just military units and hardware. Sympahthizers in every country in the Americas provide entry for Cuban ideas and agents. This support is particularly pronounced at universities and in intellectual circles. Conversely, Cuban efforts to win allegiance have generally found little backing among organized labor and small farmers. An effective mechanism has been "Solidarity Brigades" of teachers, medical personnel, and technicians sent as aid teams following disasters or to aid consolidation of new revolutionary governments. These brigades have been prominent in Angola, Ethiopia, Nicaragua, and Grenada and presumably will be sent also to Suriname if the ties with Havana grow stronger (Martin 1983, pp. 1, 20). Cuba has also been a conduit for arms from the communist world destined for rebel forces in the Caribbean Basin, although the scale of this movement is disputed. In this connection Castro has been reported to have taken a role in organizing and coordinating as well as training these subversive movements. The tactics and timing are reputed to be directed from Havana (U.S. State Department, December 14, 1981, 1–2).

Success of Cuban-backed movements in Nicaragua and Grenada—and their strength in El Salvador—tends to obscure some serious diplomatic setbacks. Panama, which in 1974 was one of the first OAS members to restore normal relations with Cuba, withdrew its ambassador in 1980 to protest Cuban activities in postrevolutionary Nicaragua. This same factor as well as Cuban meddling in its domestic affairs caused Costa Rica to do likewise. Relations with Peru were strained by Cuban actions in April 1980 when 10,000 people crammed into the Peruvian Embassy in an effort to escape from Cuba. Similar events led to a diplomatic break by Ecuador. Colombia broke relations after uncovering evidence of Cuban training and arms for the M-19 insurrection movement in its country. An unprovoked attack by Cuban Mig-21s on a Bahamian patrol boat within national waters caused The Bahamas to sever relations. Blatant Cuban interference in Jamaican affairs, especially during the 1980 election campaign, caused the victorious Edward Seaga to expel the Cuban ambassador in 1980 and to end relations the next year. Unlike the near blanket diplomatic estrangement of the 1960s, these reactions were not orchestrated from Washington. Rather, they reflected individual national displeasure over Cuban actions.

This growing regional isolation was made sharper by other events in 1980. A few busloads of refugees crashing through the gates of the Peruvian Embassy in Havana in April snowballed into a mass exodus that exceeded 130,000 dissatisfied Cubans by midsummer. Castro's attempt to dismiss them as merely loafers and criminals was only partially successful. The spectacle of frantic throngs of people of all ages willing to risk drowning at sea to escape from a reputed socialist paradise sent an image throughout the Caribbean that will not easily be erased. Most refugees went to the United

States, but others ended up in nearly every country in the hemisphere. Their stories of life under the rule of Castro did much to damage the carefully constructed official Cuban version of the achievements of the Revolution.

As a power center, then, Cuba has a number of strengths. These include location, a superpower ally, strong armed forces, and an influential leader. Cuba's progress in social areas such as education, health, housing, and equitable income distribution has won esteem, as have its successful sports performers. Even dedicated democrats hesitate in public to criticize its system (Seaga 1978, p. 30). Its weaknesses are numerous also and appear to be growing. Cuba's leader, not necessarily its people, is a dedicated adversary to the most powerful country in the world. This position brought about a U.S. economic boycott over two decades old that daily has affected quality of life in the country. It also is recognized as a police state with a stagnant economy, more dependent on the Soviet Union than it ever was on the United States (Paz 1982, p. 42). Cuba is increasingly resented by its neighbors because of its obvious willingness to interfere in their internal affairs. Long directed primarily at the United States, this last attitude tends both to lessen Cuban and to raise U.S. influence. The United States, despite its occasional abuses of diplomatic power, at least is known to be a free society at home, whereas Cuba is a dictatorship.

Cuban influence in the ministates is widespread but not politically strong, Grenada excepted, of course. Leftist perspectives, more Marxist than Leninist, are *de rigueur* among segments of the island intellectual communities. Calls for a new economic order to bring greater justice for third world countries, for example, appear to serve Cuban interest even where their motivations are genuinely nationalist. Besides the emotional appeal of Fidel Castro's leadership, the Cuban model also offers the prospect of destruction of privileged interests and an end to sharp income disparities. Thus, despite general absence of popular support for radical positions as demonstrated in open contests, elected officials in the islands avoid open confrontation with Castro enthusiasts. Lacking strength to impose its programs, the left has leverage sufficient to make public criticism of Castro politically unwise. This aspect of Cuba's influence deserves notice by policy makers in Washington.

Mexico

Other power centers also diffuse U.S. influence in the Caribbean basin. Mexico is fundamentally the most significant although because it is not hostile and has no foreign military ties it has a less unsettling effect than does Cuba. With a rapidly growing population of over 70 million and an extraordinary abundance of mineral resources, it has become one of the world's most important countries. Mexico has three particularly notable geopolitical features aside from a large population. It has a half-century of stable, constitutional government, a long and friendly border with the United States, and some of the largest petroleum reserves in the world.

The long record of political stability has enabled Mexico to adopt an international position independent of that of the United States. This stance preserves popular support at home and enhances its world status, yet leaves the government free to cooperate with its neighbor on mutual issues. The long border has encouraged an influx of tourist and investment dollars from the north and provided an outlet for job seekers from the south. This latter issue has generated political concern in the United States, particularly during the recent period of economic stress. The growing voting strength of Mexican–Americans and a desire to maintain good foreign relations, however, induce caution in U.S. efforts to restrict border crossings.

Discovery of major petroleum deposits in Mexico in the 1970s coincided with belated awareness in the United States of a dependence on oil imports from the Middle East. The initial assumption in Washington that the Mexican energy was available on request was disabused by the Mexican government, although by 1983 it has become a major U.S. supplier. The mood in Mexico was to charge high prices in order to finance domestic development and to limit production in order to extend the period of resource exploitation. Materialization of an oil glut in the early 1980s after development commitments had been made caused extreme economic distress, including one of the world's largest international debts. Just how the financial crisis will be resolved was unknown at the time of this writing. Regardless, massive energy reserves near the world's greatest market provide geopolitical influence. Provision by Mexico and Venezuela of low-cost oil to the small, poor importers of the Caribbean, for example, has added greatly to the prestige of each in regional matters.

Whether political stability will continue in Mexico has been a subject of speculation in the United States. One view of wide acceptance is that the *Partido Revolucionario Institucional* (PRI), which has controlled the government since the 1910 Revolution, no longer represents the masses and instead has become a tool of the privileged to maintain the status quo. Without doubt there is a great disparity of wealth in modern Mexico. Also, the political process in which only the internally selected candidate of the PRI ever becomes president differs from the politics in democracies elsewhere in the hemisphere. From these facts, commentators have projected a scenario in which the domino effect of successive leftist rebel victories in El Salvador and Guatemala would then destabilize Mexico and create major foreign policy difficulties for the United States.

These conjectures notwithstanding, Mexico's political system is more representative and more responsive than a cursory view suggests. For example, other political parties function openly and despite their electoral weaknesses provide vehicles for alternative ideological expression. A benefit is the nourishment of intellectual vitality in what otherwise might become a conformist environment reminiscent of one-party rule elsewhere in the world. More important functionally is the presence of recognizably different factions within the PRI. Presidents serve a six-year, nonsuccessional term, and although chosen from within the party, the ideological stance of a new president often differs markedly from that of his predecessor. In addition, despite the certainty of election, by tradition the PRI candidate campaigns actively around the country. The purpose is as much to determine the national mood as to persuade the voters.

It is well to recognize that the political hierarchy in Mexico does keep in touch with its constituents and over the years has demonstrated considerable flexibility. The leadership is not encumbered by rigid ideology and has shown an ability to coopt issues and personalities which give evidence of political strength. The fact that the system is uniquely Mexican and stems from the first successful popular revolution in modern times adds the benefits of nationalistic sentiment to its leaders. These attributes provide a political resiliency seemingly overlooked by those analysts who foresee that economic inequities will bring peasant uprisings and crippling domestic strife. Armed rebels, after all, have never been completely absent from Mexico. It seems unrealistic to fear that a foreign ideology (Marxist–Leninism) can infiltrate north by way of Guatemala and gain a following sufficiently strong to unseat the authentically Mexican system now in place. A more practical assumption is that no major political change will complicate future relations with Mexico, even though disturbances and adjustments may take place.

Mexico's role as a power center is based to a considerable degree upon its policies. It was the first country in the hemisphere to nationalize foreign holdings, specifically mining industries in the 1930s. Its ability to gain U.S. acceptance of this action established its image as a neighbor to, but not a lackey of, its powerful neighbor. This reputation for an autonomous position was furthered by a consistent unwillingness to be identified with the various power blocs of the world. Despite its oil potential, for example, it is not part of OPEC. It refused to join the OAS-sponsored diplomatic isolation of Cuba in the 1960s and has consistently maintained close relations with Havana. Mexico lent considerable diplomatic and logistical support to the forces opposed to Somoza in Nicaragua and has been active in the quest for a negotiated solution to the killing in El Salvador.

These and other positions have made Mexico a reputable power broker with access to all factions in the conficts of the Caribbean Basin. It is in this context that it was invited to be part of the Nassau Group that participated in development of the Caribbean Basin Initiative. Mexico's principal contribution is slated to be continuation of its existing programs. Included are subsidized oil shipments to El Salvador, Guatemala, Honduras, Costa Rica,

Nicaragua, Panama, Barbados, Jamaica, and the Dominican Republic. Import rebates have been granted for the principal exports of El Salvador, Guatemala, Costa Rica, Panama, and the members of the Caribbean Common Market. Mexico also had financed over 200 individual technical assistance grants within the region (U.S. State Department 1982c, p. 9). Mexico's influence in the Caribbean comes not from military strength or a flamboyant ruler, but rather from size, resources, stability, and a reputation for an independent course and concern for its smaller neighbors. It is respected by the smaller countries rather than feared.

Venezuela

The emergence of Venezuela as a regional power center is recent. The status rests much like that of Mexico on strategic location, size, wealth in oil, and stable government. Although smaller in population than Mexico, its high rate of natural increase and massive immigration rate are expected to produce a total of over 25 million people by 1990. Situated on the northeast corner of South America, it is both an Andean and a Caribbean country. Venezuela has been a leading producer and exporter of petroleum for over 60 years. Despite reserves now believed smaller than Mexico's, both its trade partners and petroleum infrastructure are better established. As noted, it also has aided regional economic stability through subsidized sales of oil to needy neighbors. Its role as a founder and leader of OPEC, on the other hand, made it a major contributor to the economic problems that created a need for petroleum subsidies.

Venezuela has had a stable democratic government, more open and competitive than that of Mexico, but not for as long. It dates from 1958. Indeed, Romulo Betancourt and Fidel Castro took office on the same day in 1959, each following popular ouster of a right-wing dictator. In contrast, however, Betancourt was chosen in a competitive election, left office after a constitutional term, and has been succeeded by five other elected presidents. This respect for due process and a vibrant, open society that attracts immigrants rather than produces refugees contributes to Venezuela's stature throughout the Caribbean basin.

As a cofounder and the richest member of the Andean Pact, Venezuela in the past participated little in Caribbean affairs. Even its perception of itself as a Caribbean nation is little more than a decade old (Pastor 1982, p. 1039). Since that time it has taken an increasingly active part in regional concerns, especially in Central America. Along with Panama and Colombia its aid for popular forces against Somoza was as great as that of any country, including Cuba. Like Mexico it has agreed to be involved in the multilateral Caribbean Basin Initiative as one of the Nassau Group. The stance is not recent. Between 1974 and 1980 Venezuela used its oil income to provide $6.5

billion in foreign economic assistance, much of it to Caribbean basin countries. These contributions represented up to 2.2 percent of Venezuela's GNP. It has also assisted by means of deposits in several development banks (U.S. Department of State 1982c, p. 10).

Less recognized as a figure in world affairs than Mexico and Cuba, Venezuela has increasingly strong influence with the governments of the island ministates. Factors that contribute to this situation are proximity, well-established migration links, and compatible economic and political systems. The ties with the Netherlands Antilles are especially close due to over six decades of integration of Venezuelan petroleum production and the refining and export facilities on the islands. Elsewhere in the Caribbean, subsidized Venezuelan oil shipments were important even though the aid was understood from the start to be only a temporary expedient. The factors listed above represent the basis for more enduring interregional relationships.

Although hardly a match for those of Cuba, Venezuela's armed forces are sufficient to protect its frontiers, patrol its shores, and maintain internal security. The planned sale by the Reagan administration of F-16 fighter/ bombers was justified by both governments on the basis of geopolitical factors (U.S. Department of State 1982e). Venezuela has been supportive of U.S. efforts to contain Fidel Castro, but to a growing degree asserts postures on international issues different from those of the United States (Seib 1981). In addition to its leading role in OPEC, Venezuelan leaders have pressed for a basic restructuring of the world economy in favor of the third world, and they were vociferous in criticism of the United Kingdom and United States during the Falklands/Malvinas conflict.

Canada

Although not a power center in the usual sense of the term, Canada's presence in the Caribbean has increased greatly since 1970. Linked by commonwealth ties, migration streams, tourism, and investments, expansion of the role of the Canadian government has been mainly in the area of economic assistance. In 1981 Canada agreed to more than double its aid to CARICOM by 1986, to $90 million. In addition, and as part of the Caribbean Basin Initiative multilateral concept, Ottawa announced plans to extend development assistance to Central American countries (U.S. Department of State 1982c, p. 9). Motivated more by humanitarian than geopolitical considerations, the aid plans conform with an objective shared by many Caribbean countries, namely, the diversification of foreign dependence. In February 1983, Canadian Prime Minister Trudeau joined with leaders from 14 Caribbean countries in St. Lucia to discuss the economic crises caused by recession. The immediate call was for emergency action by the International Monetary Fund. Canada's participation was clear evidence of its influential position.

In terms of strategic location or military capability, Canada is not an important geopolitical factor in the Caribbean. This very circumstance, however, combined with the aforementioned economic and cultural links as well as common experience of exploitation by the United States, gives Canada a distinctive status among the ministates of the region. As an interested outsider, Canada has played the role of a "helpful fixer" with respect to the peaceful resolution of disputes in the region. This function is not likely to decrease given Canada's demonstrated concerns and the trust engendered in many countries by its actions in the past. Because Canada's reputation for integrity is high not only among the island ministates but also in Cuba as well as the United States, its geopolitical function is particularly useful.

Colombia

To a lesser extent several other countries exert influence beyond their borders within the Caribbean. Colombia was a significant contributor in the multinational support apparatus against Somoza. It also has expressed willingness to participate in the Nassau Group supporting the Caribbean Basin Initiative. Despite large size, nearly 30 million people, and a two-ocean location, it has neither significant economic nor military capabilities. With a functioning democratic government it shares regional values, however. Armed revolt by M-19 guerrillas covertly trained and armed by Cuba has caused Colombia's government to identify strongly with U.S. efforts to curb Cuban influence within the Caribbean. It also was the only Latin country openly critical of Argentina's armed occupation of the Falklands/Malvinas. On most international issues, however, Bogotá pursues its own interests and does not predictably back U.S. positions.

Panama

The country of Panama acquired greater regional stature under the leadership of General Omar Torrijos. Panama's location as the site of the canal and as the land-link between the American continents are geopolitical constants. The variables during that period of increasing international prominence were the force of personality of Torrijos and the prestige that resulted from the conclusion of a treaty with the United States providing for eventual return of Panamanian sovereignty over the canal. In addition, Panama was one of the most active suppliers of money, arms, and training sites for the popular forces that overthrew the Somoza regime in Nicaragua.

The death of Torrijos in a plane crash in 1981 and the fading luster of the canal treaty accomplishment have diminished Panama's status somewhat, although it remains active in regional affairs. As a member of the self-appointed "Cantadora Group"—named after a Panamanian island on which the respective national leaders met—Panama, along with Colombia, Mexico, and Venezuela, became involved in efforts to achieve peaceful solutions to conflicts in Central America.

Others

During the 1970s both Jamaica and Guyana became influential countries in the nonaligned movement. The attention stemmed mainly from positions on world issues counter to those of Western powers and imposition of domestic measures described as socialist. Manley of Jamaica won praise for espousing a development model like neither Cuba's nor Puerto Rico's (Young 1980). The goal of an authentically Jamaican program struck a responsive note in new countries eager to establish distinct identities. Forbes Burnham of Guyana attracted some following with a similar brand of anti-imperialist rhetoric. In the case of Jamaica this prestige in the nonaligned movement virtually disappeared with the election of Seaga, who was viewed as a tool of the right. However, Jamaica's long leadership in law of the sea issues and establishment of its administrative headquarters in Montego Bay can be expected to maintain the country as a third world speaker at least on marine issues.

Despite its status as the largest, most populous, most economically advanced, and most militarily powerful country in Latin America, Brazil in the past has not acted as a power center in the Caribbean. The reasons are many but reduce mainly to the fact that few of its vital interests—economic or political—were involved there. It has only slight dependence on the canal, for example, and its exports have been more competitive than complementary. Even its language is unique in the hemisphere.

Nonetheless, in recent years Brazil has increasingly inserted itself into Caribbean affairs notably along with Mexico as a mediating agent in the political turmoil of Central America. Brazil's involvement can be expected to increase, in part due to its growing awareness of its world economic status. In addition, Brazil has attained a stage of development in which it is an exporter of advanced manufactured goods and technology, and as consumer economies the countries of the Caribbean represent potential trade partners. There is a cultural link as well. Perhaps a third of all Brazilians have an African heritage, and an increased awareness of this past is now operative in that country as well as on the Caribbean islands. Regardless of the motivations, however, Brazilian involvement in the Caribbean will be greater during the 1980s than it was during the 1970s.

RECENT U.S. POLICIES TOWARD THE CARIBBEAN

U.S. policy toward Latin America and the Caribbean rarely has focused on the small islands. A major exception was the concern in 1940 that Nazi conquests in Europe might lead to unwelcome transfers of possession of the colonies. It was that same year that the lend-lease swap of destroyers for bases laid the foundation for an American military presence on the outer rim of islands for the first time. Until very recent times the islands' status as dependencies caused decisions on their behalf to be made elsewhere. Thus policies formulated for the United Kingdom, France, and The Netherlands at times had implications for the Caribbean. As a rule, U.S. policy was directed toward the larger countries of Cuba, Haiti, and the Dominican Republic, or to the rimland states; the small islands received at best peripheral consideration. The increased thrust toward independence beginning in the middle 1970s and changing political circumstances in the basin as a whole have caused reconsideration of that approach in Washington.

U.S. interest in Latin America and the Caribbean for decades has exhibited a series of peaks and valleys. Policy shifts have tended to reflect events and public consciousness, with continuing interests obscured by immediate circumstances. The 1970s were, by and large, a period of low U.S. concern. Contributing to the mood was an absence of dramatic events in the Caribbean during a time when major troubles were occurring in the Middle East and Southeast Asia. A Foreign Service officer with long experience in the region offered the following off-the-record examples of the lack of U.S. interest in Latin America at that time. In a 1975 talk at the War College the Assistant Secretary of State for Latin American Affairs asserted that a security threat from Latin America no longer seemed credible; Castro had been contained. The agenda of the National Defense University in 1978 did not even include Latin America. Writing in a respected journal on foreign affairs, in 1979, one scholar maintained that continuation of a U.S. policy of "benign neglect" was prudent and and probably in the best interests of all concerned (Astiz 1979, p. 89). A Foreign Service officer confided that even in 1980 the incoming Reagan administration asked that a report on the significance of Latin America be limited to seven pages. It was only a few months later that Central America became a region of major U.S. concern.

This history of fluctuation in levels of diplomatic focus notwithstanding, there remains a basis for constant interest in the region on the part of the United States. Most fundamental is security of the continental United States, with protection for our Caribbean territories and use of sea routes vital to our economy holding only a slightly lower priority. For example, not only does a major part of our imported crude and petroleum products come by way of Gulf/Caribbean waters but also roughly half of the supplies for U.S. troops in NATO reaches Europe by way of the Straits of Florida. In the event of military action in the Indian Ocean or Persian Gulf, the southern Caribbean passages to the Atlantic would increase in importance. Also, despite considerable decline in strategic significance, ocean routes connecting with the Panama Canal remain important, both economically and militarily.

A related national interest of long standing is the degree to which nearby governments are friendly, politically and economically stable, and democratic. Because national security is understandably the primary concern, the first of these qualities is of top importance. This application of realpolitik at times has led to cordial relations with unsavory regimes. Yet despite public objections to such associations, the diplomatic logic is that as a neighbor a friendly dictator is preferable to a hostile dictator. The choices too often have been between these two, although most preferred in the United States have been friendly representative governments near its borders. In this context it is well to recognize that neither in the hemisphere nor anywhere else in the world are there democratic governments unfriendly to the United States.

Access by American business to foreign areas has also been an integral, if not always avowed, element of national policy. With a tradition of overseas commerce that predates our revolution, the United States government as a general practice has supported open trade contacts, especially in Latin America and the Caribbean. This priority is especially high where access to strategic minerals is involved. In the islands of the Caribbean this last interest has application only to the bauxite of Jamaica and is not vital even in that case. Alternate sources of bauxite exist, a fact that helped to defeat the attempted formation of a bauxite exporters' cartel by Prime Minister Manley of Jamaica in the 1970s. Despite the long-time presence of valuable U.S. investments in the Caribbean, however, rarely have the interests of U.S. businesses taken precedence over the more fundamental national concerns of the United States and the other American republics (see Cornell-Smith 1976, p. 140, on this issue).

For over two decades, the Cuba of Fidel Castro has been the central factor in U.S. diplomatic strategies in the Caribbean. As both a communist state allied with the Soviet Union and as an unfriendly state actively seeking to undermine regional political stability, containment of Cuba has been a major diplomatic goal. The strategy of containment rather than overthrow dates from the missile crisis agreement with the USSR in late 1962. For most of the rest of that decade, activities by Castro sympathizers and Cuban agents throughout the hemisphere led to U.S. embrace of a number of repressive governments in the name of anticommunism. Democratic rule in the region dropped to its lowest level in 50 years during this period. It was with the aim of containment that intervention in the Dominican Republic in 1965 was authorized. Whether or not one agrees that it was the day the United States lost the Cold War in the third world (Wiarda 1980, p. 248), the action unquestionably revived wide suspicion of U.S. motives in the region.

During the late 1960s and early 1970s, Cuba's interventionist activities in the hemisphere subsided. The change in strategy was motivated largely by widespread failures, especially the one in Bolivia that resulted in the death of Che Guevara. The military overthrow of the leftist Alléndé regime in Chilé in 1973 was also a major disappointment. Yet over the later part of this period Cuban forces were successful in comparable efforts in Africa, specifically in Angola and Ethiopia. Involved evidently was less a change in objectives than a shifting of targets. The reaction in Washington to the comparative quiescence of Cuban subversion in the hemisphere was a comparable decline in diplomatic attention. It was during this time that a number of OAS members ended their diplomatic boycott and resumed normal relations with Havana.

Attention to Latin America was revived as a result of two major initiatives during the Carter administration. Of most immediate significance was the successful conclusion in 1977 of the long languishing Panama Canal Treaty negotiations. This accomplishment over bitter domestic opposition carried a political cost that contributed to Carter's election loss in 1980. In Latin America, however, the treaty was of enormous geopolitical benefit to the United States. The agreement was viewed as a fundamental change in U.S. policy and defused a major source of tension within the Americas. Besides peacefully abolishing the Canal Zone, which was regarded widely as a foreign colony, Latin Americans were pleased by the fact that the main effort for completion of the canal agreement came from the United States. The absence of civil disturbances and obvious Cold War issues as motivations also aided the credibility of the Carter initiative. Another diplomatic benefit was that the canal settlement freed the nations concerned to attend to other issues of more recent origin.

The other Carter move was to make the concern for human rights in other countries an integral part of U.S. foreign policy. Although treated with scorn then and still by many critics in the United States and Europe, the emphasis was regarded seriously in Latin America. Its most direct application was in successful pressures to preserve a peaceful election in the Dominican Republic, but it was influential as well in the progress toward elected government in Ecuador, Peru, and Bolivia. The policy also eased repressions on hundreds of dissidents throughout the hemisphere. It even saved the lives of some (Samper 1983 and Maldonado 1982). In combination these Carter initiatives did much to restore the image of the United States as a supporter of freedom and nationalism. One consequence was to make public identification with the United States politically easier for elected leaders in the hemisphere.

During the Carter administration another change of importance resulted from the fiasco known as the Soviet Brigade Crisis. Presumably in order to demonstrate for domestic political purposes an image of toughness in the face of the Soviets, the Carter administration made a diplomatic issue of the presence of a Soviet mechanized brigade in Cuba. The comic aspects came from the fact that the unit had been on the island for roughly a decade and had neither recently been reinforced nor moved in a threatening way. Despite much noise the Soviet response was slight, the brigade remained, and Carter was embarrassed. The incident led, however, to increased electronic surveillance of Cuba and the Caribbean, a review of defense strategies for the region, and creation of the Caribbean Joint Task Force with headquarters in Key West. Although the reorganization created no new forces—any tactical units it might direct were to come from existing mainland strategic reserve forces—it did make available a command structure focused fully on the region. The existence of such a contingency headquarters shortens greatly the potential reaction time needed to deploy military forces and makes more believable U.S. expressions of deep concern on various issues. Viewed from other capitals it makes the United States either a more menacing neighbor or a more reliable ally.

The late 1970s also were marked by renewal of Cuban involvement with antigovernment forces in the Caribbean basin. According to State Department reports, Fidel Castro brought to Cuba the leaders of rebel factions from several countries in an effort to coordinate their subversive efforts. During their visits Castro is described as having forged unified directorates, having advised on how best to manipulate nonleftist opposition groups, and having begun a global propaganda campaign. The aim was eventual destruction of established institutions and governments (U.S. Department of State 1981b, p. 2). The accuracy of this account is difficult to verify but the timing did coincide with renewal of leftist guerrilla activity in Nicaragua in 1978, El Salvador and Guatemala in 1980, and Colombia in 1981. Regardless of the actual causes of these internal flare-ups, the diplomatic reality was that Cuba supported the variuos antigovernment forces. In reaction the strategies adopted in Washington were based on geopolitical perceptions that were colored by the events of the early 1960s.

The measures adopted or proposed first by the Reagan administration clearly were prompted primarily by alarm over the strength of the armed rebel forces in El Salvador. Although the extent of actual participation by Cuba and Nicaragua was in question, there was little doubt of their involvement in terms of advice, training, clandestine supply, and sanctuary. Early in 1982, for example, members of a U.S. congressional delegation met with representatives of the El Salvadorean rebels in Managua. Although the presence of the two groups in the city at the same time was made to seem coincidental, it gave evidence on two points. The rebels did receive sanctuary and at least advice from Nicaragua, and there was conscious effort by the rebels to influence congressional policy makers outside normal diplomatic channels.

The early U.S. reactions were in keeping with the conventional Cold War interpretation that political discontent anywhere in the world was directed in some fashion from Moscow and was best met with force. Hence the initial responses were military in nature in the form of arms and training for government forces throughout Central America. The policy was formulated to enhance the state of preparedness of allies and friends, to demonstrate an enduring and legitimate U.S. interest in the security of its friends, to improve the ability of the United States in concert with allies to project power swiftly in the face of threats, and to help foster regional and internal stability (U.S. Department of State 1981a, p. 3). This policy became controversial due to its premises, its military emphasis, and also to the harsh rhetoric employed by then-Secretary of State Alexander Haig.

In March 1982 President Reagan sent to Congress a new program of regional economic cooperation termed the Caribbean Basin Initiative. Primarily economic in content, the plan featured free entrance of Caribbean products in the United States, tax incentives for private investors, $350 million in economic aid, technical assistance, cooperative assistance with Canada, Mexico, and Venezuela, and special help for Puerto Rico and the Virgin Islands (U.S. Department of State 1982d, p. 4). Its proclaimed goals were to achieve a region free from both internal and external threats and able to devote its energy to economic progress and development of democratic political institutions. Security, democracy, and economic development were presented as being clearly linked (Stoessel 1982, p. 1).

The Caribbean Basin Initiative was a distinctive proposal in several ways. It was the first by the Reagan administration that was not primarily military in nature. In addition, the strong emphasis on the desirability of democratic government in the hemisphere was a new theme for the administration. Although unstated, this emphasis constituted an extension of the Carter human rights approach. However, the greatest change was the official designation of the various countries as part of a single region with related economic interests. In the past, Washington had treated the Caribbean as a region only for strategic considerations. The initiative was proposed because of the recognition that the economic and political problems of the different countries were related in ways that required comprehensive response and that the United States had a concern for the region's future (Pastor 1982, pp. 1041–42). Never before had the United States offered a preferential trading arrangement to a region.

Indeed, part of the resistance in Congress stemmed from unwillingness to accept its areal extent. Senator Zorinsky questioned inclusion of Pacific-facing El Salvador as a Caribbean Basin state. The Black Caucus urged that Central America be excluded entirely but that Guyana and Suriname be added. During a visit to Barbados, Congresswoman Shirley Chisholm attacked the plan and suggested that separate initiatives for the islands and for Central America be drawn. These last two ideas were transparently racial in motivation. Other objections included concern that despite its announced economic goals, the initiative contained too much military assistance and that too much of the aid was for Central America. The AFL-CIO expressed strong opposition to the free trade and tax incentive components in a time of economic distress at home, whereas the Virgin Islands and Puerto Rico sought further assurances that their past duty preferences would not be compromised. The effect of this combined criticism was to slow implementation of the plan. Although Congress approved an initial $350 million economic assistance appropriation in 1982, passage of the entire initiative package was delayed at least into spring 1983.

Despite the economic emphasis, the initiative was in practical terms a geopolitical and strategic approach. It was designed to further both short- and long-term U.S. foreign policy objectives. In the initial proposal the greatest amounts of aid were designated not necessarily for the poorest countries but rather to those where contemporary U.S. interests seemed most in need of bolstering. Thus disproportionate sums were allocated for El Salvador where the threat of a triumph by leftist-led rebels was most immediate and to Jamaica where the Reagan administration had an ideological stake in the success of the market economy policies adopted by the newly elected Seaga government.

Whatever its limitations, the Caribbean Basin Initiative did demonstrate two important changes in U.S. policies for the region. For the first time the small island states were put on record as part of an economic region identified by the geographic extent of the Caribbean. These entities differing in size, ethnicity, and historical associations were accepted as part of a melange important to the interests of the United States, individually and as units in an interrelated whole. One reason the concept is new, of course, is that only recently have most of the states become independent. Involved also, it seems, is realization that their loyalties and economic orientations are not unalterably linked with the United States. Although historically their connections have been almost exclusively with Western Europe and the United States, increasingly there are other options, and not only with the Socialist bloc. Latin America, the Middle East, and East Asia all offer economic opportunities. It is a concern for possible switches in political alliances, however, that most claims attention in Washington.

Another U.S. policy change was to make attainment or preservation of democracy a central element in the regional policy. After many decades of rhetorical posturing, evidence suggests increasing official commitment to the position that a self-determined representative government makes a more stable and compatible neighbor. Social reform and economic development in societies with shared values are clearly regarded as in the best interests of the United States. Adoption of this policy stance was influenced by several factors. One was the fact that the majority of the countries in the basin already enjoyed democracy. The vigor and resiliency of established democracy in the face of adversity manifested by Costa Rica, Venezuela, Jamaica, and the Dominican Republic have been impressive.

This new concern was formalized in October 1982 in an eight-country agreement signed in Costa Rica and dedicated to the launching of a democratic initiative in the region. Invitations were issued to all democratically elected governments in the Caribbean Basin. Signers included Belize, Colombia, Costa Rica, Dominican Republic, El Salvador, Honduras, Jamaica, and the United States. Notable among those not attending were Mexico and Venezuela, as well as the ministates of the Lesser Antilles. Reasons for the absences were not offered. The purpose of the agreement was to establish an organization to help countries that seek advice and support in efforts to carry out democratic elections. Under what circumstances a country would ask for such aid is unclear; however, its propaganda role in an ideological conflict seems obvious.

The extent to which the professed commitment by the Reagan administration to self-determination and democratic rule is genuine or merely a strategy awaits further evidence. There is some basis for believing that the concept is accepted among middle-level professionals at the State Department. Less clear is whether higher level Reagan appointees share that view. At the same time one encounters among congressional foreign relations staff members considerable cynicism regarding prospects for democratic development in Latin America, and in Central America in particular. To paraphrase one staff member, the best interests of the United States are foremost and the nature of a foreign government is secondary. Awareness that the two elements might be interrelated was not expressed. To what degree this staff mood influences legislators or applies to the island ministates was not determined. The presence of such attitudes among legislative assistants does suggest, however, that support on Capitol Hill for a foreign policy based on an ideological identification with democratic governments is somewhat shallow.

As policy the Caribbean Basin Initiative was unusual in that it was a multilateral effort from the beginning. Consulted were Mexico, Jamaica, Canada, Venezuela, Japan, and several European countries. The Nassau Group resulted from meetings held in The Bahamas in July 1981. Consisting of Canada, Mexico, Venezuela, and the United States, the Nassau Group agreed to a coordinated approach to regional development that combined multilateral efforts, consultations with area countries, and bilateral assistance. Colombia was also a prospective member. The willingness of these countries to be involved in the endeavor notwithstanding, countries such as Canada, Mexico, and Venezuela insisted on taking part on their own terms, not as parts of the U.S. Caribbean Basin Initiative.

Curiously absent from these plans was a specified role for the United Kingdom, France, and The Netherlands. With both present and former holdings in the region, these metropolitan states have more than mere interests in the Caribbean. Like the United States, they are politically a part. The extent to which cooperative involvement by these European countries was scheduled was unclear in mid-1983. It does seem as if the successful long-term economic developments on the islands would be more difficult without their participation, although the United States could fill the gap.

New economic initiatives notwithstanding, for most countries in Latin America and the Caribbean the key issue remains intervention. No matter how well-conceived or applied, U.S. policies ultimately are measured against this standard. Even the diplomatic pressure in 1978 that prevented the military from aborting an honest election in the Dominican Republic was construed by many as interference (Wiarda 1980, pp. 258–59). In this context, the ill-concealed U.S. involvement in military pressures on Nicaragua by way of Honduras were viewed with concern, even by governments themselves displeased with increasing political repression by the Sandinistas.

In the eastern Caribbean the litmus test of U.S. policy was its actions regarding Grenada. The government in power there took office through violence and soon after imposed arbitrary restrictions on its citizens. Within the region unqualified support for the personalized regime of Maurice Bishop was confined to Cuba, Nicaragua, and Suriname. Yet despite ties with Cuba in terms of technical aid and foreign policy positions similar to those of the Soviet Bloc, Grenada had not acted externally in a threatening manner. Its strategic location north of Trinidad and Tobago and expansion of its airport to accommodate large jets did give Grenada potential military significance, even though no such installations were in place. The possible use of this airfield as a forward base for attack aircraft or as a refueling stop for Cuban transports bound either for Africa or for operations in northern South America caused uneasiness not only in Washington but also in a number of other hemispheric capitals (see Map 8). These and other "worst-case" scenarios (such as emergence of even more radical leadership) notwithstanding, as of mid-1983 the worst offenses by the Bishop government were against the civil and political liberties of its citizens. Thus the level of tolerance displayed by the United States toward a nonfriendly but nonmenacing ministate can be expected to influence greatly the success of other U.S. policies in the eastern Caribbean.

Opinions differ regarding the modern significance of the Caribbean to the defense of the continental United States. The most serious threat clearly consists of a missile attack, yet missiles can be launched from the Soviet

Union itself or from submarines lying in the Atlantic, Pacific, or Arctic oceans. Access to the Caribbean by Soviet forces is unnecessary. On the other hand, presence of Soviet offensive capabilities there would make defense of the mainland even more difficult. More important than the increased military danger, a Soviet military presence in a region regarded by all factions as the U.S. "backyard" would have the geopolitical impacts of enhanced fears in the United States and a simultaneous drop in U.S. prestige and rise in Soviet influence in Latin America.

Evidence indicates that the Soviets have honored the 1962 missile crisis settlement in which they agreed not to base offensive capabilities in Cuba. As verification, the United States employs satellite imagery, overflights, surface electronic surveillance, and informants. A diversity of electronic sensors also monitor the ocean passages to warn of surreptitious intrusions by submarines. Such devices do not prevent entrance and are not entirely effective, but they contribute important verification. Of major diplomatic significance is the fact that the 1962 understanding that precluded introduction of offensive weapons applied only to Cuba, not to any other country in the hemisphere (U.S. Department of State 1982b). Emergence of regimes unfriendly to the United States and ideologically compatible with the Soviet Union, in Grenada, Nicaragua, and Suriname, gives the issue a sense of urgency. This apprehension is intensified with the prospect that comparable governments may come to power elsewhere. Yet a measure of the success of past policies is the fact that aside from regimes linked with the Soviet Union, the United States does not have even a potential security threat in the Western Hemisphere.

Current defense strategies are designed mainly to counter air attack from potential sites in Cuba, Grenada, and Nicaragua. An operating radius for the Mig 23 of 600 hundred miles is assumed against targets in the southern United States, Puerto Rico, the canal area, and in key shipping lanes. Security of navigation in the Florida Strait and Yucatan Passage in case of war would be particularly difficult to achieve. U.S. bases in the Caribbean are limited to those at Roosevelt Roads in Puerto Rico, Guantanamo Bay, Cuba, and near the Panama Canal. However, the installations at Guantanamo Bay are more symbolic than strategic; defense there against a determined ground assault is not possible. In the event of war the base would serve mainly to provide a justification for retaliation. In the canal area there is a small naval facility for coastal patrols and Howard Air Force Base on the Pacific side has a small number of combat aircraft. Many more bases would be available through mutual defense treaties with Commonwealth countries in the unlikely event of a prolonged general war.

Military aid missions, training in the United States of military personnel from Caribbean countries, and joint exercises also help U.S. security interests. Because these arrangements further the defense objectives of other countries as well, they have diplomatic as well as strategic benefits. The major, and most justified, criticism of such assistance is that the governments involved seek more to strengthen their forces against internal dissenters than against outside attack. In the case of democratic governments, on the other hand, the complaints have slight basis, and democratic rule is the most common condition in the Caribbean Basin.

In essence, then, aside from naval forces that vary in size and composition, the U.S. military presence in this most strategic part of the world is neither particularly large nor offensive in capability. Several factors account for this low profile. Aircraft based in the continental United States can reach the area or forward airfields in a matter of hours and airborne troops soon after. The same proximity that makes the region strategic also makes it accessible. The basing of forces with a Caribbean mission at home increases deployment flexibility, reduces costs, and lessens anxieties in neighboring countries. Periodic and publicized training exercises within the region, however, maintains awareness of U.S. capabilities and concerns. A small number of Soviet naval craft also are deployed in the Caribbean, supplemented at times by a larger "show-the-flag" contingent comparable in mission to the highly visible U.S. vessels that on occasion steam into the Baltic and Black seas.

REFERENCES

The Almanac of World Military Power. 1980. San Rafael, CA: Presideo Press.

Astiz, Carlos A. 1979. "U.S. Policy and Latin American Reaction." *Current History*, 74:no. 434, pp. 49–52, 89.

Banks, Arthur S. and Overstreet, William (eds.). 1981. *Political Handbook of the World: 1981.* New York: McGraw-Hill.

Bath, C. Richard. 1974. "Latin American Claims on the Living Resources of the Sea." *Inter-American Economic Affairs*, 27, Spring, pp. 59–85.

Caribbean Secretariat. 1973. *The Caribbean Community: A Guide* (June 20). Georgetown, Guyana: Author.

Cornell-Smith, Gordon. 1976. "Latin America in the Foreign Relations of the United States." *Journal of Latin American Studies*, 8, Part 1, pp. 137–50.

Crossette, Barbara. 1982. "In the OAS, Cultural Rift." New York *Times*, April 16, p. A 11.

Drewry, H. P. 1981. *Caribbean Oil Trades.* Number One Hundred in a Series. London: HPD Shipping Publications.

Exxon. 1975. *Very Large Crude Carriers (VLCC'S)* (Exxon Background Series, November). New York: Author.

Freedman, Rita and McColm, R. Bruce. 1981. "Grenada Stirs Discontent Among Socialists." *Wall Street Journal*, August 24, p. 12.

Gastil, Raymond D. 1983. "The Comparative Survey of Freedom." *Freedom-at-Issue*, 70, pp. 3–14.

Hodgson, Robert D. and Smith, Robert W. 1979. "Boundary Issues Created by Extended National Maritime Claims." *Geographical Review*, 69, pp. 424–33.

Hufford, Bonnie. 1982. "Comparative Press Freedoms of Countries of the Caribbean Rim." Term Paper. Bowling Green, Ohio: Bowling Green State University Geography Department.

Leiken, Robert S. 1981. "Eastern Winds in Latin America." *Foreign Policy*, 42, Spring, pp. 94–113.

Maldonado, A. W. 1982. "Haiti's Last Hope for Press Freedom." *Christian Science Monitor*, September 13, p. 23.

Manspach, Richard W., et al. 1976. *The Web of World Politics: Nonstate Actors in a Global System*. Englewood Cliffs, NJ: Prentice-Hall.

Martin, Everett G. 1983. "Cuba's New Caper." *Wall Street Journal*, January 26, pp. 1, 20.

Montaner, Carlos. 1979. "20 Years After the Cuban Revolution." *Caribbean Review*, 8, pp. 4–10.

Pastor, Robert. 1982. "Sinking in the Caribbean Basin." *Foreign Affairs*, 60, pp. 1038–58.

Payne, Richard J. 1980. "The Caribbean and the Law of the Sea." *Round Table*, Issue 279, pp. 322–29.

Paz, Octavio. 1982. "Mexico and the U.S.: Ideology and Reality." *Time*, December 20, p. 42.

Population Reference Bureau. 1982. *World Population Data Sheet, 1981*. Washington, DC: Government Printing Office.

Rabkin, Rhoda Pearl. 1980/81. "U.S., Soviet Rivalry in Central America and in the Caribbean." *Journal of International Affairs*, 34, pp. 329–52.

Rangel, Carlos. 1971. *The Latin Americans: Their Love–Hate Relationship with the United States*. New York: Harcourt Brace Jovanovich.

Reid, George L. 1974. *The Impact of Very Small Size on the International Behavior of Microstates*. Beverly Hills, CA: Sage Publications.

Riding, Alan. 1982. "Some Latin Nations Said to Discuss Breaking Ties with Britain." New York *Times*, May 23, p. 16.

Samper, Daniel. 1983. "Muckraking South of the Border." *World Press Review*, 30, pp. 33–35.

Seaga, Edward. 1978. "The Role of the Opposition in Jamaica." *Caribbean Review*, 7, pp. 27–30.

Seib, Gerald F. 1981. "Venezuelan President in Washington, Warns Against U.S. Latin Intervention." *Wall Street Journal*, November 20, p. 26.

Smith, Robert W. 1980. "Trends in National Maritime Claims." *Professional Geographer*, 32, pp. 216–23.

Stoessel, Walter J. 1982. Deputy Secretary of State in Statement at Hearing of Senate Foreign Relations Committee, March 25. Mimeographed.

Suman, Daniel Oscar. 1981. "A Comparison of the Law of the Sea Claims of Mexico and Brazil." *Ocean Development and International Law*, 10, pp. 131–73.

U.S. Department of State. 1982a. *Cuban Armed Forces and the Soviet Military Presence* (Special Report No. 103, August). Washington, DC: Goverment Printing Office.

_____. 1982b. "U.S. Interests in the Caribbean Basin." *GIST*, May. Washington, DC: Government Printing Office.

_____. 1982c. *Background on the Caribbean Basin Initiative* (Special Report No. 97, March). Washington, DC: Government Printing Office.

_____. 1982d. *Caribbean Basin Initiative* (Current Policy No. 370). Speech by President Ronald Reagan before Organization of American States, February 24. Washington, DC: Government Printing Office,

_____. 1982e. *Democracy and Security in the Caribbean* (Current Policy No. 364, February 5). Washington, DC: Government Printing Office.

_____. 1981a. *Arms Transfers to Latin America* (Current Policy No. 349, October 22). Washington, DC: Government Printing Office.

_____. 1981b. *Tasks for U.S. Policy in the Hemisphere* (Current Policy No. 282, June 3). Washington, DC: Government Printing Office.

_____. 1981c. *Cuba's Renewed Support for Violence in Latin America* (Special Report No. 97, March). Washington, DC: Government Printing Office.

_____. 1980. *National Claims to Maritime Jurisdictions* (Office of the Geographer, No. 36. 4th Revision Limits of the Seas Series, May 1). Washington, DC: Government Printing Office.

_____. 1981d. *Strategic Situation in Central America and the Caribbean* (Current Policy No. 352). Washington, DC: Government Printing Office.

_____. 1981e. "Territorial Status: Quito Sueno, Roncador, and Serrana." *Treaties and Other International Acts Series*, 33 (No. 10120). Washington, DC: Government Printing Office, pp. 1–28.

_____. 1971. "Nicaraguan Canal Route (termination of convention of August 5, 1914)." *Treaties and Other International Acts Series* (No. 7120). Washington, DC: Government Printing Office, pp. 663–66.

Wiarda, Howard J. 1980. "The U.S. and the Dominican Republic: Intervention, Dependency, and Tyrannicide." *Journal of Inter-American Affairs*, 22, pp. 240–60.

WISA Secretariat. 1981. *Explanatory Handbook on the Organization of Eastern Caribbean States* (February). St. Lucia: Author.

World Bank. 1981. *World Development Report 1981*. New York: Oxford University Press.

Young, Andrew. 1980. "In Jamaica, They Say, No Problem." *New York Times*, January 16, p. 25.

EXPLANATORY NOTES

1. The idea for the map was based upon maritime boundary maps put out by the Office of the Geographer, U.S. Department of State. Despite information and advice received from that office concerning maritime boundaries in the Gulf/Caribbean area, responsibility for the patterns shown is mine alone.

2. Efforts to obtain official confirmation from diplomatic sources in both countries were unsuccessful.

5

FOREIGN POLICY OPTIONS IN A
REGION OF CHANGE

Formulation of effective policies benefits from a framework of realistic perceptions. Much of the critical national dialogue regarding U.S. policies over the years has centered more upon their premises than their content or conduct. Yet even given common assumptions, there remain options as to how best to achieve defined objectives. On the following pages various options are set against perceptions that seem personally to be realistic. That biases as well as evidence are at play is admitted. To do otherwise, however, means acceptance of the prejudices of others about whose thought processes, intellectual experience, or motivations I know little. If errors are to be made, I prefer them to be my own.

The vital interests of the United States in the Caribbean can be stated simply: protection of the continental homeland from attack and security of essential sea lanes and strategic resources. To the American public and its elected leaders, these interests are not subject to compromise. The fact that actual threat of attack from the south has rarely existed makes the concern no less valid. Evidence of this attitude was the wide national approval of the readiness of President Kennedy to chance major war over such a threat in the 1962 Cuban missile crisis. The virulence of the opposition in the debate over the Panama Canal Treaty attested as well to the depth of feeling regarding possible dangers to the sea routes through the region. Related to these basic interests is maintenance of friendly relations with neighboring states, as much to exclude possible enemies as to facilitate commerce and peaceful travel.

Development of U.S. policy toward the Caribbean ministates involves selection from among different concepts. Basic is the matter of group versus individual consideration. The ministates are a product of natural and political fragmentation, yet custom and logic suggest that some degree of consolidation for diplomatic purposes has merit. These choices can be made at several levels. Are they collectively to be regarded as a subgroup, or as part of a Caribbean region? The Caribbean Basin Initiative makes use of the latter view and has encountered difficulties in Congress on that very basis. The regional outlook emphasizes broad strategic and economic relationships. Application of such a policy entails cooperative approaches to common issues. The counterposition lays stress on differences between the small, English-speaking states and the larger Latin countries. A consciousness of black versus brown racial qualities also surfaced although no one had yet been candid enough to state it openly. Even in the second view, a group perception was operative.

If a decision is made to subdivide the Caribbean Basin for diplomatic purposes, several different approaches are possible. A non-Latin zone of interest that includes Belize, Guyana, and Suriname is one approach. Another is to give individual attention to these three states, as well as to The Bahamas, Jamaica, and Trinidad and Tobago, and to address the smaller island countries as a single unit. The latter option is currently employed, with a single ambassador accredited to the small countries in the eastern Caribbean. Yet this administrative convenience need not preclude policy formulation for each state individually. It is essential to keep in mind that despite many similarities, each tiny country has unique circumstances and, even more important for diplomatic aims, an individual self-image. In the Caribbean the latter trait appears intrinsic to insularity and its significance should never be ignored in matters related to foreign relations. Regardless of the decisions made regarding collective or separate representations to the small islands, logic suggests that The Bahamas, Barbados, Jamaica, and Trinidad and Tobago merit individual foreign policy consideration. More than just greater size justifies this position. Each is not only different in detail and location but each also exerts influence beyond its borders. Influence gained with one of them offers the potential to influence others as well.

It is at this point that small size offers considerable diplomatic challenge for the United States. Every state in the world is sensitive with respect to prestige, but the matter is of particular concern to ministates. Although custom, logic, and practicality favor policies that consider the eastern Caribbean entities in particular in a collective sense, the approach runs counter to island sensibilities. To people and states with little power, dignity is a powerful emotion. A policy that by design treats each tiny state as "one of those" can be self-defeating on issues of substance. Grenada is a case in point. Because of its radical government it has acquired distinctive stature in strategic assessments of the Caribbean. Yet Grenada's location on the northern flank of the Galleon's Passage is no more significant with respect to the oil tanker routes that serve the United States than are the locations of its democratic neighbors of Barbados, St. Lucia, and St. Vincent, for example. As with the earlier case of Cuba, the lesson that a recalcitrant posture with respect to the United States brings international status is one that American policies ought not encourage.

Whatever scale of relationship is employed, it is desirable that both official and popular conceptions of the Caribbean avoid the sort of stereotype that continues to hamper understanding of conditions in Central America. Much larger and with longer histories of independence than the island states, the countries of Central America continue to be thought of in the United States as a cluster of tiny, similar, and unimportant places. The perception has been voiced in Congress as well as by the public at large. Admittedly the actual importance of each to the United States remains in dispute, but to consider them as indistinguishable entities is to ignore significant differences. Application of a similar set of conceptual blinders to the almost obstinately diverse Caribbean states could hamper national policy in a region that *is* accepted as being strategic.

In the dependencies, despite self-rule in nearly all domestic matters, foreign relations remain the province of the metropolitan power. Yet each has regional interests in common with its neighbors and distinct from those of the European center. The Crown Colony of Montserrat and the Associated State of St. Kitts–Nevis are members of CARICOM, for example. In addition, devolution has not ended. Aruba plans to become independent, St. Kitts–Nevis holds the option as a matter of contract, and both Guadeloupe and Martinique are sufficiently populous in the context of the Caribbean to seek sovereignty. Both decorum and legality insist that diplomatic channels in their regard be by way of the metropole. Encouragement of their participation in regional associations, on the other hand, seems neither improper nor imprudent, particularly in light of generally close U.S. relations with each European state. Because British, French, and Dutch international interests often parallel those of the United States, inclusion of their dependencies in Caribbean councils is more an asset than a detriment.

More than mere courtesy suggests that policies framed in Washington take account of the interests of the Caribbean states. The essence of diplomacy is an exchange of views, with the level of success contingent upon the amount of mutual accommodation realized. One hesitates to define for other countries their own interests, but several seem self-evident. Most basic of these is survival as a state. All countries share this interest, yet it is a particular apprehension to small, newly independent ones. Related but separate from survival is preservation of the right of independent action in domestic and international affairs. Poland is an example of a country that in the early 1980s retained national integrity at the expense of autonomy. In the Caribbean there also is a strong sentiment favoring democratic rule.

Admittedly a dictatorship can protect the first two of these interests equally well. It cannot, however, offer the individual freedoms and participatory government that were part of Caribbean societies even before attainment of sovereignty.

In an atmosphere of secure national integrity, economic interests became paramount on the islands. Whether labeled underdeveloped or lesser developed, each of the countries is dissatisfied with its level of economic achievement. This concern became an anxiety during the world recession of the early 1980s. It was a period not just of inadequate rates of growth but for some of them actual economic decline, a time when aid from richer countries diminished because they, too, were in financial distress. Demand for their traditional agricultural exports lessened and their expanding labor-intensive manufactures met increasing import resistance led by mainland labor unions. An effect of this economic crisis was to place in jeopardy two other interests significant on the islands. One was reduction of foreign control of their economic structure, along with demands for greater parity in trade relationships. The other was assurances of continued migration opportunities to the developed countries of North America and Western Europe. The first of these is an issue worldwide among third world countries, whereas the latter reflects a Caribbean custom that long predates independence.

Reconciliation of these interests with those of the United States encounters few areas of incompatibility. Protection of the territorial integrity of hemispheric states, especially of friendly ones, is both a treaty obligation and a long-held policy objective in Washington. A characteristic of ministates is a limited capacity for self-defense. In the same vein, however, they are even more constrained in the ability to threaten others. It is in this context that defense treaties with neighbors, with a superpower such as the United States or the Soviet Union, or with a former metropolitan state offer security. In the Caribbean the greatest security comes from agreements with the United States, a circumstance agreeable to Washington and thus far accepted by most ministates. Questions following coups by radical leaders in Grenada and Suriname remain unanswered. Projection of Soviet or even Cuban power in their support would be difficult and is unlikely. Unclear yet is the extent to which Grenada and Suriname are viewed in Washington as externally threatening and hence themselves endangered by U.S. retaliation.

Preservation of the right of independent actions represents an area where U.S. policies long have been ambivalent. In a region where hegemony has traditionally been claimed and has been exercised numerous time, U.S. forebearance of independent foreign policy positions has not been unlimited. Despite a public posture favoring democratic rule, American tolerance of domestic repression by rulers with compatible foreign policies has been notorious. It is conceivable that Fidel Castro could have imposed an identical totalitarian regime without condemnation had he not sought rapprochement with the Soviet Union and instigated subversion among his neighbors. In this regard there are few illusions within the small countries in the Caribbean. On the other hand, most foreign policy positions of the United States with respect to regional security are shared by the present governments. Divergence on other sorts of issues are likely to produce American reactions that are more awkward than threatening.

One of the strengths of the Caribbean Basin Initiative was that it addressed a problem both of special concern in the region and one with which the United States in normal times is well-equipped to deal, that is, economic development. Its emphasis on an increased role for private investment in countries already fearful of loss of their economic integrity, on the other hand, produced mixed reactions. To many in the Caribbean, aid at the governmental level, whether bilateral, multilateral, or through international financial organizations, was preferable. This position was more ideological than practical, however, considering the spotty success record of that aid approach in the Third World and a conservative political mood in Washington. The initiative along with a weak world economy also blunted somewhat the call for greater economic justice, the so-called North–South Dialogue. The one-way free trade provisions of the initiatve fit poorly the charge of unfair exploitation. Assuming a revival of world economies, the subject of international price differentials can be expected again to be an area of contention between the United States and Caribbean states.

The matter of continued immigration is perhaps the most sensitive issue between Caribbean and developed countries. The United States, Canada, United Kingdom, France, and The Netherlands all contain political factions urging imposition of stricter limitations on the entrance of immigrants. Involved are fears of job competition and changing ethnic composition. In the United States these concerns were aroused in the 1970s and early 1980s by publicized mass flows from Mexico, Cuba, Southeast Asia, and to a lesser extent from Haiti. As noted above, however, the collective migration from the rest of the Caribbean has been as great as from any other area aside from Mexico. To the island governments such outlets ease population pressures, earn money through remittances, and enhance political stability in that many who are dissatisfied for various reasons can choose to leave. Reconciliation between the various governments of the political dimensions of these human and economic problems will be especially difficult because domestic considerations in every country are involved. Unilateral approaches are unfair and perhaps even unworkable.

In the early 1980s the prospects for continuing strong United States influence in the Caribbean ministates were favorable. A surge in American investments over the previous three decades had strengthened historic economic ties and large migration flows over the same span had reinforced cultural attachments. Awareness of interrelationships with the United States was well-developed on the islands and there was increased consciousness in Washington that the United States had become a Caribbean nation in human as well as in geopolitical terms. Conversely, independence initiated a gradual loosening of bonds with Britain. The victory in contested elections of a number of leaders favorably disposed to the United States also was auspicious. The commitment to political pluralism on the islands was in accord with the ideological objectives of the United States. It may even have swayed the Reagan administration to place greater emphasis on strengthening democracy in its global policies.

The timing, content, and manner of development of the Caribbean Basin Initiative also enhanced the U.S. position in the region. Elected leaders from the region were consulted regarding the concept early in the planning stages. This participatory approach increased the sense of status of the small states and ensured that their views at least were heard before the details were announced. At the same time it provided an opportunity for the U.S. negotiators to apprise potential recipients of the limitations of American resources and of domestic political constraints. In terms of timing it must be recognized that although economic crisis was not new to the Caribbean islands, it was their first experience as independent states with worldwide recession.

The diplomatic position of the United States vis-à-vis the ministates was aided also by a decline in prestige of the Soviet Union and its client state of Cuba. Soviet armed aggression in Afghanistan and its role in the crushing of the Polish Solidarity movement weakened its world posture as a champion of third world autonomy and friend of the working class. Cuba's record of interference in the internal affairs of other states made its motives suspect in a hemisphere where fear of foreign intervention is perhaps the most widely shard national sentiment. This view of Cuba was especially strong in Jamaica, which in turn was regionally the most influential of the ministates. The advantage here was not that the United States was blameless in this regard, but that its competitors were no better. The effect was to place the positive aspects of association with the United States in more favorable perspective by reducing the appeal of the alternatives.

In addition, in countries eager to develop but facing unprecedented financial difficulties, stagnant economic conditions in the Soviet Union and Cuba offered neither prospects for aid nor models for emulation. Circumstances in Cuba were reported to be especially grim with double-digit inflation, rising unemployment, zero industrial growth, and trade deficits of up to $1 billion annually. The situation was expected to worsen as world sugar prices dropped, Western bankers pressed for debt payments, and Eastern bloc allies cut $3 billion in annual trade subsidies (*World Press Review* 1983, p. 6). Concurrent conditions in Western countries also exhibited economic downturn, unemployment, and debt but to a lesser degree and from a higher level of achievement. In addition, one of the propaganda themes of the Soviet Union long has been that under socialism depression was impossible, that it was a disease of capitalism. Contrary evidence weakened their credibility in this and other areas.

Despite these advantages, U.S. foreign relations in the Caribbean were hampered by its record of intervention and a propensity for insensitive pronouncements by public officials. The greatest burden, however, is derivitive of its greatest geopolitical asset. Economically and militarily the United States is the world's most powerful nation, a standing that is magnified when surveyed from the prospectives of the ministates. When such a colossus is inclined to be cooperative, the benefits for tiny neighbors can be generous, yet if offended its capacity for causing harm is considerable. The relationship is exacerbated by a disproportionate economic involvement by American business. This situation induces resentment and distrust even among sectors of island society inclined to be sympathetic. For leftist elements it fuels the image of an imperialistic devil to be cast out and shunned.

As of early 1983 political support on the islands for the latter point of view was vocal but narrow. Yet, though latent, the sentiment was persistent. Anti-Americanism exists to some extent everywhere in the region and on each island requires only propitious circumstances to become a potent political force. The rhetoric of Michael Manley in Jamaica employed it with effect during his tenure as prime minister. His defeat in the 1980 election resulted more from economic failures and public perception of foreign (Cuban) meddling than from rejection of his anti-imperialist stance. A similar mood is expressed by leaders of the opposition United Labor Front in Trinidad and Tobago, by politicians in the smaller islands, and in The Bahamas. Indeed, it sustains the independence movement in Puerto Rico and radical groups in the U.S. Virgin Islands.

In other dependencies, elections in March 1983 won majority seats in regional councils for a coalition of Communists and Socialists in Guadeloupe and French Guiana. As the Communist Party on the French island since 1968 has argued in favor of autonomy, emergence of a new, leftist-led Caribbean country there is conceivable (Lasserre and Mabileau 1972, p. 98). Concern in the Netherlands Antilles has been with satisfaction of the aspirations of young, university-trained technicians and bureaucrats in the event of economic distress. With the advent of a world oil glut and a depressed banking business on the islands, apprehensions in this respect have grown.

U.S. foreign policy options for the Caribbean are not complex in concept. Application of a given course of action is quite another matter. Under the Reagan administration the approaches changed little from those of

Jimmy Carter with two obvious exceptions. One change was almost full acceptance of the viewpoint that political instability was caused mainly by subversion directed from Cuba at the behest of the Soviet Union. Featuring harsh language by then-Secretary of State Haig, political pressures were put upon both countries to cease and desist. Within the threatened countries aid was in large part for military-related items, such as transport, training, and arms. Efforts to enlist neighboring countries in the effort also stressed military measures. Economic aid cut-offs to Nicaragua and Grenada were accompanied by bombast, nearby military build-ups, and maneuvers: in short, a near classic application of great power projection within its perceived zone of hegemony.

The other policy change was the Caribbean Basin Initiative which was in many ways a nearly opposite strategy to the great power approach and which was innovative at least in its regional outlook. In mid-1983 the two were different in another way as well. The administration had implemented a number of military measures whereas key provisions of the initiative were still stalled in Congress. A combination of interests provided opposition for the initiative, although one powerful House member remarked privately in March 1983 that once President Reagan gave the initiative his full attention, it would pass. At the same time, both the overt and covert aspects of the military approach in Central America drew increasingly congressional resistance. Presumably forms of military coercion directed toward Grenada and Suriname would provoke similar opposition. On the basis of the trend of the mood in Congress, then, the prospects for expansion of a peaceful U.S. policy approach were greater than for a military one.

Elsewhere in the region cooperation with Panama proceeded as scheduled toward the goal of complete relinquishment of U.S. control of the canal by the year 2000. This progress was made despite the fact that as as presidential candidate Ronald Reagan had argued against ratification of the canal treaty then before Congress. The Reagan administration made little change either in the level of U.S. military strength stationed within the Caribbean or in the status of Headquarters of the Caribbean Task Force. The latter measure—aimed at increasing the responsiveness of U.S. military capabilities, like the Canal Treaty—was a Carter initiative. The expression of U.S. support for elected governments was also a continuation of Carter policy, altered rhetorically but similar in effect. Indeed, a major bonus for the Reagan administration's foreign policy objectives was the almost simultaneous election of Edward Seaga as prime minister of Jamaica. Once in office Seaga's emphasis on the role of free enterprise in develoment and a personal antipathy for Cuba was a ready-made entree into the Caribbean for economic concepts favored by President Reagan. Subsequent voter rejection of candidates from the left in other island countries further encouraged advocates of greater private sector investment but were less influential in the development of U.S. policy than were the results in Jamaica.

A drastic change in current U.S. policies toward the Caribbean would be a move toward normalization of relations with Cuba. Regardless of the relative merits of such an action it would be, in the words of former diplomat Wayne Smith, "the one approach that has not yet been tried" (Smith 1982, p. 173). There seems little doubt that resumption of normal trade with Cuba would offer economic benefits to both countries, and to Cuba in particular. It also might reduce incentives for Cubans to migrate and ease that contemporary concern, although evidence from other friendly countries of the region suggest that perhaps migration might even increase with the easing of restrictions. Carlos Montaner (1979, p. 9) speculated that renewal of what he regards as the natural interrelations between the two countries would unavoidably introduce pluralistic elements into Castro's police state and lead to a loosening of Cuban dependence on Moscow. In this scenario, the inevitable aging of Castro and his entire generation of leadership would make likely the emergence of a less repressive and, to the United States, a less threatening government. It is his view that neither the traditional character of the Cubans nor the reality of close U.S. proximity supports the ideological assumption that a communist dictatorship there is irreversible.

Reopening peaceful relations with Cuba could indeed have the benefits envisioned, especially if concessions by Castro on the matter of overseas subversion activities could be obtained. The latter achievement would unquestionably ease security concerns in the United States and neighboring countries. On the other hand, the economic impact on the ministates could be devastating. Normal economic contacts between the United States and Cuba mean for the most part trade in sugar plus tourism. The 1962 U.S. economic boycott was a major stimulus to tourism on the other islands and has aided sugar growers on a number of islands, cessation of the boycott presumably would harm touirst and sugar economies elsewhere in the Caribbean. In terms of imports, the material needs of Cuba are mainly machinery, transportation stock, appliances, high technology, and petroleum. With the partial exception of appliances, few such items are exported by the region's other island states. The trade benefits from such a diplomatic opening would accrue mainly to the United States. In addition, in the event that such a U.S. action stimulated a revival of the Cuban economy with Fidel Castro still in command, to what extent would this improvement of the quality of life in a socialist Cuba weaken the ability of elected leaders nearby to withstand political challenges from the left? It is conceivable that an end of the U.S. diplomatic and economic quarantine would contribute to a regional political destabilization contrary to current foreign policy objectives.

The question of whether extension of economic aid and adoption of a conciliatory posture toward avowedly Marxist–Leninist governments will modify their domestic and international behavior has yet to be answered. It is the issue that perhaps most divides policy makers in Washington. The best arguments in its favor were events in Yugoslavia after 1948, yet in this instance Tito has already broken with Stalin and had little choice but to turn to the West. Cuban sympathizers long have maintained that Castro turned to Moscow only after rejection by Washington. Similar reasoning was advanced regarding the leftist stance taken by the Sandinistas in Nicaragua and currently is gathering momentum with respect to Grenada. Evidence to support these interpretations is not persuasive, but is not disproven either. Under the Reagan administration, however, debate over the option of an opening with Cuba seems academic. Given his domestic political base he cannot openly accommodate leftist governments. By 1985 political consolidation by Marxist–Leninist factions in Nicaragua, Grenada, and perhaps even Suriname may have progressed to the point that even resumption of U.S. aid under a different and more flexible president would be insufficient to protect a degree of pluralism.

Regardless of the advisability and even possibility of initiating more friendly relations with present regimes in Cuba, Grenada, and Nicaragua, adoption of a position of greater tolerance toward political mavericks would seem to offer diplomatic rewards. Fairly or unfairly, the United States is regarded around the world and even by many at home as an opponent of social change. The fact that many of these same critics deny the legitimacy of any change other than one toward Leninism—*the* revolution—is less significant geopolitically than is the perception of a diplomatically rigid United States. This image is to some degree self-imposed. Spokesmen in Washington—Alexander Haig for one—gave every evidence that U.S. policy was based on the premise that anyone dissatisfied with the status quo had been manipulated by a communist power. This simplification may indeed by unjust, but it is a plausible reading of Haig's pronouncements. Rhetoric has eased under Secretary Schultz, although evidence that policies had also moderated was less apparent. Adoption of an attitude of greater flexibility manifested more by deeds than words would seem to give greater credibility to U.S. positions favoring social progress.

The choice of a lessened U.S. presence and greater reliance on mutlinational approaches to Caribbean problems has already been made part of the Caribbean Basin Initiative. Certainly the opportunity for extension of this approach existed with respect to Central America. Mexico, Panama, and Venezuela had made clear their willingness to act as mediators there. The Socialist International also signaled a desire to become more active in efforts to achieve a nonmilitary solution. Rigidity within the Reagan administration and domestic political constraints, however, make acceptance of these offers unlikely. The rejection, regardless of its logic, tends to reinforce a negative world view of the Untied States both as a peacemaker and as an advocate of social progress.

The prospects are much more favorable for a cooperative approach to dealings with the island ministates. Peaceful conditions there give no incentive to "send a message to the Kremlin." The islands already have economic commitments elsewhere, as well as political links with the British Commonwealth. Deeply felt on the islands is both a degree of apprehension regarding too close an embrace by the United States and a desire to diffuse their dependency to as great an extent as is practical. Available also are alternative power centers in Mexico, Venezuela, Canada, and Colombia. These countries have growing national interests in the island Caribbean and a desire for greater international prestige. Involvement of one or more in the achievement of common objectives could both strengthen the regional system and lessen apprehensions regarding the motives and power of the United States.

The suggestions here are not new, although they are framed in an unconventional context. My personal biases are evident. Profound political, economic, and social changes have occurred and continue in the Caribbean. Unchanged, however, are the primary security concerns of the United States. The task of policy makers in Washington is to devise approaches that achieve national objectives in a region of newly independent ministates. It seems logical that the most promising attitude in a search for solutions is one that regards change as an opportunity rather than a peril. Diplomatic flexibility, however, has greater prospects of success when sustained by a principle.

A principle that appears to offer great promise in this regard was enunciated in the 1982 State Department Survey of Human Rights, "Human rights is at the core of American foreign policy because it is central to America's conception of itself" (New York *Times*, 1983, p. A 22). Applied in consistent fashion in international affairs this position could well serve the long-term interests of the Untied States, especially in a region of ministates. It is an option that is strongly recommended.

REFERENCES

Editorial. 1983. New York *Times*, February 15, A 22.

Lasserre, Guy and Mabileau, Albert. 1972. "The French Antilles and Their Status as Overseas Departments." In *Patterns of Foreign Influence in the Caribbean*, edited by Emmanuel de Kadt, pp. 82–102. London: Oxford University Press.

Montaner, Carlos. 1979. "20 Years After the Cuban Revolution." *Caribbean Review*, 8, pp. 4–10.

Smith, Wayne S. 1982. "Dateline Havana: Myopic Diplomacy." *Foreign Policy*, 48, pp. 157–74.

World Press Review. 1983. March, p. 6. As translated and adapted from *Neue Zurcher Zeitung*, Zurich.

APPENDIX

COMPARATIVE PRESS FREEDOMS OF COUNTRIES OF THE CARIBBEAN RIM: CRITERIA

The countries of the Caribbean rim are classified according to the degree of press freedom they offer. They are grouped from most to least free.

Category 1 Both print media and broadcast are privately owned and independent of government control. Constitutions guarantee freedom of the press and it is respected in practice. Media are free to criticize government without fear of retribution.

Costa Rica, Dominican Republic

Category 2 Print media are privately owned but there can be government regulation of broadcast media. Constitutions generally guarantee freedom of the press and it is respected in practice, although minor restrictions may vary from state to state or province to province. Such restrictions may not necessarily be written "laws." Media are free to criticize government, but restrictions may demand equal time and/or space for opposing views.

Bahamas, Barbados, Belize, Jamaica, Mexico, St. Lucia, St. Vincent and the Grenadines, Trinidad and Tobago, United States (for comparison), Venezuela

Category 3 Some government regulation over print and/or broadcast may exist, from limitation on newsprint importation to carrying news or information only about party candidates over broadcast media. Constitutions may indicate press freedom is afforded the journalists, but journalists are forced to join a collegium, or be licensed by the state, and are therefore restricted. Isolated incidents of censorship, or terrorism against journalists, have occurred.

Colombia, Dominica, Guyana, Honduras, Panama, Suriname

Category 4 Free Press may be guaranteed constitutionally for print and broadcast media, but media do not operate freely and independently.

Journalists may be censored or practice self-censorship due to fear of retribution; such retribution may range from loss of reporting privileges to jail to exile to actual physical harm. Media laws or codes are vague, open to interpretation, and are often manipulated by the government to serve its own purposes. Newspapers may be shut down temporarily or permanently.

El Salvador, Grenada, Guatemala, Haiti, Nicaragua

Category 5 No press freedom exists. All print (including magazines, books, and pamphlets) and broadcast media are tightly controlled by the state, and dissenting opinions are not allowed.

Cuba

Source: Bonnie Hufford, *Comparative Press Freedoms of Countries of the Caribbean Rim*, Bowling Green State University Geography Department (1982), unpublished report.

INDEX

ABOUT THE AUTHOR

Thomas D. Anderson is Professor of Geography at Bowling Green State University, Bowling Green, Ohio, 43403. Born 9/23/29 he holds A.B. and M.A. degrees from Kent State University, Kent, Ohio, and a Ph.D. from the University of Nebraska at Lincoln. He has broad professional interests with most stemming from his training in cultural geography. From this perspective he has done research and published on such varied topics as agriculture, land use, population, maritime boundaries, shipping routes, and especially on politics, both U.S. and international.

Professor Anderson also taught at the State University College at Geneseo, New York, and held summer positions at Kent State University, University of Virginia at Charlottesville, State University of New York at Albany, and Western Oregon College at Manmouth. In 1974 he was Senior Fulbright–Hayes Lecturer in Agricultural Geography at the Institute of Geography and Regional Development of Central University of Venezuela in Caracas. During 1953–55 he was an Infantry lieutenant with the U.S. Army with service in Korea. He also has been an elected City Councilman in Bowling Green, Ohio.

In addition to a book, articles, and research reports intended for the geography profession, Professor Anderson has been a consultant with private industry on projects related to industrial development. His articles of interpretative commentary have appeared in *The Nation, Current History,* the *Toledo Blade*, New York *Times*, and *Christian Science Monitor*.